LIFE STREAMS

SUNY series in Latin American and Iberian Thought and Culture

Jorge J. E. Gracia and Rosemary Geisdorfer Feal, editors

LIFE STREAMS

ALBERTO REY'S
CUBAN AND AMERICAN ART

Edited by

Lynette M. F. Bosch

and

Mark Denaci

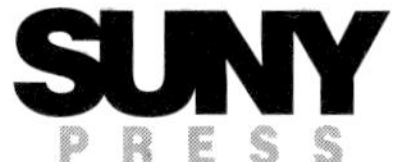

Cover image courtesy of Alberto Rey.

Published by State University of New York Press, Albany

For information, contact State University of New York Press, Albany, NY
www.sunypress.edu

Production by Eileen Nizer
Marketing by Michael Campochiaro

Library of Congress Cataloging-in-Publication Data

Life streams : Alberto Rey's Cuban and American art / edited by Lynette M.F. Bosch
    and Mark Denaci.
        pages cm. — (SUNY series in Latin American and Iberian thought and culture)
    Includes bibliographical references and index.
    ISBN 978-1-4384-5056-8 (pbk. : alk. paper)
    1. Rey, Alberto, 1960—Criticism and interpretation.   I. Bosch, Lynette M. F.,
editor of compilation.   II. Denaci, Mark, 1969– editor of compilation.
III. Rey, Alberto, 1960– Works. Selections.

N6537.R44L54 2014
709.2—dc23   2013019603

10 9 8 7 6 5 4 3 2 1

*To all those who made their way here to build lives,
to those who will come,
and to the ones who have gone*

—Lynette M. F. Bosch

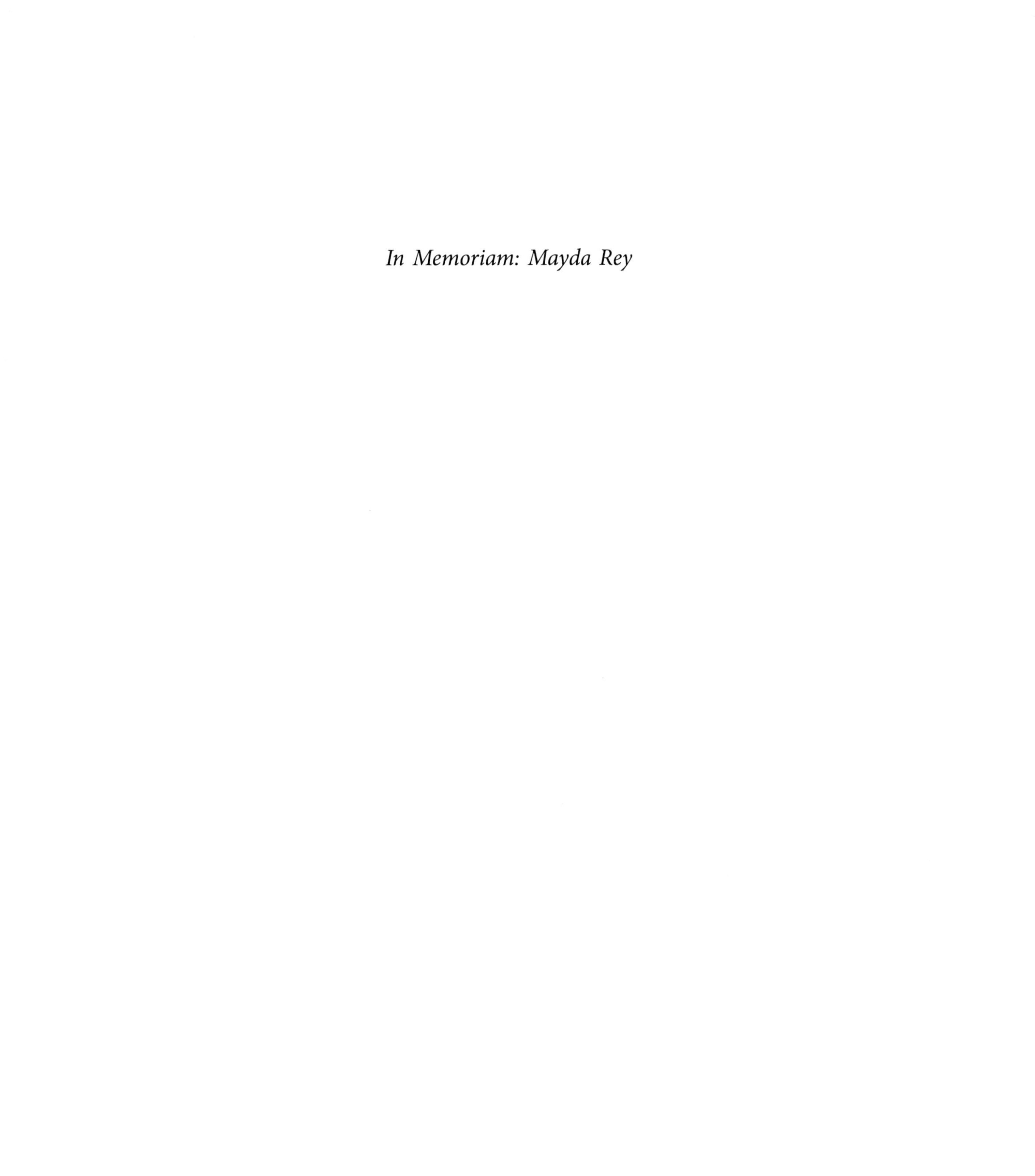

In Memoriam: Mayda Rey

Contents

This book would not have been possible without the support of the following:

SPONSORS

State University of New York, Fredonia, New York
The Burchfield Penney Art Center, Buffalo, New York
State University of New York, Geneseo, New York
The Geneseo Foundation, Geneseo, New York
Will Kelly, CFP, Managing Director, United Capital Financial Advisors, Buffalo,
  New York
St. Lawrence University, Canton, New York

REPRODUCTIONS SPONSOR

The color reproductions were funded by a generous subsidy, courtesy of Professor Jorge Gracia, holder of the Samuel P. Capen Chair in Philosophy and Comparative Literature, University of Buffalo, New York.

Acknowledgments

The formation of an artist is the product of inborn talent, hard work, ambition, and support that comes in many forms and from many sources. Alberto Rey would like to thank the following for their unstinting support over the years: Janeil Strong Rey, Graciela Rey, Diego Rey, Mayda Rey, Enrique Rey, and Olga Rey.

Alberto Rey, Lynette M. F. Bosch, and Mark Denaci are grateful to the director and the curatorial staff of the Burchfield Penney Art Center for the support they have given to this project. We thank: Anthony Bannon, executive director of the Burchfield Penney Art Center; Scott Propeack, associate director and chief curator; Tullis Johnson, associate curator and manager of Archives; Don Metz, associate director of Public Programs.

We especially thank for additional support: Dennis Hefner, president, State University of New York at Fredonia; Virginia Horvath, president, State University of New York at Fredonia; John Kijinski, dean of the College of Liberal Arts and Sciences; David Tiffany, vice president for University Advancement and executive director of Fredonia College Foundation; Anne Baldwin, director, Sponsored Research, State University of New York at Geneseo; Savi V. Iyer, dean of Curriculum and Academic Services and chair of Art History; and Dorothy Limouze, professor of Art History, St. Lawrence University.

We also thank contributors to this volume: Jorge Gracia, Isabel Alvaréz Borland, John Orlock, Sandra Firmin, and Benjamin Hickey.

A special thank you from Alberto goes to those special individuals who have knowingly or unknowingly supported and inspired him through their work, their friendship, and their lives: Johanna Drucker, Robert and Elizabeth Booth, James and Andy Hurtgen, John Straight, Jim Wilcox, Mirta, Pepe, and

Joel Alvarez, Mirta and Greg Rice, Omar and Leysa Alvarez, Jorge Santis, Doug and Ann Manly, Chuck McKinney, Mike and Fran Filkens, Jason Dilworth, Mike and Ethel Suchar, Tim Frerichs, and Matt Dorn. For friendship and support the editors of this volume thank: Dorothy Limouze, Larry Silver, Annette Bosch, and Arielle Marcus.

For personal support, the editors of this book thank Charles E. Burroughs, Elsie B. Smith Professor and Chair of Classics, Case Western Reserve University, whose observations about Alberto Rey's work made us think more and better; and Paul Dwaine Fournier, whose continued personal help and support has been valuable toward the completion of this project.

Foreword

SCOTT PROPEACK

The Burchfield Penney is committed to recognizing cultural integrity and to celebrating the excellence of our artistic community.

—Mission Statement, Burchfield Penney Art Center

Science asks us to test and retest hypotheses and learn, over time, whether our original ideas hold true. Alberto Rey is a scientist who communicates in visual terms, which is undeniable in his most recent series of works in *Biological Regionalism*. While the essays in this book—contributed by Lynette M. F. Bosch, Mark Denaci, Jorge Gracia, Isabel Alvarez Borland, John Orlock, Sandra Firmin, and Benjamin Hickey—allow the artist to take precedent, flipping this alignment from artist/scientist to scientist/artist is necessary when introducing the artist.

Rey visually documents circumstances over time, and reconsiders the motivations that started processes—evolutions that initiate and complete works of art, or movements of individuals from location to location, or biological realities and their transformations over time. With Rey's paintings, videos, installations, and sculpture, we gain visually stimulating information that becomes part of our shared record. But what remains is greater than a data set or a pie chart—it's a compelling visual statement that helps us find the artist, our community, and ourselves in the world.

The premise of examining change is also the perfect way to understand the relationship between Rey and the

Burchfield Penney Art Center. In addition to the series, *Biological Regionalism: Scajaquada Creek, Erie County, New York, USA* exhibited in conjunction with the publication of this book, Rey's work has been in several exhibitions at the Center over more than two decades. So, too, have Rey and his work become subjects of study at the Center: with the acquisition of *Holy Angels Church and Chair*, 1987, the Center was the first museum to collect his work. The museum has made four additional acquisitions since, and each of these—*Binary Forms: Floating Between, 1991; Appropriated Memories: Vinales, Cuba, 1996–97; Waters of Caibarien, Cayo, Brujas, Cuba, June 14, 2004;* and *Aesthetics of Death VII, 2008*—have contributed to our understanding of the scientist/artist and his work.

In his series, *Biological Regionalism*, Rey achieves what we hope to find in science and celebrate in the arts; by extrapolating information from accumulated data, we better understand a subject—and that subject helps us come to know ourselves.

On behalf of the Burchfield Penney Art Center, we are proud to present this catalog in conjunction with the exhibition titled *Biological Regionalism*. The Board of Directors wish to acknowledge the support of all of those who have made this publication possible, notably Will Kelly and United Capital Financial Advisors.

Scott Propeack
Associate Director, Chief Curator
Burchfield Penney Art Center

LIFE STREAMS

Introduction

Life Streams: The Cuban and American Art of Alberto Rey

LYNETTE M. F. BOSCH

This book is a collaborative project intended to provide an overview of the life and artistic career of Alberto Rey, a Distinguished Professor at the State University of New York at Fredonia. The catalyst for this volume is a projected exhibition of Rey's work at the Burchfield Penney Center for the Arts in Buffalo, New York, titled *Biological Regionalism: Scajaquada Creek, Erie County, New York, USA* scheduled for March 14–June 22, 2014. The art historians and curators contributing chapter essays to this volume are an interdisciplinary group composed of the book's editors, Lynette M. F. Bosch (State University of New York, Geneseo, Department of Art History)

and Mark Denaci (St. Lawrence University, Department of Art and Art History), along with contributors Jorge Gracia (Samuel P. Capen Chair, SUNY Distinguished Professor, University of Buffalo, Department of Philosophy and Department of Comparative Literature), Isabel Alvarez Borland (Murray Professor in the Arts and Humanities, College of the Holy Cross, Spanish Department), John Orlock (Samuel and Virginia C. Knight Professor of Humanities, Case Western Reserve University, English Department), Sandra Firmin (Curator, University of Buffalo Gallery), and Benjamin Hickey (Curator of Collections and Exhibitions, Masur Museum). Each of the essays in this volume reflects an aspect of artistic, literary, critical, or historical theory that addresses aspects of the complex artistic trajectory that Alberto Rey has traveled in his life and career.

Rey's work includes painting, sculpture, video, and installation, and is currently focused on exploring issues of ecological sustainability through imagery related to fish and fishing and the waterways in which fish live. Throughout his career, Rey has focused on giving visual form to his concerns with identity and identities, an aspect of his work that springs from his hyphenated identity as a Cuban-born American. Rey is an indefatigable traveler, who has extensively explored the United States, Cuba, Europe, Latin America, the Caribbean, and Iceland, searching for ways in which he can relate the individual human experience to the larger universal life of our world. As an artist whose work is part of major national and international museums and collections (Brooklyn Museum, Albright-Knox Gallery, Bronx Museum, Fort Lauderdale Museum of Art, Extremaduran and Latin American Museum of Contemporary Art, Badajoz Spain, and the Burchfield Penney Art Center, among others), Rey has achieved a significant level of recognition in the world of contemporary art. The exhibition at the Burchfield Penney Art Center is a meaningful opportunity for Rey to bring his work to his home community. Rey's paintings are of fish and landscapes that function as symbols and metaphors for the people he has met and the places in which he has lived. The allegorical possibilities thus created by this network of associations opens a space for the spectator to engage with Rey and with the cultural environments represented in his work.

Rey is an artist, a husband, father, son, brother, and active community activist and conservationist, with strong memories of his late sister, and his home is in Fredonia in Western New York State. He is also a transnational Cubanborn American, who has lived his life in the United States on the hyphen of two identities. Brought out of Cuba at the age of three, Rey went, with his parents and sister, first to Mexico, then Miami, then Barnesboro, Pennsylvania, before settling in Fredonia, in 1989, to become a professor of drawing and painting. Cultural diversity is part of his identity, and a personal search for meaning has generated his desire to know and understand different people and cultures. This desire stems from his identification with different groups and cultures, from his Cuban origins to his present life in Western New York State.

In Cuba, Rey's family belonged to a self-identified group of Cuban *criollos*, who had settled in the small, rural town of Agramonte, where they owned a small farm that they worked on themselves. They were a diverse family of mixed ethnic roots, who considered their home culture beyond Cuba to be Spain, because most of the family had come from Spain, with a few coming to Cuba from the Canary Islands. Consistently, Rey's family on all sides had always lived in small, rural villages. As a result, the family had practical skills that assisted them in surviving and adapting in Cuba and in the United States. Always, Rey's family worked hard in both countries at a range of manual jobs, from farming and small manufacture to small business, along with hunting and fishing as pastimes and to supplement their diet. Rey's father, who had an exceptional talent for mathematics, earned a PhD in education at the University of Havana, which enabled him to retrain in the United States as a teacher of Spanish. The family settled in Barnesboro, Pennsylvania, and slowly rebuilt their lives to the same modest level of comfort they had in Cuba, and with the same practical skills. Rey's current life has combined aspects of his family's history. He is a professor of art and a professional artist, the first in his family, and he lives in the small, rural town of Fredonia, where he continues to fish (although he releases his catch), as part of the set of skills that his family traditionally possessed. As a result of his experiences of assimilating from a mulatto Cuban culture into a mainstream American culture in Barnesboro, Rey's initial problematic encounters with early discrimination taught him to accept difference in himself and others. He also learned how to relate to different cultures, being neither fully Cuban nor fully American or even Cuban American, as he lacked a Latino community, while growing up in Barnesboro. Presently, Rey has achieved a level of comfort with international culture that enables him to connect to different groups at every level of society that he meets as he travels for his work. The desire to extend his understanding of people and cultures that he learned from his personal experience of being outside both his home cultures has brought him, after a long trajectory, to the study of fish and their worlds. The path that led Rey to this juncture of his life started, in 2000, with a series titled *Trout Encounters* and two other series, *Biological Regionalism* and *The Aesthetics of Death*. The series were a way for Rey to address recent changes and losses in his life by connecting his life to the natural environments we share with the animals living alongside us. It is *Biological Regionalism* that is the focus of the Burchfield Penney Art Center exhibition.

For Rey, trout have become a symbol of a variety of personal and global issues. For the directorial staff of the Burchfield Penney Art Center, and for the artist and the authors of this book, one major goal of this exhibition and book is to communicate Rey's intentions so that all can understand the meaning of his images. A secondary goal is to enable the spectator of this exhibition and the reader of this book to relate their own life experience and personal concerns about our place in the natural world to the images Rey has created. Part of Rey's intention is to provide a communicative structure in which participant spectators can increase their understanding of their lives by looking at Rey's work. Hence, a meditative dimension is intended to bridge the solipsistic gap that separates us from one another by providing a link through his images.

Another part of Rey's desired outcome is that, by seeing the streams, countries, and the biodiversity of trout, the active spectator can have a direct experience of nature akin to that which was Rey's catalyst for this series. Through Rey's paintings, this exhibition, and this book, engaged spectators can learn about environments they might not otherwise see, and participate in experiences of nature they might otherwise miss.

One goal of this book, in conjunction with Rey's past, current, and future exhibitions, is the establishment of a renewed understanding of American cultural and environmental diversity in relation to the global; Rey's desire is to connect specific manifestations of these aspects of human experience to the universal whole. The authors of this book have written a series of essays that trace Rey's trajectory so that his process and his artistic intentions can be transmitted. Each of the essays forming the book's chapters was selected to contextualize a different and individual aspect of Rey's art and life, with the goal of presenting a unified and cohesive explanation of Rey's work.

The first essay in this volume is Lynette Bosch's "Alberto Rey: Intersections," which provides a biographical overview of Rey's life, his artistic concerns, and the different stages of his artistic career. The essay presents Rey as an artist who connects his experience, observations, and research to the works of art that he creates. Initially and primarily a painter, Rey's artistic repertoire expanded as he explored different subjects and concerns, and Bosch's essay traces how the changes in his artistic expression respond to the events of Rey's life.

Jorge Gracia's essay, "The Construction of Identity in Art: Alberto Rey's Journey," specifically addresses, from a philosophical perspective, the formation and definition of identity—national, cultural, individual, or familial—in all of the aspects conveyed by the word *identity*. Gracia focuses on discussing the balance that hyphenated identity requires of an individual who moves between two cultures as he describes how Rey has fused the different aspects of his identity into a cohesive body of work. Drawing from philosophy, critical theory, and personal experience as a Cuban-born American, Gracia addresses the subject of identity from a scholarly, yet personal, perspective, producing an essay that is layered with interpretive possibilities for individual works by Rey. As a scholar of philoso-phy, Gracia employs authors as diverse as St. Augustine and David Hume to explicate the process of being and becoming that is intrinsic to the definition of self.

Isabel Alvarez Borland brings her experience as a scholar of literature and specifically of Cuban American literature to bear on her exploration of meaning for Alberto Rey's works in her "Alberto Rey's *Balsas* Series in the Cuban American Imagination." Alvarez Borland's essay follows a chronological and thematic progression as she relates Rey's work to that of other Cuban American writers and artists, thus contextualizing Rey within his peer group of Cuban Americans who employ art (literary and pictorial) to address and communicate their experience as bicultural Americans and transnationals. The essay focuses on the iconic use of rafts as metaphorical vehicles for escape, transition, travel, exile, immigration, danger, and expectation. For Cuban Americans, as for other groups (Haitians, Laotians, Vietnamese), for whom rafts or *balsas* represented escape and a new life, images or descriptions of rafts and voyages on rafts resonate as a major cultural markers of their Cuban identity. But Alvarez Borland's essay does not confine itself to Rey's *Balsas* series, as she addresses the symbolic, metaphorical and allegorical aspects of each of Rey's progressive groups of works that trace his patterns of thought. Thus, from an interdisciplinary perspective, Alvarez Borland addresses Rey's artistic trajectory, employing a variety of critical approaches.

Mark Denaci's essay, "Absent Presences and the Living Dead: Alberto Rey's Haunted Aesthetics," contextualizes Rey within the history of aesthetics and art criticism as he analyzes Rey's visual strategies for creating meaning in his images. Denaci places Rey within the parameters of debates about art and representation in which Clement Greenberg, the critic who arguably reinvented painting, and Martin Heidegger, the controversial philosopher who attempted to redefine art itself, play crucial roles. Greenberg's questioning of the validity of thematic subject-oriented painting is well known, and Denaci's analysis of how Rey comments on, subverts, and moves beyond Greenberg's strictures provides an understanding of Rey's subtle engagement with issues of presence and absence in representing ideas and identities. Denaci's overview of Rey's response to these aesthetic debates begins with Rey's early series, which are directly about identity, and ends with Rey's cur-

rent concerns with environmental issues and mortality. Denaci's essay is a bridge for this book's first three chapters to the remaining text, which is more focused on Rey's interest in painting fish, a project that he began in 2000.

Lynette Bosch's "Trout as Form and Symbol" initiates a concentrated emphasis on Rey's three most recent series: *Trout Encounters*, *Biological Regionalism*, and *The Aesthetics of Death*. To provide an art historical context for Rey's work, Bosch gives an overview of landscape painting and the painting of fishing and angling that includes consideration of sixteenth-century scientific naturalism and continues to contemporary painters of fish, who are Rey's peer group. Bosch also provides an analysis of how Rey's recent artistic focus on fish is connected to his earlier series, making the argument that Rey's path to his current work is continuous and cohesive with his personal and artistic accomplishments. Bosch's essay segues into John Orlock's essay, which provides a very different approach to the subject of fish and the history of fishing from that taken by the other contributors to this book.

John Orlock's "Reading the Waters: Early Works of Influence on the Literature of Fly-Fishing" is an essay that does not seek to directly address Alberto Rey's work, but which concludes with a "Postscript" from Rey that responds to Orlock's evocative essay. Orlock begins his discussion of the cultural significance of the literature on fly-fishing in Classical antiquity and concludes with Ernest Hemingway's Nick Adams stories and Norman Maclean's *A River Runs Through It*. Sir Izaak Walton's *The Compleat Angler* is central to Orlock's discussion, as it is the singule most important manual of fishing that exists. First published in 1653, *The Compleat Angler* was and is the summation of knowledge about how to fish and how to think about fishing. Orlock's discussion emphasizes the philosophical and spiritual aspects of fishing and the role that these elements play in both the culture of fishing and its literature. Thus, even though Orlock's essay is not about Rey's work (because Rey has only rarely illustrated any literary work about fishing), Orlock provides a larger understanding of the nature of fishing and the literary contribution that helps us to understand why fishing became so important for Rey. Orlock also touches on concerns that parallel those of Rey in the areas of resources, changing attitudes toward landscape, and environmental issues that are part of the literature of fishing. Therefore, this essay provides a window into the ideology of fishing that is the foundation for Rey's personal and professional exploration of this human endeavor.

Following Orlock's essay, Rey provides an "Artist's Statement" that addresses the exhibition he has designed for the Burchfield Penney Art Center. In his *Biological Regionalism: Scajaquada Creek, Erie County, New York, USA*, Rey explains why he has focused on this particular body of water and what it means to him as a member of its community and as an artist. For Rey, the Scajaquada is part of a globally connected system of waterways close to his home. And in his "Artist's Statement," Rey communicates his artistic intentions, goals, and reasons for why his current work continues to follow the path on which he decided in 2000, when he began *Trout Encounters*.

Sandra Firmin's "Time Submersion: A Portrait of Two Creeks" analyzes, describes, and interprets two of Rey's exhibitions belonging to his *Biological Regionalism* series. Firmin's concentration on *Biological Regionalism: Ellicott Creek, Amherst, New York, USA*, 2010 and

Biological Regionalism: Scajaquada Creek, Erie County, New York, USA, 2013 enables her to reach back to Classical literature, the literature of fishing, and the representational history of fishing contextualized within contemporary ecological concerns in a way that supplements previous considerations of these topics by this volume's other contributors. Firmin's goal is to meticulously examine Rey's working process from idea to display. In so doing, she explains how Rey researches each area and each part of his ongoing series so that he can become a part of the community and the environment he has chosen for his next investigative and artistic journey. Firmin's essay takes us directly into Rey's creative process and into the message he wishes to communicate to his audience.

Benjamin Hickey's "Alberto Rey: Beneath the Surface" focuses on Rey's project for the Masur Museum in Monroe, Louisiana. Hickey begins his essay by contextualizing the Louisiana project in connection with the exhibition *Biological Regionalism: Largemouth Bass, Ellicott Creek, Amherst, New York, USA* and the painting *Biological Regionalism: Brown Trout, Hosmer Creek, Hosmer, New York, USA*. The essay describes the Louisiana project, *Biological Regionalism:*

Bayou Desiard, Monroe, Louisiana, USA, from its inception to its enactment, and it traces Rey's research process from his asking for maps, objects of significant local resonance, books, and images of the area, to the many trips required for his personal exploration of the environment on which he will focus. Hickey also emphasizes Rey's scientific interests and his collaboration with local scientists and area organizations, populations, and research resources. Hence, Hickey's essay is a pragmatic portrait of how Rey enacts his work. Additionally, it contextualizes Rey's imagery within the ongoing dialectic of "high" and "low" art.

This thematic subject category, where species of fish connect Rey to universal realizations about our place in the cosmos, has been the focus of Rey's creative energy since 2000, when he began the series *Trout Encounters* as an extension of his interest and developing skill as an angler. *Trout Encounters* was also developed from Rey's desire to break out in new directions as an artist. For Rey, the representations of fish became a way whereby he could address the different stages of life and a new visual medium in which he could think and communicate his personal life experience. As someone who always felt culturally "different" from others because he was Cuban in the United States, Rey has always been interested in cultural difference and the interaction between individuals and their environment. Because he grew up in Barnesboro, without either a Cuban American or a Latino group to ground him in his Hispanic identity, Rey learned to connect to the landscape around his home as a way of defining himself. Early hostile encounters, as he was learning English, that were the result of how he looked and his different ethnicity, led him to appreciate building bridges between different cultures. In painting fish, Rey transfers the skills he learned early into learning about a different cultural environment—the world of fish and their surroundings linked to the local cultures that share habitat with the fish he studies. By incorporating the differences between humans and fish into his work, Rey addresses communal identity through that which is shared—life and death and a world of survival and adaptation.

Because the lives of fish are short, precarious, and filled with danger, the vulnerability of these creatures brought Rey to confront his own mortality and that of his close family, affected by illness and death during the years when he began to paint fish. *Trout Encounters* led to the current series *Biological Regionalism*, in which Rey records his observations of fish populations and their environments, as well as *The Aesthetics of Death*, which deals directly with evanescence and mortality. It is the *Biological Realism* series that provides the works for the Burchfield Penney exhibition. Through his renditions of fish and their environments, Rey addresses the spectator on a variety of subjects, such as personal identity, the trajectory of life, death's proximity, the impact that our actions and behavior have on our environment, and how through the observation of one fish a universal connection to life's significance can be understood.

In his work, Rey enables connections and meaning for the images he creates, which are, first and foremost, works of art of great aesthetic beauty, through his ability to represent the forms of the natural world he has come to know as an angler and fisherman. In Rey's paintings, we see trout and other fish living within their natural environments. We experience their perception of their world and we come face to face with the realization of the value of their existence for us. One need not ever have fished to understand the validity of the lives presented by Rey or to connect to the experience of being in these landscapes and streams. The encounter with the varieties of trout and other fish represented by Rey reminds us that we are part of a larger biosphere and that what happens in each of its parts affects the whole.

Rey's paintings of fish are also about memory, time, and a reminder that what is here now may be gone. In the evanescent, transitory, and diminishing populations of fish, there is a reminder of the plenitude that once existed. In painting these fish, Rey paints an America of the past, and brings us back to a time when the national identity was based on a concept of never-ending bounty—a message that was clear in the paintings of American artists such as Thomas Doughty or John James Audubon. Rey's fishing grounds cover territory once fished by Native Americans, who fished for subsistence. These populations became displaced as European settlers took over the territories, and subsistence fishing became sports fishing in the European traditions, as industrialization and leisure changed the nature of the activity. Yet, even these early artists, who worked when the landscape was relatively untouched and the birds and animals were plentiful, were aware of the vanishing resources they were recording. Even as Audubon created his series, he understood that he was preserving them at the peak of their already threatened abundance.

Rey's paintings evoke the varieties of life experience that we share with all other species: the desire to survive, hunger, reproduction, existence, being in the moment, and the tension that exists between competing drives. It is the competition between the human need for food and the fish's instinct for survival that is the crux of fishing. This contest is the catalyst for Rey's observations about the environments in which these contests unfold, which he explores in his work and in this exhibition. At this point in his career as a guide and naturalist, Rey knows that the scarcity and vulnerability of trout means that wild trout should not be harvested, as each death depletes the population. In some cases, such as that of the Scajaquada Creek, the depletion is critical, as trout seldom swim there. For Rey, fishing is now concentrated in the process of angling and not in the taking or eating of fish. Thus, Rey continues to fish because, for him, it provides a level of spiritual satisfaction that enables him to make sense of his life's trajectory and its complicated essence. This exhibition is Rey's way of communicating what he has learned as an artist who observes and records, and as someone who lives in present-day realities that have developed from his and our collective and historical past.

As Rey has worked on this series, he has developed his interest as an angler and guide into concerns about the environments in which trout live and the erosion of these environments resulting from global pollution and unregulated urbanization. Rey's intention in the creation and presentation of this series, whenever and wherever it is exhibited, is to draw attention to the natural environment that is being slowly but inexorably compromised and to create a record of what we now have that might someday disappear.

Biological Regionalism varies in locale and has become global in localization of the specific diverse species and landscapes Rey represents. The nature of the images Rey has created has changed over time, as the main theme has expanded to address Rey's life, his identity as a Cuban American artist, the illness and death of members of his family, and his concern that the increase in environmental destruction that is happening will cause the loss of our connection to nature. In essence, *Bio-logical Regionalism* is about life and death, the personal and the universal, and the complex ways in which we either engage with or destroy our natural environment. Such connections are also a reflection of how we relate to ourselves and the people who form our lives and with whom our destinies are linked.

Each of the authors of the articles found in this book understands the connections between Rey's life and his work as an artist. It has been our goal to bring to the reader of this book and the participants in Rey's ongoing body of work an understanding of Rey's life, his intentions, and his goals. Rey represents the citizen-artist who chronicles his life as he observes and explains our world, as a member of the global and local academic, artistic, and conservation communities; a citizen of this country; and someone who lives and works in Western New York State with his wife, Janeil, and their children, Graciela and Diego. Rey is an artist who is engaged in making a record of the time in which he lives so that future generations can connect to our experience and understand how we became them in the same way that Rey seeks to explain through his art how the past became our present, as "they" became "us."

1

Alberto Rey

Intersections

LYNETTE M. F. BOSCH

Alberto Rey is a Distinguished Professor of Painting at SUNY Fredonia.[1] He is also an internationally recognized Cuban-born American artist who works in a variety of media that includes painting, sculpture, installation, and video. In the middle of his life, and after decades of searching for personal and cultural identity, Rey has found the nexus where the diverse facets of his personal and professional life come together. This center is located in the quiet, Western New York State town of Fredonia, where Rey lives with his wife, Janeil Strong, and their two children, Graciela and Diego. This convergence of his personal and professional lives is the catalyst for Rey's current artistic expression, linked to his outreach work for the community in which he lives.[2] At this stage of his life, Rey's art has brought him through a series of transformations that have altered the works he creates and the philosophy whereby he lives, and this process of change and discovery is a central theme of this book about his life and work.

Alberto Rey was born in Havana, Cuba, on August 7, 1960.[3] His mother, Olga Guerra Rey, had traveled there from the family's home in Agramonte, three hours from Havana. Enrique Rey, Alberto's father, was a principal of high school and a teacher of mathematics, with a PhD in education, whose lack of sympathy with Fidel Castro's revolution was

"

known in his hometown. On April 18, 1961, the day after the Bay of Pigs invasion failed to remove Castro from power, Enrique Rey was jailed on a chicken farm for ten days. Olga Rey's two brothers and her father were also jailed.

In March 1963, Enrique Rey obtained political asylum in Mexico, where he worked for Monsanto, saving enough money by August, to bring his wife, daughter Mayda, and son Alberto, to Mexico. The family settled in Tlalnepantla, a suburb of Mexico City. A year later, Rey's immediate family immigrated to the Unites States and settled in Miami, where they joined other members of their extended family. In Miami, Rey's father and mother worked a series of jobs: his father worked in a sugar refinery, as an airplane mechanic, and for a fiberglass boat manufacturer. He cut aluminum sheets for a window manufacturer, and he also worked at Ancel, the makers of Hispanic food products, in the packaging department and as representative for the company. Rey's mother worked at home, as a seamstress doing piecework, as an Avon salesperson, and as a builder of fishing rods. Rey's early childhood was spent in Miami's Cuban American enclave, and as other members of the family joined the original exiles, they settled into a community that kept their Cuban culture alive, though transplanted to the United States.

When Rey was seven years old, his father accepted a job teaching Spanish at Northern Cambria High School and moved the family to Barnesboro, Pennsylvania (population 2,500). Adjusting to this new life wasn't easy, as the family's English wasn't yet fluent, and they were the only Cuban family in town. Rey endured some harassment from town locals because he spoke English haltingly and didn't look as though he could fit into the white, American mainstream that defined Barnesboro. Barnesboro lacked a Latin American community; hence, the Rey family was alone in an American culture they barely understood. The closest and only Cubans the family knew in this area were the friends who had helped them to settle in Barnesboro, who taught at Indiana University of Pennsylvania and lived an hour away. Rey assimilated to American culture as quickly as he could, and he describes growing up in Barnesboro as living in a small, rural, coal-mining town of 5,000 residents and two traffic lights" by the time he was an adolescent. He remembers that "in front of the house was a large mound of leftover dirt from an old coal mine, and behind the house was a forested hill, where we hunted, slept out, and ran up and over on the way to the town swimming pool." As he recalls it, it was like "a scene right out of Michael Cimino's *The Deer Hunter*, which was filmed in 1978."

It was in 1978 that Rey received an appointment to West Point Military Academy, which he left with an honorable discharge to study biology at Indiana University of Pennsylvania. Rey had joined West Point after being invited as a result of his accomplishments as a scholar and as a football player, but oceanography appealed to him more than a military career, and he sought and received the honorable discharge that enabled him to pursue his interest in science. Although he had always been interested in drawing and copying images, Rey had not considered a career as an artist until he took some art courses and was encouraged by Professor Paul Ben-Zvi and Professor Vaughn Clay to pursue art as a course of study. While in college, Rey took different jobs each summer along the Jersey Shore. With hindsight, Rey's current series is the natural outgrowth of his diverse interests in marine biology, oceanography, landscape, fishing, and art.

In 1980–1981, Rey moved to the Pittsburgh area, where after attending classes for a year at the Visual Communication Program at the Art Institute of Pittsburgh, he eventually received a BFA in drawing and painting from Indiana University of Pennsylvania. During this period, he worked as a darkroom technician and messenger for Focal Point Photography, while he studied the Carnegie Museum of Art and Natural History's collection. After graduation, Rey moved to Boston, where he worked briefly doing cutting and pasting for a design firm and created illustrations for the *Christian Science Monito*r.

Soon thereafter, Rey moved to Miami, where he lived with his aunt and uncle and where he worked for Christo on the "Surrounded Islands Project." Rey became involved with this project after he observed some of the work that had been started by Christo's group, while drawing from hotel rooftops. After doing a little research, he found that the headquarters for the project was located on Pelican Island, and, after interviewing, he was hired. He worked full time with Christo and Jeanne Claude in an international community of artists and nonartists that made him realize the potential for working as an artist. On a personal level, living in Miami connected Rey once more to his Cuban culture, with which he had only sporadic contact during summer visits, after his family moved to Barnesboro.

In 1984, Rey moved to Rochester, New York, in what was his first move to the general area of Western New York State, where he now lives. In Rochester, he lived on South Goodman Street and worked for Light Impressions and for Lichtenstein Marketing Communications. A year later, he began graduate study at the University of Buffalo and received his MFA in 1987.

Soon after he completed his studies, Rey traveled throughout Spain and Morocco before returning to Buffalo, where he taught Spanish at an inner-city school. Travel in Spain meant that he was able to see many of the works he had studied as he explored the home culture for Cuba's Hispanic population. The trip was professional and personal, as Rey's ancestors had come from Spain to Cuba from Santander, Escalante (near Santander), and the Canary Islands, hence, this trip enabled him to return to his family's home country and to explore his family's primary culture, so closely linked to Spain. On this trip, Rey visited Escalante (near Santander), in 2007, but not the Canary Islands, places to which he could trace his family's origin and which were especially meaningful to him.

By 1985, Rey had moved twenty times, each time making new connections and friends and adapting to the local culture of each place that became a temporary home. His frequent moves and trips in between relocations created increasing numbers of memories that he felt needed organization so that he could begin to understand the trajectory of his life. From his desire to map his life in a way that could produce order out of seeming chaos, Rey began his first two significant, coterminous, distinct, yet connected series: *Autogeographical* and *Floating*, on which he worked from 1985 to 1987. The *Autogeographical Series*, which incorporated drawings of experiences Rey had while in graduate school, focused on places the artist had known and lived in, one example being *Holy Angels Church and Chair* (fig. 1), a record of a church in the Lower West Side of Buffalo on Porter Avenue. The *Floating* series connects to a series of dreams that Rey had for a number of years, where he floated over the rooftops and landscapes of locations where he had lived: "The higher I floated, the easier it was to make sense of all the locations where I had lived—over these floating images, I incorporated the drawing and painting of other memories." Rey tried to capture the ephemeral and transcendent evanescence of these dreams in works such as *Transitions* (fig. 2). The floating and suggestive forms of this work create a visual effect comparable to changes in dream sequences, and are evocative of how memories of events past pass through our minds.

Boston was once again Rey's home when he moved there, in 1988, to teach at Lincoln Sudbury High School, the Education Department of the Museum of Fine Arts, the Art Institute of Boston, and the New England School of Art and Design. Simultaneously, Rey started taking art history classes at Harvard University, and he traveled to Mexico: Isla de Mujéres, Valladolid, and Chichen Itza. This year also marked Rey's first solo exhibition at the New York City Museum of Contemporary Hispanic Art (MOCHA).

At this point, he began work on the *Black Lace* and *Nuptial* series, which began in1987 and continued until 1989.[5] These two intertwined series were early explorations of spirituality, eroticism, and marriage. Rey initiated the *Black Lace* series with the goal of capturing the fascination that Catholic ritual and the lives of the saints exerted on his imagination. Intermixed with the imagery of Roman Catholicism were references to the "Orishas," or deities, of Santería, Cuba's version of the syncretism that exists in Latin America between African religions and Catholicism. Santería is a syncretic religion, in which the gods and goddesses of Africa were given new names and identities by the slaves brought to work Cuba's plantations. The new names were protective, as slaves were forbidden to practice their own religious traditions and were forced to accept Catholicism. Gender slippage was also a factor in the concealment of the Orisha's identities when they later were renamed after Catholic saints. Thus did Chango, a chief and male deity, become St. Barbara, as Chango's warrior aspect was represented by St. Barbara's attribute—the sword. Hidden within the matrix of the Catholic cult of the Saints, the Orishas continued to be worshiped by Cubans, whose families preserved the African traditions within European Christianity. Santería is a cultural marker for Cubans, who know that both traditions coexist in Cuba and among exiled Cubans, and its blend of African and

Cuban resonates especially with Cuban Americans, whose families were considered to be of the same mixed ancestry. For Rey, Santería is another marker of his Cuban and family identity.

Rey's interest in ritual and in the use of veils, worn by women in churches as a sign of ritual dress and, in intimate settings, for the purpose of seduction, caused him to employ the shapes and forms of black lace in the *Black Lace* series, seen in *Black Lace Series: Fertility* (fig. 3). Gold was equally important, as the precious metal of which liturgical vestments are made and with which statues of saints were gilded. In *Post-Nuptial Gold: Time*, gold is used to indicate the precious quality of this metal and its association to church ritual and to marriage as a rite of the Catholic Church.

These two series flowed into another, *Binary Forms* (1988–1992), which addressed the same issues as the previous series while becoming more focused on personal themes after Rey married Janeil Cam Strong in 1989.[6] Rey had met Janeil, who grew up in Gloucester, Massachusetts, while he was living in Boston. *Binary Forms* was intended to incorporate references to a number of concepts and motifs: Rey's marriage to Janeil; the religious context of marriage; the juncture of spirituality and eroticism; the overlap of present and past found in memory; and the links between memory and spirituality that Rey sought to clarify through the abstract forms he employed in this series.

Rey and Janeil married in the same year that Rey accepted a position as an assistant professor of art at the State University of New York at Fredonia. With Janeil, Rey made a home in Western New York State and they explored the region to which they had moved, even as they traveled to Isle de Sainte, St. Kitts, Antigua, and Guadalupe in1989, and then to Italy in 1990 to see Rome, Florence, Capri, Sorrento, Venice, and Ferrara. In 1991, Rey worked with Christo again, as a crew captain on the *Umbrellas* project in Tejón Pass, California, after which he returned to Mexico. These early trips, the local and the international, began a pattern of life and travel for Rey that continues, as he is always in motion, regionally, nationally, and internationally.

The exploration of the region around Fredonia in which Rey and Janeil engaged after their arrival in the area led to two series of interlocking significance for Rey: *Madonnas of Western New York* (1991–1993)[7] and *Madonnas in Time*

(1993–1995).[8] In the first series, Rey built small, open-backed wooden boxes, on the front of which he painted small images of buildings, statues, monuments, or markers that represented cultural icons for Western New York State, an example of which is the Niagara Mohawk plant (fig. 5). Rey's intention in this series was straightforward: he wanted to create a record of the sights and places that grounded communal identity in the area where he had made his home. Because he connected culture to spirituality, he rendered the selected regional sites into the equivalent of votive images. The painted scenes are reminiscent of ex-voto offerings, where recipients of miracles rendered an image of gratitude to either a saint or God as an offering. Such images are part of Mediterranean and Latin American culture, and they were a means for Rey to link his Cuban cultural identity with his new home.

The *Madonnas of Western New York* series brought about an important stylistic change for Rey, as he moved from a predominantly abstract style to one of realism. He so changed because he wanted the content of his images to be clear and accessible to the spectator. His abstract paintings emphasized emotion and spirituality, but by being abstract, they sacrificed clarity to personal expression. In this new series, Rey wanted to make sure that the content and symbols were defined and recognizable. Because the exploration of his new identity, as someone who lived in Western New York State, was based on visual markers that needed to be recognized, Rey's choice of realism was necessary to convey the intention of this sequence of works. To this end, he developed an iconographic and symbolic system that incorporated local monuments with evocative relocations of these objects into the sites of his past life.

Paradoxically, the more that Rey and Janeil explored their locale, the more Rey's thoughts turned toward Cuba, and by 1993, he was working on his next series, *Madonnas in Time* (1993–1995). In this group of works, Rey continued to create the same type of boxes he had employed in the previous series, but the images now combined the abstract shapes from *Binary Forms* with painted scenes the backgrounds of which were copied from old landscape photographs of Cuba from the 1910s and 1920s. The old photographs were copied in paint and painted in black-and-white; in circles or ovals in the skies of these landscape views, Rey painted, in color, images of various monuments and buildings of Western New York State, as seen in *Madonnas in Time: Viñales* (fig. 6). Some of these monuments were iconic, while others were meant to be more reflective of the everyday, even mundane life of the area: according to Rey, "I wanted to bring spirituality to everyday experiences and, by so doing, to bring spirituality into my own life." The black-and-white represented the unreal—that which Rey had not experienced—and these were images in which nostalgia played an important role. The combination of visual registers was also Rey's way of connecting to both Western New York and Cuba; thus, the series combined his actual and his inaccessible homes. With the *Madonnas in Time*, Rey began a graphic and focused exploration of his Cuban identity that would continue until the year 2000, when he would completely change his thematic concerns to those he now pursues.

The images of Cuba's landscape, chosen because they were apolitical and free of the controversies that are part of Cuban twentieth-century history, caused Rey to actively question what it meant to be Cuban and what it meant to him that he did not have any memories of his birth country. Cuba, for Rey, was Miami, and the years he had spent in Miami with his Cuban relatives—the only place in his life where he was surrounded by Cubans and where he could become part of a Latino community. His knowledge of Cuba was filtered through the family stories that his parents, aunts, and uncles told, and his relationship with Cuba was secondhand, but also primary when it came to the consumption of the foods that Cubans consider their national foods. Hence, Rey decided that in order to explore his Cuban identity, he needed to start by painting monumental images of the foods that meant "Cuba" to him, and he thus embarked on his *Icon* series from 1993 to1995, simultaneously with his *Madonnas in Time*.[9]

Reminiscent in size and concept to Andy Warhol's *Campbell's Soup Cans*, Rey rendered individual Cuban foods as monumental single images that, so depicted, became inescapable signifiers of identity. The large size of these works was important, because by increasing their size Rey transformed mundane foods into icons that symbolize a culture. *Icon Series: Ancel Guava Paste* (fig. 7) provides a good example: the bar of Ancel guava paste is a staple in Cuban homes and a reminder, to Rey, of his father's and uncle's time spent working for Ancel in Miami. Every Cuban who sees Rey's monumental bar of guava immediately imagines the taste of the sticky and sweet tropical fruit paste that reminds them of home, if they have personal memories of Cuba. For those who lack such memories, the same image is a metonymic substitute for memory and the sign for home and Cuba, which remain the set associations.

The years between 1992 and 1996 were ones in which Rey was moving ahead with his career while engaged in the creation of the his succeeding series of works. In 1992, he was promoted to Associate Professor at State University of New York at Fredonia and awarded tenure. Some of his paintings became part of the collections of the Albright-Knox Museum, the Brooklyn Museum, and the Bronx Museum of Art. In 1994, he received the William T. Hagan Young Scholar/Artist Award from SUNY, Fredonia, for distinguished scholarly and creative activity, and the Minority Visiting Scholar Award from Central Missouri State University. In 1996, he was promoted to Professor of Painting. Simultaneously, his parents retired to Miami/Perrine, and he and Janeil began a series of annual visits

to see them. In the same year, Rey accepted an additional position as the director/curator of the Chautauqua Center of the Visual Arts at the Chautauqua Institution in Chautauqua, New York. Rey's travels continued and he returned to Europe and to Mexico, where he exhibited at the Nina Menocal Gallery in Mexico City.

At this point, Rey was acknowledged as an international Cuban American artist of distinction within the contemporary art world centered on Latin American and Latino artists. From his home base in Fredonia and his professional affiliation with SUNY Fredonia, Rey reached out to become part of the global landscape of contemporary artists known for their work on issues of identity, cultural multiplicity, and the exploration of diverse ethnicity. He had established himself in this world as an artist of significant status, represented and exhibited by the Galería Emilio Navarro in Madrid, Spain, and Miami, Florida. Yet, Rey never rested; he continued to be productive, and the recent emphasis he was placing on his Cuban identity manifested in new series of works.

The monumental scale of the *Icon* series emboldened Rey to give larger form to his renditions of old photographs of Cuba's landscape, and in 1996 he began to work on the *Appropriated Memories* series (1996–1997), of which *Appropriated Memories: Viñales, Cuba* (fig. 8) is an example.[10] In *Appropriated Memories*, Rey concentrated on Cuba as the geography and topography of an island (instead of on its history, people, and cities) and began to paint Cuban landscapes based on old black-and-white photographs. By painting the land, Rey avoided Cuban politics, and he pursued his visual exploration of a Cuba he had never seen, filtered through time and the medium of photography. Rey also felt more connected to Cuba as he painted its appearance, which was an act of creation, and he felt connected to other Cuban painters who had painted the same or similar landscapes. In solving the aesthetic and technical issues created by these paintings, Rey felt that he walked the same artistic and conceptual territory with Cuban artists who had gone before him and who had faced the same challenges. Yet, even though these landscapes were emotionally charged for Rey, he maintained a distance by not engaging with current events in Cuba or with recent Cuban history.

In 1980, Rey's grandmother, Mercedes Rey, left Cuba in a raft that capsized, and she was among those who drowned during this event. Enrique Rey, Rey's grandfather, died in 1986. These two deaths meant that the knowledge his grandparents had about the family would remain unknown to the rest of the family, and Rey began to think about what else he would not learn about his family and his personal history. The neutrality of the landscapes of *Appropriated Memories* began to give way, however, after these family deaths, which caused Rey to begin work on two series devoted to the rafters or *balseros* who risk their lives escaping Cuba, hoping for a better and freer life in the United States. Thus, between 1996 and 1999 Rey created *Las Balsas (The Rafts)*, *Las Balsas (The Rafts) Constructions* and *Las Balsas (The Rafts) Artifacts*.[11]

While Rey did not immediately respond artistically to the deaths of his grandparents, his grandmother's death on a raft was eventually processed into the *Las Balsas* series, comprising Rey's contribution to a genre reflective of contemporary exile experience. Cubans are not the only group that employs rafts to escape to freedom, as Vietnamese, Laotian, and Haitian refugees also use them. These international refugees are known to all through images that are broadcast in news reports and photographed in newspapers and magazines. Although Rey's *Las Balsas* series is specifically Cuban, it also references international experience and reality. Despite the personal element in the *Balsas*, Rey's goal was to create a body of work that could speak about all groups who have had the courage to launch themselves into the unknown in an act of defiance and a search for a better life. In the series and subseries, such as the *Artifacts* series featuring the objects found in the abandoned *balsas*, Rey sought to create works that would bring the spectator to confront the reality of the people who made and traveled in the rafts. His three-dimensional *balsas* and his paintings of these rafts evoke the human presence and experience without particularizing that experience with individual representation. Who arrived or did not arrive in the rafts is not enunciated, but is left to the imagination of the spectator, who must complete the image by visualizing individuals and their stories. By requiring this empathetic response, Rey spurs spectators to engage deeply with his images as they think about the passages of their ancestors responsible for their existence right up until they moment that they stand in front of Rey's works.

While for every Cuban the image of the Cuban *balseros* is a marker of identity, for those who have been—or whose relatives and/or friends have been—on these rafts and survived, the reality of the *balsas* takes on a different, more urgent and immediate meaning. Rey began the *Balsas* series after he made a trip to Stock Island, in 1996, to conduct research at the Cuban Refugee Center, now called the Transit Center for Cuban Refugees. While there, he saw some of the preserved rafts that had been abandoned by *balseros* and this became the catalyst for all of the *Las Balsas* series. With the image of the actual rafts embedded in his mind and connected to his grandmother's death, Rey was able to move to give his emotions and research visual form and thus the series began.

The *Balsas* series were two- and three-dimensional, with some rafts being sculpted and others painted. For paintings such as *Balsas II* (fig. 9), Rey painted the *balsa* images on wooden panels suspended inside of black, opened boxes; as with most actual *balsas*, the panels and boxes were made from discarded, found wood. The *Balsas Constructions* were small sculptures that Rey displayed on high pedestals made out of clay, wire, and flour. The *Balsas Artifacts* series were close-up explorations of the objects found inside the rafts, and in *Las Balsas (The Rafts) Artifacts: Caridad del Cobre* (fig. 10), Rey represented a statue of the patroness of Cuba, the Virgin of Cobre, that had been brought in a raft as a prayer for safe deliverance.

The year 1998 was an eventful year for Rey: his daughter, Graciela, was born; he returned to Cuba with his mother; he founded the Buffalo-area Sportfishing and Aquatic Resource Educational Programming (SAREP) Youth Fly Fishing Program, in which he works with inner-city and local youths to develop their connections to nature; and he was selected to the New York Foundation for the Arts' Advisory Board. His connections to his birth country of Cuba, as well as his relationships with his local community, with the artist community of his home state, and with his growing family, all deepened in a year that changed his life and gave it new directions.

In 1999, a stumbling block occurred when Rey was diagnosed with chronic migraine, even as he moved to a new home in Fredonia, set up a new studio, and began working on his first sixteen millimeter film, *Seeing in the Dark*. The

illness, which was not immediately diagnosed and which greatly incapacitated him for the better part of a year, made him reevaluate his life and work. The aftermath of his first Cuban trip began to resonate, and he slowly understood that his search for identity had been a romanticized search for a past that had never existed. Rey felt that he needed to clear his life and find a way to make art that was more integrated into who he was, instead of who he might have been had he not been brought to the United States by his parents.

Even as he began to understand that he needed to move in new directions, he completed the last of his directly Cuban series, *Cuban Portraits* (1998–1999). Inspired by the work of the Mexican portrait painter, Hermenegildo Bustos (1832–1907), Rey began the series prior to his trip to Cuba.[12] His goal was to create a record of the faces and personalities of individual Cubans in exile and on the island. Whereas Rey's previous work had been a focused exploration of his internal world, in the *Cuban Portraits*, he turned his attention outward as he created a record of the Cuban people in and outside Cuba. Rey no longer painted memories or meditative explorations of possible and past lives, and the visceral immediacy of the *Cuban Portraits* is evident in the rendered presence of the individuals Rey encountered in the United States and on his first trip to Cuba. Suddenly, Cubans and Rey's Cuban identity were real, grippingly realized, and alive.

In the Cuban part of this series, Rey wanted to represent those Cubans who had endured and survived the hardship of being Cuban in the aftermath of Castro's Revolution. Both *Cuban Portraits: Hilda, Agramonte, Cuba* (fig. 11) and *Cuban Portrait Series: Alberto, Agramonte, Cuba* (fig. 12) belong to the Cuban part of this series, and they each reflect Rey's goal. Hilda is Afro-Cuban. She is simply dressed and she gazes out of the frame at us with an expression of resigned strength that speaks of a lifetime of hard work and struggle. No island paradise for her, says the set of her lips, the deep furrows on her face, and the dark shadows under her eyes. Alberto of Agramonte, a mechanic, is Rey's name's alter ego, who has lived the life Rey might have experienced if he had remained in Cuba. His expression is very similar to that of Hilda, despite the difference in their gender, race, and age. Coming from a family of mixed ethnicity, each of these portraits addresses part of Rey's

family identity, as his family incorporated Cuba's diverse population among its members. The Cuban Alberto and Hilda are resigned and resolved to continue to endure what life brings. While not overtly political, these portraits summarize what Rey learned about contemporary Cuba— that the island was not a tropical cruise, but was a place where life was difficult, resources were few, and life was a constant search for the most basic necessities.

While in Cuba, Rey visited his family. In pre-Castro Cuba, Rey's family wasn't rich, or highly placed in society, influential, or powerful. They were country people, who worked hard for their modest lives. In Castro's Cuba, Rey's relatives were not members of the Communist Party, so they did not have access to superior food, material goods, or housing. Neither did they work in the tourist business, where foreign currency and black-market goods could ease their life. Rey's family were average Cubans, still trying to make their living from agriculture, assorted jobs, and the controlled amounts of foods and goods that the government doled out to the general population. Rey understood when he returned that Cuba was nothing like the nostalgic image he had formed from old photographs, but that it was a place where people struggled every day for material goods that even many underprivileged Americans assume will be readily available to them. As a result of his experiential knowledge of Cuba, Rey understood when he returned, that his previous search for Cuba had reached an end and he needed to explore new venues for his work.

To purge himself of the Cuba series, Rey launched into *Studio Retablos* (1998–1999), a series of works in which he painted new paintings onto old, discarded works by anonymous artists.[13] This series represented a transition that enabled Rey to sort through past experiences unrelated to past series, and to explore new artistic horizons. Rey found the old paintings in flea markets and antique shops for a few dollars. Their faded appearance appealed to him, and on the surfaces of these old pictures, he painted brightly colored scenes that related to his life and to the environment in which he lived. Characteristic of this work is *Studio Retablos: Mexican Figure* (fig. 13). The paintings were sanded down and stained to show a faded impression of their original state, partially erasing their previous creator, but not entirely: they still maintain a connection to the past artists. The point of the new work was to expunge the imagery

of the old work from his system and from future related directions; he succeeded in achieving this goal, because at the end of the *Studio Retablos*, Rey was clearheaded, freed from his past work, and ready to move in a new direction.

As the century turned, Rey's life was changed by a series of events that included the birth of his son, Diego (2001); his being awarded the Kasling Lecturer Award for distinguished creative and scholarly activity (2001); travel to Montana, Wyoming, Idaho, Yellowstone Park, Tucson, Sedona, and the Grand Canyon; a second trip to Cuba with *Fly and Fish Magazine* (2002); acceptance as an Orvis-Endorsed Guide (2002); travel to Iceland; a Chancellor's Award for Excellence (2003); travel to England and Wales; a return trip to Iceland; a promotion to State University of New York Distinguished Professor; and additional travel to Alaska, Spain, and the Bahamas. In 2000, just before the birth of his son, Rey began his new artistic direction with *Trout Encounters*, a series that focused attention on his interest in fishing, biology, ecology, and environmental science, and that brought him back to his American childhood in Pennsylvania, where he spent hours exploring the woods and streams near his home.[14]

Part of what made Rey understand that he needed a new direction for his work was the juxtaposition of his visit to Agramonte, in 1998, with his mother—who was seeing Cuba again after thirty-five years of exile—with the coincidence of the birth of his daughter, Graciela. These events biologically linked the past to the present and the future in a way that caused Rey to reconsider his previous ideas about Cuba, about family, and about his identity or identities. The trip to Cuba gave Rey concrete and actual form for the stories he had always heard and the faded photographs through which he had studied his native country. Now, Rey had his own memories of Cuba and his own observations about the island, and he understood that his family's past in Cuba was gone, even as that past was juxtaposed with the future of his family in the United States as represented by his daughter.

The year 1999, when Rey began to suffer from recurring migraines, was a watershed moment for him, and as the debilitating migraines recurred, the illness shook his confidence, interfering with his ability to physically continue his work and life as he was accustomed to doing. Rey emerged from this prolonged stage of illness affected by the experience, yet committed to continuing to link the diverse parts of his life into a whole. The renewal of his health meant a renewal of his commitment to his life and to his work, and in the year 2000, Rey brought together aspects of his life and work that he had not yet explored in the series *Trout Encounters*, where he began to incorporate his long-standing pursuit of trout fishing, from which he had begun, in 1998, the SAREP Youth Fly Fishing Program for inner-city youths in Dunkirk, New York. Rey had seen this program as a way to connect troubled young people with nature and with an opportunity for skilled, yet meditative, activity that could produce a sense of accomplishment and connection for those who felt otherwise disconnected from their environment and from society on the whole. At a time when illness severed Rey's sense of self and identity, his ability to empathize with those who were dispossessed of culture and place meant that as he recovered, he turned to the occupation he had identified as being restorative and that could bring a renewed sense of purpose to his life. The new series, which accomplished Rey's new goals, was *Trout Encounters*.

In 2000, Rey began an almost microscopic scrutiny of the trout for which he fished, and he began to paint portraits of trout in the various stages of their life cycle in the streams that he fished. For Rey, it was important to re-create the proportions, color, and texture of trout, identifying the specific species found in a specific place. Each native species looks different and is reflective of the body of water in which the trout live. Hence, the trout portraits are metonymic of their environments—their streams, the topography of these streams, and the larger landscape through which these streams flow. Yet, while a hyperrealistic style manifested in these trout "portraits," there was also an attempt to capture the identity of the fish as an animal and as a sentient being. The meditative regard that Rey had for the act of fishing, and the manner in which he responded to the actualization of the trout from the streams in which he fished, meant that he functioned as the recorder of their existence and experience. As with his other work, centered on identity, Rey's work with *Trout Encounters* began to transform into an enactment of the essential nature of the trout he preserved in the paintings where the trout swam, leapt, lived, and died in their natural environments.

Identity studies turned outward, as Rey used his experience as a participant and observer to bring the spectator into the private world of the experience of fishing and of fish and to the natural world that he could share through sight. In so doing, he took the first step toward becoming an advocate for these silent environments that are vulnerable to destruction, as the contemporary world expands its destruction of the natural environment. In making us think about the degradation of the natural habitat for fish and other animals, Rey makes us think about the consequences of this loss for us because we too are becoming an endangered species, as we pollute our world.

Trout Encounters was the original and regional/local version of the later series *Biological Regionalism*, which would take Rey on a national and international exploration of the connections between trout and the landscape the trout inhabit. In both series, Rey seeks to represent the biological reality of his thematic subjects juxtaposed with an aesthetic exploration of the symmetries, proportions, and colors of the depicted fauna and flora. Through *Trout Encounters: Brown Trout, Hosmer Creek, Sardinia, New York, USA* (fig. 14), Rey addresses his early interest in nature and science and his later interest in oceanography. *Trout Encounters* is also a series grounded in the transitional phase, where Rey, as a child and adolescent, became more American than Cuban, as he assimilated to the American culture of Barnesboro, Pennsylvania. *Trout Encounters*, therefore, indicates a change of interest on Rey's part from exploring Cuban culture to an exploration of his American identity and his personal interests prior to the decision he made to become an artist instead of a scientist. In effect, *Trout Encounters* is Rey's way of knitting his multiple identities together into a new pattern of visual representation that expresses who he is beyond his Cuban identity. Viewed as such, *Trout Encounters* appears to be a series toward which Rey was inexorably moving, as it incorporates diverse aspects of his interests and his life.

In 2004, *Trout Encounters* morphed into another series titled *Biological Regionalism*.[15] As a series, *Biological Regionalism* was simultaneously more specifically targeted and more universally comprehensive; in this series Rey employs the images of *Biological Regionalism* to address the current appearance and ecological condition of individual waterways. His paintings, videos, installations, and informative wall-texts are meant to bring these bodies of water and their life into the exhibition space, so that spectators can connect to the natural settings through their participatory encounter with Rey's work.

Each part of *Biological Regionalism* reflects the locale where Rey does his research and where he explores the local culture of which specific natural and biological forms are a formative element. Rey once traveled to urban centers in search of insight about his Cuban identity, and he now travels to multiple natural sites, searching for the connections that exist between all natural environments and the peoples who live near and far from nature. In this series, Rey found a way to combine all of his interests and to explore all sides of his multiple identities. As can be seen in figs. 15 through 20, Rey's paintings reflect his travel to Cuba, Montana, Iceland, and Alaska, these being a tiny sample of the wide range of *Biological Regionalism*.[16]

While *Trout Encounters* and *Biological Regionalism* are two of the series that ground Rey in Western New York State, they also connect to his past, to his interest in global culture and environments, to his birth in Cuba, and to his identity as a Cuban-born American. For Rey, Western New York State represents his home base, where he established his married life with Janeil and where his children Graciela and Diego were born. Rey's exploration of the area's natural resources, then, is an extension of his recognition that he has a home in Western New York State and an identity as an American angler developed in the decades he has spent in the region.

Yet, the tradition of fishing that has localized his life and his work has definite and overt links to his Cuban past, as fishing for food and sport is also a marker of Cuban identity. Rey's trips to Cuba enabled him to fish in Cuba and to connect his experience as a Western New York State angler to his Cuban past through this activity. Therefore, when Rey paints trout and other types of fish, some of which also swim in Cuban waters, he is creating a network of associations that is as fluid and changeable as his hyphenated identities as a Cuban and an American can be when Rey moves from his Cuban family to his American life. The fish he paints are both form and metaphor for home, for travel, and for his dual identity, symbolized by the fish's movement across zones and spheres of existence.

Rey's work, throughout his life, has been about memory, travel, relocations, finding a home, and finding the spiritual in the everyday. This duality, based on his self-perception as a Cuban American, extends to the way in which Rey practices fishing: as an everyday activity that is part skill, part sport, and part hunt, but one that also involves an inherent, meditative spirituality. This quality has long been associated with fly fishing, at the very least since the first publication of Isaak Walton's *The Compleat Angler* in 1653; to this day, Walton's book maintains its iconic status among fishers, and at over six hundred editions is the third-most published book in the English language, behind only the Bible and Shakespeare.

Rey's artistic mission has always been to create intellectually accessible and visually captivating images that evoke the act of memory and remembrance, and through which the spectator can travel in place and time. This is especially strong in his images of Cuba's landscapes and people, and particularly true of the landscapes, which are large paintings that extend the spectator's visual field into a participatory experience. In the *Icon* series about Cuban food, there is found the precedent for the presentation of the iconic trout, reified on a monumental scale in a manner comparable to that which Rey employed for the bars of guava and pastries that define his Cuban identity. The paintings of trout and their landscapes are about Rey's present life and the realities of that life.

Today, Rey has joined to his other identities, his involvement with his community and his activism about environmental issues, which includes working with young people teaching them about fishing and ecological concerns. He is an artist, a professor, and an involved member of his community, who works with young people teaching them about fishing and ecological issues. He is also an Orvis fly-fishing guide and keenly aware of the scientific issues that are part of his interest in fish and the environment. His work as an artist and a professor take him outside, as he works outdoors and requires his students to also work outdoors in traditional plein air painting techniques. It is from these multiple roles and from the manner in which Rey connects his life to his work that each of Rey's series came into existence.

As the process of exploration of New York State that began with the *Madonnas of Western New York* continued with *Trout Encounters* and *Biological Regionalism*, the work created a focus for engagement with the people who surround Rey in Western New York State. Simultaneously, Rey expanded his engagement with his community to connect to other regions in the United States and in other countries. This type of engagement extends even farther as he creates site-specific work around the country and the world, most recently at the Masur Museum of Art in Monroe, Louisiana, as is discussed in Benjamin Hickey's and Sandra Firmin's essays in this book. There is an inherent reciprocal process at work between life and art that is important for understanding what these site-specific exhibitions represent for the artist and for the spectator, who sees Rey's world and perceives this world from the perspective of the experience of the fish Rey paints.

To a degree, the change in subject represented by *Trout Encounters* and/ or *Biological Regionalism* was a deliberate attempt on Rey's part to break with the past and with what he considered an overly nostalgic introspection and retrospection about his past. The trout represent a dynamic present that incorporates Rey's long-standing interest in biology and science with his career as a visual artist, thereby joining two previously separate aspects of his personal identity.

The search for identity through the representation of trout and their environments has followed a parallel process to those of earlier series by taking Rey from his home in Western New York State to other places and countries, most recently to Italy, where Rey fished at the headwaters of the Tiber. For Rey, the process of travel, research, and exploration of new places and cultures is more important than bringing the series to a close or an artificially defined end. As he puts it, "The work in its entirety allows me to extend the outer boundaries of my aesthetic and intellectual knowledge, and therefore creates a more fulfilling existence."

Thus, the trout paintings became a new topos and a new format that began with local specificity and quickly moved to a global perspective that incorporated his earlier interests in identity and community. The change, however, though continuous with his earlier work and interests, is not immediately perceptible as such. Hence, when Rey moved from an overt exploration of his identity and the markers of his life as a Cuban American, the initial reception of his new work was less than enthusiastic. At first, some of the venues that had welcomed him previously would not exhibit the new work. The series lacked an obvious political edge, although it is undeniably political in intention and impact. The works were considered by some to be too straightforward and naturalistic, and because they were paintings of fish, they were perceived as being too narrow in scope to attract a general audience.

Yet Rey persevered, and he began to develop a circle of interested spectators and curators who appreciated his presentation of local wildlife and landscapes. His big break came from Johanna Drucker, at the University of Virginia, who didn't see a disconnection between Rey's earlier and current work, and who saw the potential for the series thought to be too tame and traditional by other curators. Drucker's insightful and groundbreaking essay on Rey's fish paintings opened up the territory within which Rey's trout could be critically assessed. Drucker's essay, and essays on these series by others, are discussed in this book in Lynette M. F. Bosch's piece, "Trout as Form and Symbol."[17] Since art museums and galleries were not interested in exhibiting this work, Rey began exhibiting in alternative spaces. Because he could no longer be pigeonholed as a Latino artist, Rey found a new identity as an American artist, fully exploring the American side of his identity through this new vein of transformation of the specific into the universal. In so doing,

Rey found a new identity for himself and for his work, and this metamorphosis is inscribed and inherent within the message and meaning of *Trout Encounters* and *Biological Regionalism.*

With these two series, Rey also gained a new definition of the purpose of his work when he found that people who were not familiar with the art world or with contemporary art could be reached in a way that was new to him. Rey found a new audience for his writings and artwork in the world of fly-fishing and travel literature. Using his experience as an immigrant who had learned at a young age how to open new doors and to overcome his fear of the unknown, Rey transformed himself through his American work and his Cuban exile experience, crossing into different spheres of interest and adding new hyphens to his identity.

Consequently, his art brought new meaning and context to his life, and these changes enabled him to look at his work—past and present—from a new perspective. In short, in painting trout, Rey found a whole new life as an American artist based in Western New York State, from which he could reach out to the rest of the world. In establishing new connections, Rey fully realized the intentions and desires that were the catalyst for his first work: to understand the world and his place in it, and to enable his experience to connect him to other people, so that they in turn could relate their lives to those of one another.

The exhibition at the Burchfield Penney is the point of connection for Rey and his audience, because the Burchfield Penney is an area museum able to create links to and among all the intersections of Rey's life, even as it enables such connections to expand globally. Through this book, Rey can engage the spectator in a participatory experience, where the spectator is invited to come along on Rey's fishing expeditions and share in his thoughts and observations about his process as an angler and an artist. Thus, while the Burchfield Penney exhibition is transient, the book will remain to document Rey's progress and his engagement with his world as an artist with a multi-faceted perspective on contemporary life that is the result of the specific circumstances of his historical place in twentieth- and twenty-first-century history.

Rey remains the same person, but since he began to paint trout in the year 2000, he has gained multiple new perspectives and different interests, and has reached a broader audience than he would have if he had not taken the chance to change his work and life. The new subjects enable Rey to explore all of his interests and to read widely about biology, angling, history, contemporary art, the history of art, environmental studies, and local and global politics as he explores new places. These forms of knowledge, which initially can seem to be disconnected, all converge in the multiple centers of his interest in fish and their environments. For Rey, the increase in communication with new audiences plays a part in his desire to continue the series, because the work is accessible to everyone and has something to say to all who see it. This work relates to contemporary concerns about ecology, preservation, sustainability, and appreciation—all issues that have history and immediacy beyond art. For these issues, Rey's art is a medium of conveyance where the message is much larger than the medium, yet the vehicle for this message is particularly effective as a result of his artistic expertise and cumulative knowledge. Painting fish freed Rey from a too-tight binding of his identity, enabling him to join one of the centers of contemporary art through a redefinition of his multiple identities into a combined statement about our world, its natural resources, and their spiritual importance.

From an initial periphery as a Cuban-born artist living and working in the United States, Rey has moved into the mainstream center of current cultural concerns about our world. That he began in 2000 means that Rey was ahead of the wave of environmental art that has increased in the past decade. Rey arrived at this central place of artistic and cultural development, then, through a very personal exploration of home and self. Rey is very aware that by going outside the identity issues of his earlier work, the center grew to encompass the periphery, and his artistic and personal story became multicentric, containing multiperipheries in an ongoing exploration of new subjects and issues. The spectator of the Burchfield Penney exhibition and of Rey's other exhibitions finds that his current work is large in scale. This monumental size is deliberate and very important: it is a technical challenge for the artist and a way for the spectator to become part of the artistic vision, and Rey wanted to make work that people could not dismiss. The large size of these paintings also responds to Rey's intention to make them resonate with large-scale religious art, because these paintings also have a spiritual dimension in their connection to nature.

The large scale, moreover, is crucial for understanding the work, because the size of each painting creates fascination, immersion, and absorption. Through the monumentality of the paintings, the spectator plunges into the depicted worlds, and the plunge moves the spectator from the mundane to the sublime regions of mind and experience. Size matters, because it enables absorbed communication with the presented fish—in their world, on their terms, as observed and recorded by the artist, who brings them to those participating in their display. Large paintings cannot be overlooked, and Rey is adamant about making sure that his message is not overlooked. Size is important because size generates fascination, and it enables the absorption of the spectator into the subject represented: the plunge into the mundane. The more something may be overlooked, the more reason to paint it large, so it can't be overlooked.

Rey connects to the present public by painting fish in an aesthetic style and manner that is intentionally meant to be reminiscent of devotional art. His images are imbued with spirituality because they relate to the sublimity of nature and of life, and his intention to link the spectator to this fundamental connection informs the meditative quality and impact that these works have on those who participate in Rey's installations. Rey's images are a link between the environments he depicts and the spectator who absorbs his representations. Beginning in 2004, Rey's perspective on *Trout Encounters* and *Biological Regionalism* changed as a result of a series of events that would transform his life.

In 2004, Rey's life changed irrevocably when his sister, Mayda, died at the age of forty-seven from pancreatic cancer. A few months later, Rey's father-in-law, Neil Strong, died from lung cancer, and in 2006, Janeil was diagnosed with a first bout of breast cancer, followed by a second cancer diagnosis in 2010. These years changed Rey's life and work, as he assimilated the series of deaths and illnesses that beset his family. Rey recalls that during these years he began to collect images of dead fish, and these images eventually became the foundation for his *The Aesthetics of Death Series*, which he began in 2006.[18]

For those who are removed from their destined cultures and who live their lives in a constancy of transitions, the idea of home is always juxtaposed with what is not home, and the touchstone for being home becomes the people who displace and replace the tangible markers of origin. The real and threatened loss of those personal anchors that form the relationships that measure and define life, and that become the only real home that the exile has, rips away a part of the personal identity that has been patched together in the aftermath of this original rupture. The potential or actual loss of family, friends, and spouses has a particular type of inescapable horror for everyone, and one that resonates with the previous hole left in the life of those who have already endured and recovered from an original loss. Rey's early life had been marked by the death of his mother's brother, his grandmother, and his grandfather, as well as the present absence of his Cuban home. Now, the cycle of loss began to repeat, and the changes brought a new need to redefine Rey's identity as someone who could absorb the new realities and incorporate them into his life and accept them through his work.

Rey's response to these years of new losses was *The Aesthetics of Death* series. The recent deaths in Rey's family and his fear for his wife's health sensitized him to the need we have to confront our deepest fears as well as to extend compassion to others who also suffer. What had become an exploration of an external world in *Trout Encounters* became internalized into a passage for absorbing sorrow and facing loss. Rey's paintings of trout had always been a metaphor for life rendered into images that were intended to alert us to experiences other than our own and to give us a perception of the world from another position. In *The Aesthetics of Death*, Rey expanded his meditations of sympathy for another life form into a medium intended to alleviate sorrow. Rey accomplishes this by minutely capturing the colors of putrefaction, the texture of desiccation, the stillness that ensues when volition and movement end.

Throughout his career, Rey had turned to his work to express the events and emotions of his life, and in the aftermath of these events, he turned to his work to mourn and to address the impact that illness and death had on his life. In so doing, Rey touched on issues that are universal, as he explored his personal grief as a window into the human experience of change, loss, and passing. No longer concerned with specific issues of personal identity or even specific geographic places or biological organisms, Rey turned his attention to what binds all forms of life as he explored death in all of its aspects, from the cessation of life in a body to its decay and its eventual dissolution and reabsorption into the order of things. Thus, materiality and spirituality are inextricably joined in Rey's *The Aesthetics of Death*, in which Rey holds up the actuality of death and decay so that spectators can see that every natural process in this world is imbued with an inherent beauty, a reminder of the transcendence of existence that enables the material to connect to the spiritual. Rey's fish are a connector to his unshakeable belief that there is something greater than us and something beyond the now, and that only through death can we know the end of things and the truth of existence. Through his visual and aesthetic meditation on the subject of death that is the foundation of *The Aesthetics of Death*, Rey brings us face to face with the final question of what happens after the death that no living organism can escape. Rey does not attempt to answer that question; he simply holds up the reality of death and its aftermath, leaving the spectator to draw meaning from what he so painstakingly places before us.

Rey's career as an artist has been grounded from the beginning in his ability to think of himself as an example of many. While he uses his individual life to address the issues that are important to him, he has always assumed that he is not alone in his investigations and that others are also on the same journey. For Rey, art is a means of dialogue in which he speaks with a community of spectators in a very intimate way about things that are very important to him and to them. Rey's paintings have always been an exchange between artist and public, and as Rey continues to work on the series that have occupied him since the year 2000, he has not deviated from his original intention. The trajectory of his life and career have led him inexorably here, where he is now engaged in the logical next step on the path he began when he decided to become an artist instead of an oceanographer, both of which were intrinsically linked to the quest for discovery originally started on the streams of his boyhood.

NOTES

1. The information on Alberto Rey's personal life and his assessment of

his work and how it relates to his life is taken from a series of interviews conducted with Rey from 1999 to April 2012.

2. Rey is involved in the following community programs: SAREP Youth Fly Fishing Program, director/founder, 1998–present. The program provides biological and conservational educational to 350 students a year, along with mentoring and a vehicle through which to make college more accessible to minority and lower-income youths; Canadaway Creek Conservation Project, founder/director, 2006–present. The program organizes an annual stream clean-up and bank stabilization project; Brook Trout Restoration Project, founder/director, 2006–present. The program teaches local, middle school students how to raise brook trout from eggs, for the purpose of introducing them into a local stream. The SAREP Youth Fly Fishing Program meets biweekly, with bimonthly fishing trips. The newest initiative of which Rey is a part is the Children in the Stream Conference, which brings together educators and community leaders from around the country to teach young people about fly-fishing, as a way to relate to literature, science, social studies, art, and nature. The Burchfield Penney exhibition would be a way for Rey to connect all of these local and community activities into an interrelated series of events that would also become part of the larger community project to clean up the Scajaquada Creek's watershed—see "Artist's Statement," for a description of this body of water and the effort to reduce its pollution.

3. For a more detailed biography, see Appendix I—Alberto Rey: Biographical Timeline.

4. Of the *Autogeographical* series and *Floating* series (1985–1987) Rey wrote,

For the past several years, leading up this point, I had been trying to organize and find effective formats for which to present the memories that had been important in my life and how they had influenced how I processed thoughts and my ideas about identity. The "Autogeographical Series" incorporated those symbols of memories in layered aerial drawings of my past 'homes' in the Pennsylvania, Massachusetts, New York, Florida, Cuba, and Mexico. The 'Floating Series' reflected the dreams I had been having for years that provided a perspective on how I had arrived to that point in my life by floating above all past twenty locations where I had lived.

5. The *Black Lace* and *Nuptial* series unfolded between 1987 and 1989. As Rey recalls his goal for these series, he said,

As I investigated past cultural memories, I remembered my fascination with the romanticism of saints, the role of rituals, and the incorporation of superstitions into popular Cuban culture and the practice of the religion of *Santería*, and the Cuban version of Roman Catholicism. Gold and black lace became the two symbols that I selected to reflect the importance of religion in my past and in Cuba culture. Black lace not only incorporated an interesting set of contradictory symbols that juxtaposed religion and seduction, but the veils also allowed for their being used as a vehicle for the layering of imagery and images.

6. The *Binary Forms* series (1988–1992) incorporated marriage and religion; eroticism; memory and spirituality. Its abstract style allowed for a freedom of expression Rey wanted at this point and his symbolic vocabulary referenced gold (marriage and religion); black lace (religion and eroticism); binary forms (marriage); overlapping forms (marriage and memory). Rey explained that he used abstraction because ". . . abstraction would allow me to combine these references together, while still reflecting a minimalist aesthetic. I hoped that this approach would examine the spirituality of memory and emotion, without the restrictions of specificity of realistic imagery."

7. About the *Madonnas of Western New York* series (1991–1993), Rey said,

After moving to Western New York, my wife and I regularly came across scenes that were mundane but seemed to symbolize the culture in the area. We kept returning to these places, as though we were receiving some spiritual enlightenment from those landscapes. I was also intrigued by Mexican and Italian retables and how the artists managed to create a relationship between their everyday lives and a sense of spirituality through their art. I wanted to create my own series of work that brought this sense of spirituality into my everyday life. The work combined realistic iconography over abstraction from the "Binary Forms," as a way to link my ongoing investigations into my life and society.

8. In the *Madonnas in Time* series (1993–1995), Rey directly addressed Cuban culture and his curiosity about his native country. As he recalls, "The 'Madonnas in Time' series incorporates nostalgic black and white landscapes from Cuba, during the 1910s and 20's and uses those images as a background to color, contemporary scenes from the United States. These realistic images were placed over abstracted images from the Binary Forms Series. Each painting was a reflection of my life and my identity."

9. The *Icon* series (1993–1995) was Rey's breakthrough series in that it was with this group of works that he began a serious artistic and personal investigation of his Cuban identity. As he has stated, "I became very interested in single objects that symbolized specific themes in Hispanic culture. These large frescoesque paintings, first dealt with issues relating to culture, history, religion, gender and inscribed in the individual presentation of these against a white background, there was an indication of the alienation experienced by the exile. The series documents Cuban food as specific everyday objects that symbolize Cuban culture."

10. About the *Appropriated Memories* series (1996–97) Rey said,

After working on the Madonnas of Time Series, I really enjoyed painting landscapes of my first home and felt connected to past Cuban painters who had painted the same scenes. I wanted to concentrate on a series dedicated to the landscape as a metaphor for a culture. This particular series tries to capture the fulfillment and spirituality found in researching, finding and painting images of what are for me a lost time. These images are an abstracted past. These images had become my memory. These are nostalgic interpretations of a country without politics or individuals; the untainted aesthetic of a country that I cannot remember and probably never really existed. When I painted this landscape, it was as though I was walking on the island.

11. Here Rey describes *Las Balsas (The Rafts)* (1995) series:

While investigating the Cuban archives at the University of Miami and in the Key West Library, for the Madonnas in Time Series, I went to the Cuban Refugee Center on Stock Island. The Cuban Refugee Center provided temporary housing for many Cuban immigrants who had arrived to the keys on rafts and housed a small collection of rafts and materials used by Cubans who attempted the 90-mile crossing. I wanted to document these objects as silent remnants of great human tragedies and of a contemporary politically social condition that is part of our time. *Las Balsas (The Rafts) Constructions* (1996) were small clay and wire rafts, covered with flour to give them a feeling of timelessness. The *Las Balsas (The Rafts) Artifacts* (1998–1999) is ". . . an extension of the Balsas Series and documents the objects found in the rafts that made the crossing and also in the rafts found empty after the crossing. This is an intimate look at the objects selected by those fleeing their homeland many of whom would never return or survive.

12. Rey said of his Cuban Portraits (1998–1999),

This series was influenced by the work of a Mexican portrait painter by the name of Hermenegildo Bustos (1832–1907), whose extensive series of portraits unknowingly created a visual document of an ethnic group during a specific period in their history. While my previous bodies of work documented objects and landscapes that symbolized a culture and a country, I wanted to now dedicate my last series on Cuba to documenting some of the Cubans in Cuba and in Miami, during this period in history. The portraits try to capture the elements of the individual's character, their economic class and their ethnicity.

13. About the *Studio Retablos* series (1998–1999), Rey explained,

As I was moving from one major direction in my artwork to another different, yet related, direction, I wanted to create a series that would incorporate past influences that were not used in any series, while also cleansing myself of influences, so that I could start fresh in the next major stage of my artis-

tic career. The Studio Retablos series incorporated inspirational images that I had collected on my research trips over the past twenty-five years, but that were not directly connected to any specific series. I painted these selected, important objects over abandoned paintings by other artists I had found over the past ten years. I was intrigued by the strange collaboration and about creating something that was relative to my past work but also addressed issues of high and low art.

14. Rey said of *Trout Encounters* (2000–2004),

In 1998, I returned to Cuba for the first time in thirty-six years and saw everything quite differently upon my arrival back in the States. The void that I had been trying to fill with my artwork was partially filled, but I was ready to move on and intellectually and emotionally investigate other parts of my life and of the society to which I belonged. I finished the "Cuban Portraits" series and decided to continue to investigate Art History, Contemporary Art and society's connections to our environment, and my interest in biology and the undervalued artistic notion of regionalism and angling art.

As most of our social and economic reliance had moved to an urban setting, the connection between nature and culture in contemporary society seemed to have been lost over the last few generations. As the Hudson River School artists had brought images of the wilderness to the general public, this series would try to mend these lost connections by presenting paintings of fish and landscapes that were characteristic to a specific region and that were local to the exhibition sites. While the regions are specific, the issues raised would be universal.

15. Rey explained about the *Biological Regionalism* series (2005–present), "This series is a national and international extension of the 'Trout Encounters' series. It incorporates paintings, video, artifacts and informational plaques that identify the landscape and the fish distinctive to a region. The installations reflect on the environment and on the social aspects that have affected specific environments. When works from this series are exhibited together, they create connections between the environments that are investigated."

16. Rey has fished and made work in the following locales (the list is not comprehensive, but is indicative of his favorite places), which he describes below:

BREIÐDALSÁ RIVER IN ICELAND

I had always wanted to experience the secluded environment of Iceland and this is one of the rivers with the most awe-inspiring scenes of raw wilderness I have ever experienced. I remember walking and fly fishing alone in a river with glaciers all around and standing in crystal clear water that had been filtered by lava fields. Other times, I'd look over a cliff at a massive waterfall and would climb down to find some slow water to fish. There was one day when I was left with a friend on a barren stretch of landscape where the river was moving at very fast flow. We worked our way out into the water as we tried to reach what seemed to be productive water as the the water moved up my waist on our waders and my foot barely stayed on top of the stream bed. I remember thinking about the danger and the unlikelihood of being able to make it out of the river if I lost my footing, but the rivers can be seductive and make you forget about the consequences.

ANIAK RIVER IN ALASKA

Looking back, it was surprising to realize what someone in contemporary society had to do to find a true sense of wilderness. By wilderness I am referring to an area with very little exposure to human interaction. After arriving at this tributary in a secluded part of Alaska, one could stand on the shore and experience a constant parade of one of the most abundant and diverse examples of fish moving upstream to spawn. Like Iceland, this was another environment that included 24 hours of daylight that, after a few days, made you reexamine your daily routine.

A comprehensive list of the places where Rey has fished are listed at the end of his Biographical Time Line.

17. Lynette M. F. Bosch, "Trout as Form and Symbol," pages 105–142.
18. Alberto said of the "Aesthetics of Death" (2006–present) series,

I began to conceptualize this series about ten years ago, when I started collecting images of dead steelhead without knowing why—until two years ago, when recent family deaths and serious illnesses had re-sensitized me to the fragility and richness of life. These paintings try to capture the aesthetics of the elegance of life in the face of death and my emotional connection to these fish and their environments in which they live and die. While I was intrigued by the idea of having the "Trout Encounters" and "Biological Regionalism" series be able to reintroduce piscatorial art back into a contemporary aesthetic dialogue, this series tries to create a venue to investigate the vitality of life and its relationship to our mortality through the contemplation of the beauty of our inevitable decay.

2

The Construction of Identity in Art
Alberto Rey's Journey

JORGE J. E. GRACIA

Alberto Rey's art not only reveals the challenges he has faced in the construction of his identity as an immigrant to the United States, but also makes clear how it has helped him to develop a coherent and functional conception of himself and his place in his family, ethnos, and nation. In this chapter, I explore the various landmarks of his artistic and personal journey in order to understand in particular how art plays a key role in the construction of his identity, becoming a paradigm of how art and identity cooperate symbiotically in the artistic life.

From the moment we are born until the moment of our death, we are engaged in the development of an identity. Many philosophers hold, with René Descartes, that the self is a thing that thinks—he called it a substance, something that stands under and supports everything else we are—whereas others, with David Hume, maintain that the self is a collection of experiences that somehow stick together.[1] Both have a point—the first, because the self has unity, not only in action but in thinking and feeling. I exist, and it is I who thinks, acts, and feels. But when we delve into our selves, we find not one thing, but a multiplicity of experiences, sensations, and thoughts, so the Humean position also has merit.

Some philosophers have taken into account this double character of a self, as both one and many. An early, ostensive example is Plotinus, who proposed a trinitarian foundation of the universe used later by Christians to explain the nature of God: one substance and three persons. This was a way to bring together these seemingly incompatible conceptions of the self, although in the end this model does not work for us insofar as we are not just one and three, but one and many. Rey is not only an individual, but also a father, a husband, a human being, a teacher, a body, an organism, a mind, a Cuban, an American, and many other things in addition.

Most significant is that he is both himself and also a member of various social groups—ethnic, racial, national, religious, and cultural, to name just a few examples—that often pull in different directions. Being Cuban, American, Latino, Hispanic, and an immigrant to boot, he finds himself, like many others who live in multiethnic, -cultural, and -racial societies in a state of uncertainty as to who and what he is. And yet, as all of us, he needs to know who he is and how to integrate his own self with those of others and with the claims that others make of him: coworkers, family, friends, religious congregation, fellow citizens, and so on. These identities are aspects of him with which he identifies, and their plurality entails that he needs to juggle them in order to keep himself as a functioning unit. A set of disparate elements cannot act as one, cannot be Rey; coherence is necessary. He can be many things, he can have many identities, but those identities must find a modus vivendi that brings them together and helps transcend incompatibilities that could lead to contradictions. Otherwise Rey's self would break down and its unity would be destroyed. Incompatibility and contradiction would paralyze him and prevent him from taking action. It is in this context that art plays a key role, serving to integrate experiences, organizing them into a whole that makes sense.

Because the self is one and multiple, it is in a permanent pursuit of balance and harmony, not just between its unity and its multiplicity, but, equally importantly, between the elements that constitute its multiplicity. Only when it integrates these elements together into an overall identity can we successfully endure. The self is like a city or a country that seeks to unite its people, resources, territory, and government into a body politic that functions as one in spite of its plurality. Or perhaps even more appropriately, the self is like a family, with many different members that share a common history but no characteristics essential to all.[2] The various identities that play roles in Rey's self share some common elements with each other, but there is not one element that all of them have.

Rey's Cuban and Latino identities have in common the Spanish language, the emphasis on the family, and a spiritual sense that integrates both Catholic and African religious traditions, among other things. This makes possible to understand both what makes him unique and also similar to others. We see how this works in his art in the depiction of cultural and historical images: a bag of pork rinds, a guava bar, an iconic fortress from Havana, a raft used by Cubans to cross the channel into the United States, a reference to baseball in Barnesboro, Mexican retablos, and a piece of lace. These and other bits of culture and history are integrated into an indirect narrative of the experiences that make up Rey's life.

The development of an overall identity is mostly unconscious and unintentional. Everything we do is a reflection of who we are, a cause of it, or both. Most of the time, we are unaware of the process of constructing ourselves. In this we are not very different from mere animals. What we become has little to do with intentions and is often fortuitous. When children are born, they are not even aware of themselves as individuals, let alone as human beings or human selves. At first they have no sense of the boundaries between themselves and the breasts that feed them. Only slowly do they begin to distinguish between the two. Time and experience are required to develop a gap between child and mother, and eventually the rest of the world that surrounds it. Fuzzy impressions and experiences turn into more precise ones, into here and there, I and the other, mine and yours. The process is long and difficult. It involves adding to, and taking away from, what we were or thought we were. The toe is mine, but the nipple is not. A sense of the I and the thou, in Martin Buber's terminology, or the I and the other in more postmodern terms, slowly emerges.[3]

We do not try to be someone in particular, but often become who we are in spite of our generally changing intentions. We are too busy making money, foraging for food, enjoying sex, or feeling pain, to be concerned with being the persons we are. And yet, our actions reveal who we are or are becoming by uncovering our likes and dislikes, what makes us happy or unhappy, our concerns, and what we seem to ignore.

Everyone travels this road, but a few of us go beyond it, by making explicit the journey of identity construction. Philosophers, writers, and artists in particular reveal our struggles in this process through our work, which becomes a set of footprints on the road we travel. Many ways of revealing it, some more direct than others, exist. The autobiography is quite explicit. Accounts of individual lives present us with the perspectives of the authors and how they came to be who they are. They mark a defining moment, an explicit reflection on self-identity. A diary is another way, although this presents a less structured view contemporaneous with the events that unfold in a personal history. A still less structured and explicit way is found in the work of artists and fiction writers, who do not intentionally try to represent the process of identity formation, but their creations indirectly tell much about them, their preoccupations, goals, desires, and moods.

Rey has not produced an autobiography or a diary, but he has created a substantial body of work that often deals directly, and always indirectly, with his journey of identity construction. It is significant in that it becomes a visual narrative of the struggles in which he has been engaged and the battles he has fought in seeking an integrated self that responds to the various social claims on him.

Perhaps it is particularly so because it has helped him to negotiate these struggles and conflicting claims. The art is not just a footprint he has left of his journey, but also a way that has played a role in the negotiation. In particular, art has allowed Rey to express and objectify dimensions of this process of which he would otherwise be unaware. The first step to a resolution of challenges is to understand them, and to do so requires their explicit formulation. Rey has been able to achieve this through his art insofar as it records key events in his life, significant factors in the cultures that nurture him, places where he has lived, and memories of events that have affected him deeply. It tells us about his relations with family and friends, the places where he has lived, the memories he has and those he wished to have, and the attempts at assimilating them into a new culture and at preserving his original roots.

The development of an identity results from the interaction between a subject and its circumstances, as José Ortega y Gasset would say.[4] Changes in the context have implications for identity. Apart from the physical environment in which we live, the contexts that influence us the most are the family, the community, the ethnic group, and the nation of which we are a part. Each of these provides a habitat in which we function. The family is most immediately influential during our childhood, but soon the community makes its presence felt, pressuring us in diverse ways. The family and the community are in turn immersed in a culture and society, our ethnos, that dictates our values, religion, and customs. Above this is the nation, with the political organization that establishes the parameters of our freedom. These factors have played roles in forging Rey's identity and have been recorded in his art.

In many cases, people live lives that experience few, if any, radical changes. The family and the community are frequently constants even when members of it die or become estranged from each other. Ethnicity also provides a certain unity, and so does the nation. The America of 1940s is not the same as the America of 1960s, but America is still America in both decades. Families, communities, ethnic groups, and nations are dynamic phenomena in a constant process of change, but those immersed in them change with them, adapting themselves to the process that takes place, preventing them from noticing.

The process of identity construction becomes more complicated when we are subjected to drastic changes in family, ethnic group, culture, or nation. Persons who experience these undergo shocks that require readjustments in identity and often a growing awareness of it. An adopted child goes through a traumatic period that takes years to complete, depending on the age when the child was adopted. One of the most radical changes is experienced by immigrants, who leave their homeland, their communities, ethnic groups, and nations in order to settle in foreign environments and different societies, among peoples who belong to alien *ethne*, cultures, and nations. This is the case with Rey, the son of Cuban parents growing up in an Anglo American society where his parents' background strongly contrasted with the context that surrounded him.

Many immigrants never recover from the shock they experience, and only some are able to blend in or assimilate into the new context. Some never learn the language of the new country, and others continue to engage in religious practices that hark back to their original culture even when they contradict the practices current in the society to which they have emigrated. A lucky minority adapts well either because of an affinity to their new social context or because they came too young to experience the kind of shock that older immigrants experience, but even these, as is the case with Rey, feel pressures that affect who they are.

A certain dialectic is frequently evident in the process through which most immigrants pass. The experience is somewhat chaotic, with different stages of mixing that follow each other in a largely unpredictable order, reflecting circumstantial factors and accidental events. Some stages seem common: an effort to integrate elements from the society the immigrant has joined; a neglect or rejection of elements of the original identity to make room for new elements; the recovery of elements from the original identity that appeared to have been lost or that had been previously rejected; and the integration of all these into a coherent, functioning whole.

Like most immigrants, Rey was thrown into the immigrant's dilemma: Should he assimilate into the new and reject his background, or should he reject the new and continue to live in the world of his parents and friends? He was predisposed to blend into the new culture, but continued many of the practices his parents taught him and still considered himself a member of the Cuban community. Family ties to Cuba and Cuban culture were not easily abandoned, although a desire to get ahead and fit in the new society increasingly pressured Rey to neglect the connections he had with his parents' community.

These forces generated tensions further fueling a desire to leave the past behind and join the mainstream of American life. But a negation of the past proved unsatisfactory in the end, generating a longing for an idealized, romanticized, image of Rey's cultural roots, which in turn gave rise to attempts at recovery, revealing an origin that could not be abandoned. The tensions between the old and the new did not cease until the past was integrated into the present and the immigrant in Rey accepted a hybrid self in which elements from the past were integrated into the present in a functioning identity.

Rey's journey is paradigmatic of the struggles of an immigrant in search of a well-integrated identity. He was born in Havana, Cuba, in 1960, in a family originally from Agramonte. His family left Cuba for Mexico when he was three years old and eventually moved to Miami in 1965. Shortly after, they settled in Barnesboro, a small mining town in Pennsylvania, where Rey grew up. Rey has no memories of Cuba, but he grew up in a Cuban family that kept in touch with relatives in Miami, visiting them often and maintaining links to the larger Cuban community there and in Cuba. The family environment had strong ties to the Cuban culture and community. Like most Cubans who have immigrated to the United States, his parents and other members of his family regarded themselves as Cuban, although they adopted the American nationality and felt gratitude to the country that gave them refuge in a time of crisis.

As with most children of immigrants, Rey was steered toward a traditional career in the professions. In college he majored in biology with a view toward becoming an oceanographer. After a stint at West Point, this goal was turned upside down when he discovered his passion for art and decided to devote his life to it. The decision did not go well with the father at first, but eventually he accepted his son's vocation.[5]

Rey started his artistic education by learning to paint and draw realistically, as many others do in art classes, but as he became more technically comfortable, he began to explore various techniques and styles other artists had used. His aim was to learn all he could so as to be able to express himself, free from technical handicaps that would limit his range as an artist and prevent him from finding his own voice. He wanted to be authentic, to be himself, but the artistic context in which he lived pulled him in different directions, which he began consciously to resist in graduate school. There, like Descartes had done in philosophy, he tried to throw out everything that he had learned and that surrounded him in order to find "his own vision," starting from scratch. This, of course, was impossible—we never begin with a tabula rasa, as John Locke mistakenly believed—but the attempt made him turn to his own personal experiences as a fertile ground of inspiration. He delved into his inner self and the memories he found there, rendering the images that occurred to him in simple, childlike drawings and incorporating floating figures mimicking his dreams. He was looking for a perspective on his life and the many places where he had lived. The work, as he puts it:

> became more layered with realistic images, then the realistic images became more abstracted. The abstract images were a reflection of the same subject matter (which was my life, my memories, my thought processes, my identity), but more symbolic, more of a metaphor for what had happened. By being less specific, I hoped to capture the emotional complexities that realism can often complicate by having the audience concentrate on each recognizable image and not experience the spirituality of the work as a whole.[6]

Rey organized the images from this period into a series that harked back to vivid memories of his life growing up in the small coal-mining town of Barnesboro, and then combined references to being Cuban and his present life in the United States. He became progressively more interested in Cuban culture, for as his relatives began to die, he realized that his opportunities to connect to Cuba were being lost. First came the investigation of Cuban music, since that was one of the most available examples of Cuban culture he could access. Very little was available from Cuban art at that time, so he concentrated on Mexican art as the closest thing to it.

Still, his inclination was to produce work that was fully in the mainstream of American art, which led him to focus on abstraction, a mode of expression devoid of connotations tied to any particular nationality, culture, ethnicity, or race. But for Rey art is an expression of the self, of who he is, of his experiences and personal struggles, so he could not separate his work as an artist from his self. Abstract art fulfilled his craving for formal creativity, but the feelings that arose from the particular circumstances that made him who he was remained unfulfilled. He needed to be more specific, to turn to the particular, both to do justice to his experiences and to make his work more accessible to others.

Here he was, in an Anglo American environment, in the international world of contemporary art, where there was no place for his Cubanness, and yet he was Cuban in spite of not having memories of a life in Cuba. He lived among people who spoke Spanish, talked about what was happening in Cuba and to Cubans, ate Cuban foods that were unfamiliar to mainstream Anglo American society, maintained strong familial ties, and was intensely spiritual in ways that differed sharply from the puritanical faith of Anglo American Protestants.

Rey could not ignore this almost overwhelming background. To ignore it would have meant to leave out a great part of himself, and authentic art cannot do that. Art must come from within, from who we are, and express the deepest corners of our selves. Early on in his career, Rey understood this and sought to relate his work to memories and formative experiences. In the first three series of works he created, he used largely abstract forms but nonetheless introduced in them stylized figures that related the work to his personal history.

In the first series, created between 1985 and 1987, titled *Autogeographical and Floating Series*, he represented vistas of the various places in which he had lived, seen from a bird's-eye view, including his past homes in the United States, Mexico, and Cuba, even though he had no direct memories of the last two. In largely stylized landscapes, figures function both as historical markers and symbols of different cultures. The drawing, *Championship Error: Barnesboro Baseball Memory* (8.5 inches by 11 inches, ink on paper), is a good example of the double duty of his art. The work depicts an error Rey made in the outfield that caused his team to lose the championship. He returned to the field late that night, in the small coal-mining town along the Susquehanna River, and with no one else around: "I got down on my knees and cried. I never cried at any sporting competition before or since. The 48 written on the back of the player lying on the ground was the number I had worn when I played football. The number was I, my identity in the town."[7] This is a piece of personal history, but the work goes beyond it, for baseball is a popular game in Cuba and the United States that ties the two countries, becoming a metaphor for Rey's longing to bring together his divided identity.

The *Black Lace* and *Nuptial Series*, created between 1987 and 1989, began when Rey was dating the young woman who was to become his wife (fig. 3). With the reference to black lace he tried to recover a sense of the sacred and profane mixture in Cuban spirituality, the version of Catholicism practiced in the island with its dose of African Santería. Delicate webs suggest not only the richness of Cuban traditions and their origins in the Spanish baroque and Africa, but also the veils, as much mental as physical, involved in religious rituals.

The reference to nuptials points to marriage before it takes place. At the personal level, it refers to the union of two separate identities coming together. At another level it can be taken to echo the union of two cultures in the immigrant, the desire to integrate them into one that is not a fusion of the two identities even though, as in marriage, they are meant to remain tied forever in a bond that changes them.

Valladolid (40 inches by 48 inches, oils, ink, and rabbit-skin glue on plaster), is named after a small town outside of the famous Mayan ruins of Chichen Itza, where Rey and his wife stayed one night while in Mexico. The town takes the name of a famous city in Spain. The intricate weave, taken from the pattern of the metal bedposts, suggesting a kind of lace, rests over a finer weave, with white lines on a clothlike background, perhaps

a cityscape or blueprint, that unites elements from Spain, Mexico, and Cuba. The work is historical, but a metaphorical interpretation of the weave leads to the self, constructed of different elements, that unite into a textured whole.

Between 1988 and 1992, Rey produced the *Binary Forms* series, which continues the exploration of the marriage bond (fig. 4). It reflects the time after a marriage has taken place when two become one, giving rise to a different form that expresses their union. Here we find a landscape of suggestions that brings together different forms into a cohesive unit: faith and the erotic, marriage and piety, memory and forgetfulness. Some forms are superposed over others. Some appear to be vegetable, as in *Steel 2* (96 inches by 48 inches by 4 inches, oils on steel), and others animal, as in *XXXI* (14 inches by 11.5 inches by 6 inches, oils and wax on linen), but in every case they stand against a recurring clothlike background. The term *binary* points to the marriage bond, but also constitutes an indirect reference to the dual constitution of identity and a desire for integration.

In 1991–1993 a more drastic change occurs with the series *Madonnas of Western New York* (fig. 5). Rey had recently moved with his family to that area of the country and the art took a more obvious geographical and figurative turn, although maintaining its usual spiritual edge. A Madonna is a holy figure and a mother, the womb from which we come, and a source of spiritual inspiration. Rey uses this metaphor to explore, in an Augustinian move, the spiritual and cultural symbolism of ordinary objects. A hotdog stand in *JC's Hot Dog Stand* (13 inches by 10.5 inches by 3 inches), an overpass in *Route 90 Overpass* (6 inches by 6 inches by 3.5 inches), and a road in *Lakeshore Drive* (13 inches by 10.5 inches by 3 inches), become symbols of America as experienced in his new home in Western New York. The works are small, oils painted on wood boxes that contrast with the natural colors of the varnished wood, and hark back to Mexican *retablos*, places of worship and meditation or objects of reverence. Cuba is ostensibly absent, but the Mexican and Cuban pasts are present in the overall metaphor expressed by the series title. Mexican art was very important to Rey at the time, because it was difficult for him to find much on the history and culture of Cuba. Mexico was a way he could connect to Cuba, functioning as a substitute for it. He traveled there several times, exploring the museums, and studying the art.

Between 1993 and 1995, Rey produced another Madonna series, titled *Madonnas in Time*. The images are presented on the surface of boxes to make them look like religious objects or icons. The boxes are painted in bright colors with oils and added simple designs, suggesting a diversity of objects. The main images are copies of black-and-white archival photographs from the 1910s and 1920s. Superposed on them, Rey painted colored images of his everyday life in rural New York State. The color marks them as real memories, different from the monochromatic images representing experiences and memories others had. The black-and-white images consist of landscapes and places, some of them quite famous, such as the Viñales Valley in *Viñales* (30 inches by 36 inches by 4 inches) (fig. 6), Havana in *Havana* (30 inches by 32 inches by 4 inches), Isla de Pinos in *Isla de Pinos* (36 inches by 48 inches by 4 inches), and various other vistas of Cuba. Here is a very explicit effort to bring together the artist's own memories with those that, as presented in the works, constitute his background but of which he had no firsthand experience.

While Rey was creating the second *Madonnas* series, he also painted ten very large works (96 inches by 48 inches by 4 inches) he dubbed the *Icon Series* (1993–1995). They were rendered in oils on a fresco technique over plaster that goes back to religious art on the walls of churches in the history of painting. Instead of landscapes, and abandoning the use of photographic models, these pieces depict objects of ordinary experience, particularly in Cuban popular culture. The most dramatic of these are pictures of food that focus on iconic symbols, capturing the everyday: a glass of sugar cane juice, *Guarapo*; a rum-soaked cone of cake in the form of a funnel, *Panetela Borracha*; a bar of guava paste and jelly, *Ancel Guava Paste* (fig. 7); a pork rind, *Chicharrón*; and a bag of pork rinds, *Bag of Chicharrones*. These images are recognizable to every Cuban, but they are foreign to anybody else. They focus on what is idiosyncratically Cuban and ethnically provincial. Whereas the pre-*Icon* series could be more intelligible to non-Cubans—landscapes and buildings are images to which most people can easily relate—how can a non-Cuban relate to what looks like a greasy paper bag or a glass of yellow-green juice titled *Guara-po*? These paintings constitute a batch of identity. They are crying out: *I am Cuban!* But they are painted by an American.

The next step was to create three series of works, *Las Balsas* (*The Rafts*) (1995) (fig. 9), *Las Balsas* (*The Rafts*) *Constructions* (1996), and the *Las Balsas* (*The Rafts*) *Artifacts* (1998–1999) (fig. 10), which focus on a painful experience, the desperate isolation of the island, and a compulsive and perilous escape from it. The series motif goes back to the tragic death of Rey's grandmother, who in trying to escape from the island in a *balsa* did not survive. Rey was directly touched by this tragedy, but he did not begin the series until he had visited a museum in Miami where remnants of *balsas* (e.g., *Las Balsas: IX*, 19 inches by 13 inches by 7 inches) and some of the objects *balseros* brought with them were displayed, things they thought they needed in the crossing and religious objects to give them strength (e.g., *Balsas Artifacts: Cross and String*, 15.5 inches by 12 inches by 4 inches). The sight of these artifacts, traces of narratives and lives, some of which had been lost, deeply affected Rey, and when he returned to his studio he began to paint. The works are encased in boxes, painted in his now-standard technique of oils on plaster, as solemn images in an altar. The *balsas* are surrounded by an aura of light; they "float in pools of silent light on glassy seas that isolate each boat," with the use of the technique of *grisaille* contributing to a mood of commemoration.[8] They are objects of reverence, sacred in their portrayal of suffering, survival, and death.

A raft is a rich universal symbol that goes beyond the portrayal of a trip. It connotes the journey of the immigrant; it suggests the loneliness of the self in the universe; it warns of the risk of chance; it signifies the life of the artist; it alerts us to the perils of human existence; and ultimately it points to Rey's journey in his search for identity as a human being and as an artist. This motif is found everywhere in world art, and many Cuban artists in particular have explored it in great detail. But Rey's rendition, with its mixture of spirituality and pathos, is unique.[11]

From 1996 to 1997, Rey went back to old archival black-and-white photographs from 1890 to 1920, using the images as models for oil paintings on plaster.[9] He called this series *Appropriated Memories*, because his aim was, more explicitly than before, to re-create memories of images from Cuba that should have been his own, but that he never had. These were places and buildings that were frequently talked about within his family and among their Cuban friends, but that he had only

seen in pictures. The black-and-white images fit the model of memories that have lost the intensity of color and have become part of the makeup of the psyche. Details are missing and the chiaroscuro in which they are rendered gives a sense of incompleteness, darkness, and lack of definition that emphasizes their character as memories and adds a somber, meditative mood. Some are of well-known landscapes he had visited before in his art, such as the Viñales Valley, *Viñales* (48 inches by 84 inches by 4 inches) (fig. 8) or Isla de Pinos, *Isla de Pinos* (48 inches by 84 inches by 4 inches). The most impacting of them is a painting of the fortress that guards the entrance to Havana Harbor and is a symbol of both the city and Cuba, an emblem of resistance and strength, *El Morro* (48 inches by 36 inches by 4 inches). The impressive structure is rendered in broad outlines, and the darkening sky and clouds suggest either a coming storm or the beginning of the night. Both can be symbols of an ominous future. With this series, the longing to fill an incomplete past, a vacuum as Herrera puts it, within a very different present became fully explicit in Rey's art.[10] These works tell Rey's story without words, but he was not completely done with the journey of recovery and integration.

Until 1998, Rey had largely focused his work on images of objects, but between 1998 and 1999, he also began to paint a series he titled *Cuban Portraits* (figs. 11 and 12). These were depictions of Cubans both in Cuba and the United States, members of his family and their friends. Apart from capturing individual differences, the portraits reflect differences in social and economic class, ethnicity, and race. These works put faces on the experiences he had been narrating before through objects and landscapes.

Also begun in 1998 and extending until 1999, is a series titled *Studio Retablos*. A *retablo* is a religious set of images or sculptures that is placed behind the altar in a church in a wooden structure, but it can also be a popular painting used for devotional purposes. The series highlights images of objects, animals, and people, placed on landscapes or undefined backgrounds. Their points of departure were often works by anonymous artists neglected by critics that Rey had found discarded. His challenge was to re-create the narratives behind the works and tie them to his own experiences.

In *Studio Retablos: Mexican Figure* (14.5 inches by 17 inches) (fig. 13), a nude woman rests on a superimposed landscape encircled by an aura of light against a larger autumn background. The image is taken from a painting found in a small, rarely visited art museum in Mexico City, not too far from the Zócalo. According to Rey the work emphasizes "the beauty of the image and the fact that many wonderful works are never published and therefore remain largely unknown."[12] He thought of this as a way of giving it life. In *Dolphin* (16 inches by 34 inches) the figure of a man, depicted in the browns of the surrounding landscape, collapses on a wire fence in which he appears entangled and trapped, while a blue dolphin in an upright position at the top is encircled in an aura of light.

Although there is nothing ethnic about this series, the name and the treatment of the images come from the same spiritual background that informed the *Madonnas* series. The series also explores the concepts of high and low art, beginning the discussion about angling art as low art and the landscape as a "traditional concept." It also questions the idea of ownership after a work is purchased, modified, and then exhibited. Finally, it concerns the life and identity of a painting after it is finished.

The series on Cuban portraits marks an end to Rey's explicit focus on his Cuban background and a beginning of a new direction. The first indication of the change occurs with the *Retablos*, for these are closely tied to his personal experiences, but no longer focus on Cuba or its culture. The move away from Cuba was prompted by a trip Rey made to the island that disenchanted him. The romantic and mythical image his family and other Cuban exiles had conveyed to him was shattered by the stark and painful reality of the Cuba of the present. He realized he had to change the course of his art and set a new goal, which he found in the connection between his interests in fly fishing, biology, and nature. Ethnicity ceased to be a major topic of his work, which shifted to nature, although a connection to Cuba remained.

The new direction branches out into three series: *Trout Encounters* (2000–2004) (fig. 14), *Biological Regionalism* (2005–present) (figs. 14–20, 22–24), and *Aesthetics of Death* (2006–present) (fig. 21).[13] The work aims to explore land-scapes, flora, and fish in various modalities. It includes landscape watercolors, such as *Great Lakes Region, New York 3: Midwinter Afternoon at the Mouth of Great Lake Tributary, New York* (6 inches by 9 inches), and oils of fish on plaster, such as *Brown Trout, Hosmer Creek, Sardinia, New York* (15.5 inches by 33 inches) in New York State. Trips to Iceland, Ireland, Cuba, and various states of the Union also inspired him to paint natural landscapes and fish from those places, such as *Abandoned Farmhouse: Skogar, Southern Iceland* (33 inches by 48 inches), and to create videos of fish in the water and other scenes and sounds not realized in paintings. Cuba still inspired some works, although it became only one more place where Rey explored his interest in nature; it ceased to be a main motif, turning into another source for the exploration of nature, while Rey's American self took center stage. As he puts it:

When I look at my work, I see it as though I am reflecting on my role in American society. To me there was nothing more American than to become a fly fishing guide. This was my final step in the acclimation to the culture, to be in some small way an expert of this particular part of American culture. Nature is part of society, and how we interact with it or not is reflective of other issues related to economy, culture, and perception. I started to think about this series when I asked myself why I was so interested in fly-fishing. Why was it of interest to me? Why were fishing programs so popular on TV when fewer people were fishing? I then started to study what had happened in art history to reflect this change. I saw the classification of regionalism, angling art, and to a lesser extent landscape painting, as forms of low art in contemporary society resulting from a cultural change. Knowing this and my role in this change became the premises from which the work evolved.[14]

The feelings toward Cuban culture and society that had inspired much of the work Rey had produced gave way to a distinctly universal interest in the natural character of the country. Not that Rey's work was ever parochial to a culture. His art has always carried a universal message, even when the message was framed in culturally particular images. Its aim was never to record the particular as particular, but rather to use the particular as a point of departure to transcend it by revealing feelings and experiences common to all humans. The emphasis on particular images dominated most of Rey's work until 2000, but with the new focus on nature, these images receded and new ones took their place. This is most significantly evident in the series on *The Aesthetics of Death*.

The paintings of this series draw a connection between the fate of various species of steelhead to the impact of humans on nature. In large canvases, such as *Aesthetics of Death: VIII* (72 inches by 120 inches), Rey depicts dead fish in various stages of decomposition, in bright, vivid colors that contrast with the somber character of the reality. As is usual with his work, the inspiration for it comes from very specific circumstances, often very personal. The work was initially intended as a reflection on death and its contrast with life. Fish become a metaphor for this dialectic. The series was started soon after Rey had experienced some health problems, his sister had died of pancreatic cancer in her mid-forties, his father-in-law succumbed to lung cancer, and his wife was diagnosed with her first bout of breast cancer. As he relates,

It was a very difficult year. It took me a while to get myself together, but seeing steelhead dead on my guide trips, it brought it all back. The dead fish reflected all that was good and had gone wrong. They reminded me of the fragility of all life and the potential for vitality in my own. I wanted to document death, not usually a popular topic, in an iconic manner, in large realistic works painted with colorful gestural brushwork that would make the work seductive and prompting us to think about death, life, and whether this was low art. I have always tried to make the message subtle and thoughtful. From the first, the environmental content was there, but the work was mostly about me. It was more about how we perceive death and, in doing so, how we perceive life. I have to tell you that my sister's death, Mayda, in 2004, dramatically changed me emotionally to this day. I still tear up just writing about it.[15]

Beyond personal experiences, and the contrast between death and life, the works present death in its stark reality and paradoxical beauty, its causes traceable to humanity and a callous disregard for our surroundings. The tragedy of an unnecessary death, the disappearance of a species, and the destruction of its natural habitat capture the attention of the observer, who is moved by the strong imagery. Dead fish become metaphors for the fate of humans themselves who, in destroying nature, also destroy our future. We are framing our own demise, just as we have framed the defiling of the landscape that surrounds us, the extinction of animal species, and the pollution of our environment. But this is not all, for looking closely at the paintings, we see that they also develop a commentary on the contrast between the fragility and vitality of life, which is emphasized by the gestural manner in which the work has been painted with thick paint and strong, vivid colors. Rey's vision is important and sad, but not pessimistic. Even in death there is beauty, and beauty leads to understanding, as Plato argued in the *Symposium*. There is hope after all, in that the recognition of our predicament and misery may lead to the exercise of our glory.

I began this essay with some thoughts about the need to integrate the various strains that make up our selves into an overall identity that functions effectively. Then I turned to the challenge that immigrants who leave their own cultures and native lands face in carrying out this task. In their effort to become whole, they go through various stages, such as the rejection or neglect of their origins, the romantic and nostalgic appropriation of the past, and the more or less successful integration of the past and the present into a coherent, functioning self. The journey is not easy insofar as it entails the union of often disparate elements that conflict with each other, what Nicholas of Cusa called *coincidentia oppositorum*. These struggles have been narrated in literature by writers and graphically illustrated in the work of artists who have struggled with their past and its integration into their present.

Rey's work is paradigmatic in this regard insofar as it eloquently illustrates the phases through which the artist, as an immigrant, goes in the construction of a satisfactory functioning identity that recognizes the value of the various elements that enter into its constitution. Immigrants are motivated by the need to blend in and be assimilated into the societies to which they have emigrated and the necessity to make room for their past culture, ethnicity, and nationality in the new. Rey's art records in captivating images the road of an artist who has successfully moved through these various stages of identity formation and reached a moment of transcendence. The various series of superb artworks that Rey created between 1985 and today constitute a clear testimony of the experience of an artist who had to face and overcome the challenges of immigration in order to become whole.

NOTES

1. For René Descartes, see *Meditations on the First Philosophy*, in *A Discourse on Method and Selected Writings*, trans. John Veitch (New York: E. P. Dutton and Co., 1951), 96 and 148. For David Hume, see *A Treatise of Human Nature*, bk, I, part IV, sec. 6, ed. L. A. Selby-Bigge (Oxford: Clarendon Press, 1975), 251–252.
2. For the Familial-Historical View of Identity, see Jorge J. E. Gracia, "Cuban-American Identity and Art," in Isabel Alvarez Borland and Lynette

M. F. Bosch, eds., *Negotiating Identities in Literature and Art* (Albany: State University of New York Press, 2009), 175–188.

3. See Martin Buber, *I and Thou,* trans. Ronald Gregor Smith (New York: Scribner Classics, 2000).

4. See José Ortega y Gasset, *El hombre y la gente,* in *Obras completas*, vol. 7 (Madrid: Revista de Occidente, 1964), 115.

5. See "Landscapes of the Mind," an interview with Alberto Rey, in Jorge J. E. Gracia, Lynette M. F. Bosch, and Isabel Alvarez Borland, eds., *Identity, Memory, and Diaspora: Voices of Cuban-American Artists, Writers, and Philosophers* (Albany: State University of New York Press, 2008), 91–101, and A. O'Reilly Herrera, "Appropriated Memories: A Conversation with Alberto Rey," in A. O'Reilly Herrera, ed., *Remembering Cuba: Legacy of a Diaspora* (Austin: University of Texas Press, 2001), 299–306.

6. This and other citations below are taken from an unpublished, electronic interview by Jorge Gracia on April 26–27, 2012.

7. From electronic interview with Gracia.

8. Lynette M. F. Bosch, *Cuban-American Art in Miami: Exile, Identity, and the Neo-Baroque* (Aldershot, U.K.: Lund Humphries, 2004), 142.

9. For the use of photography to recover the past in art, see Isabel Alvarez Borland, "The Memories of Others: Ana Menéndez and Alberto Rey," *Review: Literature and Art of the Americas*78, vol. 42, no. 1 (2009), 11–20.

10. Herrera, "Appropriated Memories," 302.

11. For another but very different example, see Emilio Falero's *Across,* oil on canvas, 48 inches by 48 inches, 2006, in Gracia, Bosch, and Alvarez Borland, eds., *Identity, Memory, and Diaspora*, 107.

12. From electronic interview with Gracia.

13. For the significance of these series, see Johanna Drucker, "A New Naturalism: Biological Regionalism and the Work of Alberto Rey," http://www.albertorey.com/paintings/a-new-naturalism/, as well as the essays by Sandra Firman and Benjamin Hickey in this volume.

14. From electronic interview with Gracia.

15. From electronic interview with Gracia.

3

Alberto Rey's *Balsas* Series in the Cuban American Imagination

ISABEL ALVAREZ BORLAND

Then I saw that the days and the nights were passing and I was still alive, drinking sea water and putting my head in the water, as long as I could, to refresh my burning face. . . . When the raft came apart each one grabbed a tire or one of the planks. Whatever we could. We had to cling to something to survive. . . . But I was sure I wasn't going to perish. . . . It was like the end of a novel, horrible. Someone had to remain to tell the story.

—Guillermo Cabrera Infante

In one of the final vignettes of Cabrera Infante's *View of Dawn in the Tropics* (1974), history becomes dramatized in a first-person narrative as life is pitted against death.[1] For Cabrera Infante (1929–2005), the use of a *balsero* perspective creates a new empathy in the reader, who is immediately drawn to the lives of those who speak and to their suffering.

Infante's *View of Dawn* addressed the lies and the violence in Cuban history, and the use of oral language and popular scenes and topics such as a *balsa* crossing provided an effective portrayal of the links between writing and repression. Thus, in the above-quoted vignette, the author changes the narrative voice of *View of Dawn* from the distant third-person of a fictional historian to the intimate first-person voice of the *balsero*. Faced with the event of an ocean holocaust, Cabrera Infante simply could not pretend objectivity before such a tragedy.

Since the late 1960s, the raft or *balsa* appeared as a tragic yet familiar icon in the visual works and narratives of Cuban exile writers. Visual artist Luis Cruz Azaceta (b. 1942), who left the island as a teenager in 1960 and has been in exile for more than fifty years, has depicted the ocean tragedy since those early years and has obsessively treated the theme from different perspectives and painterly styles. In fact, the first *balsa* images of Luis Cruz Azaceta—produced in the early 1970s, a time roughly contemporary to the writing of *View of Dawn in the Tropics*—showed depictions of this theme in its most naked stages. In an interview with Jorge Gracia (2008), Azaceta remarks that he dealt with certain themes such as the *balsa* crossings because they affected him personally and collectively: "The image of the balsero, while it is Cuban, is also universal in depicting isolation, horror, and displacement."[2] *Balsa* crossings have been going on during all of Azaceta's creative life and, for this artist, they are a Cuban experience that is very close to him and part of the exile reality. Because of the temporal proximity to the physical experience of various *balsero* exoduses, both Cruz Azaceta and Cabrera Infante display indignation and anger toward a history that changed their lives forever.

The Soviet Union collapsed in 1990, and Cuba lost important subsidies from its main trading partner. Fidel Castro declared the time a "special period" and asked Cubans to conserve and sacrifice for their country. By 1994, when Castro announced that the military would no longer hinder ocean departures, more than 30,000 Cubans took to their rafts and boats.[3] People escaping Cuba in homemade rafts was nothing new, but what was different was the number of attempts suddenly being made in 1994. During this time, the *balsas* and the *balseros* who sailed them reemerged in works by scores of younger Cuban artists, both in the United States and Cuba. Rafael Lima, a reporter and *balsero* spotter, describes what he saw in 1994:

"The impression one gets flying over the balseros at 500 feet is one of looking down at floating garbage. You cannot believe that people are crossing an ocean on these things. They are pieces of Styrofoam. Not blocks. Pieces. You lower to

200 feet and the garbage gets bigger, and then 100 feet and you see there are people dressed in rags standing on the garbage, and when you see the children being held up in the air for people in the plane to see, your heart breaks. We dropped survival packages with water and called the position in to the Coast Guard."[4]

How are contemporary immigrant experiences of community expressed through visual and literary culture? What are the different ways in which the issue of community can be engaged by the Cuban American artist? This study considers the ways in which the visual renditions and narratives of the *balsa*—some created roughly at the time of the 1994 exodus and others very recently—function as a kind of migration narrative for contemporary Cuban exile artists and how the visual and narrative representations of the raft operate within an immigrant community as a mode of storytelling or story making that seeks to unify the fragments of an exiled community. By doing so, connections are made between the visual representation of the *balsa* and other modes of narration.

The haunting images of Alberto Rey's *Balsas* series (1995–1999) and the tragic narrative of Joaquín Fraxedas *The Lonely Crossing of Juan Cabrera* (1995) were created immediately before and after the 1994 Cuban *balsero* crisis, and thus these works serve as indexical examples of how *balsa* images and narratives have evolved and reshaped our contemporary understanding of this tragic subject. In more recent years Cruz Azaceta's series *Trajectories/Trayectorias* (2010), and the novel *Cubop City Blues* (2012) by Pablo Medina, point toward the persistence of the *balsa* in the imaginary of the U.S. Cuban exile artist and address a perspective on this theme that illustrates the constantly changing visions of community in U.S. Cuban narrative and visual art. By selecting Cuban artists belonging to several generations and a variety of migration waves, we trace how these artists depict not only their own personal suffering, but also the trauma of community displacement.

ALBERTO REY'S *BALSAS* SERIES (1995–1999)

Born in Havana, Cuba, in 1960, Alberto Rey's family left Cuba for Mexico in 1963 and moved to Miami in 1965. Two years later, his family relocated to Barnesboro, Pennsylvania, a small coal-mining town where he lived until the early 1980s. In his website statements and in interviews with O'Reilly Herrera in 1998 and Jorge Gracia in 2006, Alberto Rey indicates that he felt a range of emotions and a sense of alienation from the story of the aftermath of 1959, a story that somehow was his, but that at the same time he had not lived.[5] It wasn't until graduate school when—prompted by the tragic death of his grandmother, whose raft never made it to U.S. soil—the artist felt an intense need to confront the story of his parents' exile, a story that had not yet fully resonated with him during his teens. Only then did Alberto Rey understand the degree to which his identity had been shaped by his parents' exile and, indirectly, by the 1959 revolution. Four series of paintings, all created between 1995 and 1999, exemplify Rey's most important work on identity: *Icons* (1993–1995); *Appropriated Memories* (1996–1997); *Las Balsas* (1995–1999); and *Las Balsas Artifacts* (1995–1999) (figs. 7–10, respectively). While each series of paintings is thematically and stylistically unique, they are tied together by Rey's exploration of his Cuban heritage.

As Rey observes in conversation with O'Reilly Herrera (1998), in *Icons* he want-ed to recognize "the integral function of food in preserving and transmitting culture, memory, and tradition."[6] The *Icons* series, consisting of ten large paintings of single objects (5 feet by 8 feet), evokes the aesthetics of pop art through a coded and playful visual language that allows the artist to connect with Cuban viewers and participate in the experience of a shared culture. *Bag of Chicharrones*, for instance, depicts a greasy brown bag whose contents only the Cuban viewer could identify as pork rinds (*chicharrones*), a coded way to find a connection with a community the artist felt he had long ignored. In another painting, *Ancel Guava Paste* (fig. 7), Rey appropriates the commercial label "Ancel" and the product *dulce de guayaba* (guava paste) as he speaks on different levels to Anglo, Hispanic, and bicultural viewing audiences.

Appropriated Memories (1995–1997), a series of paintings based on black-and-white archival photographs of Cuba taken between 1890 and 1920, represents Rey's exploration of the story of the 1959 exile. The memories "appropriated" are inspired by photographs of familiar representations of Cuban landscapes and landmarks that Rey had never seen. According to the artist, the use of photographic references from the late nineteenth and early twentieth century was very intentional and places the images, in the painter's words, in "a country without politics or individuals." As Rey indicates, this type of ahistorical depiction would remove the artist from the political issues that forced his family's exile, allowing him to create a separation between the imagery of the past and the reality of Cuba's present. Moreover, the artist's use of archival black-and-white photographs allowed Rey to express his inability to create from the memories of others: "I could have gone into the mid-1990s and found color images, but I wanted to work with the black and white because I wanted an untainted separation from the present."[7]

In *Appropriated Memories*, the viewer detects reverence for the image, which is bolstered by further experimentation with light on the black-and-white photograph. As in his previous works, the artist draws the viewer into an intimate relationship with the image by providing only the most meager context and by forcing the viewer to look more closely at the images due to the insufficiency of light. In appropriating and depicting the century-old images of Cuba, the artist struggles to imbue the work with a reality that he understands

was not his own, but which nonetheless is fully resident in his psyche. A lack of resolution or a blurring withholds their details and the viewer is left groping to make sense of the landscapes and monuments that characterize the series. When the artist paints the images from these archival photographs, he manipulates the light from the original images so that its source comes from only one point in the painting. Everything else is made darker in order to control the order in which the viewer looks at the painting, contributing to a clear but somber mood. For instance, in *El Morro*, the viewer is unsure if the image's darkness is produced by nighttime calm or by an ominous, impending storm. The only light available is the flat, weakened light that escapes from the low, gray clouds painted above the structure. A bluish tint further forces the viewer to struggle to see the well-known landmark that had been a Cuban prison since Colonial times. In a similar vein, in *Behind El Morro*, the viewer senses a sad evanescence to the place, as gray fog seems to be rolling just ahead of rain-bearing clouds. Another picture, *Havana Harbor*, projects a sense of uniformity as the harbor shows none of the expected signs of life from vessels, humans, or sea. Past and present blended, these images depict Cuba as a place dedicated to impermanence, spectral in memory.

The title of the series, *Appropriated Memories*, is playful and somewhat misleading, since Alberto does not transpose, enhance, or paint over the photographs as would be expected of most artists who work with photographic appropriation. According to Rey, "the paintings, although painted in a devotional sensibility, are painted in a gestural manner so that the brushwork is evident and so it is clear that the work is a painting, not a photograph. The manipulation of the image is important so that it is clear that [only] the image is appropriated and that it is a selected visual metaphor for a much larger concept."[8] *Appropriated Memories* thus explored borrowed memories as a personal reflection on time and personal identity. Alberto Rey's play with light creates an intimate, personal rendition of classic Cuban landscapes and provides an example of how a visual artist is able to appropriate only *the image* of a memory in order to re-create a geography never seen.

Yet it is his next series, *Las Balsas* and *Balsa Objects*, that becomes his most significant work on identity and community.

In fact, the *Balsas* series began a meditation on death that prevails today in Rey's current work, as the artist now explores death and loss as it occurs in the natural world. The images in the *Balsas* series were inspired by empty rafts or *balsas* that had washed ashore from Cuba, which the artist had seen on a visit to the Cuban Refugee Center on Stock Island during the summer of 1995. In the artist's own words, "While investigating the Cuban archives at the University of Miami and in the Key West Library for the *Madonnas in Time* Series, I went to the Cuban Refugee Center on Stock Island. The Cuban Refugee Center provided temporary housing for many Cuban immigrants who had arrived to the keys on rafts and housed a small collection of rafts and materials used by Cubans who attempted the 90-mile crossing. I wanted to document these objects as silent remnants of great human tragedies and of a contemporary, politically social condition that is part of our time."[9]

Lynette Bosch observes that Alberto Rey makes use of available traditions in art history that would bring additional meaning to his coffin-like rafts. In almost every work of the *Balsas* series, Rey endows his vessel with a sense of spirituality by placing it as a singular object within a spotlight and surrounding it with darkness as if it were on a stage. The image of the raft and what it represents to the Cuban memory is reinforced by the artist not affording the viewer the slightest chance for distraction. A general lack of additional information leaves the viewer quite alone with the raft, creating a sense of bearing witness to its tragic journey. According to Bosch, Rey's use of a fresco-like technique, a format that had historically been used during the Renaissance, coupled with the representation of the *balsa*s as altarpieces in the manner of the *Retablo* religious paintings and the artist's use of *grisaille* tonalities, achieved the solemnity the painter sought to attain. This technique, avers Bosch, gives the impression of a memento mori as a silent way of eulogizing the many deaths in the ocean.[10]

Rey's *balsas* provide none of the anticipated context of the subject image, as these vessels render only the essential physical elements that constitute a simple raft, yet upon these basic elements all the complexities of the loss of human life are entrusted. Here the subject is explicit and somber, and the visual language is not coded by cultural familiarity as it was in *Icons*. In *Las Balsas II* (fig. 9), the viewer faces two tires in a blue background that suggests they are floating in the ocean. Working in a slightly naive style, Rey adds a raw character to his vessels: the tires seem entirely vulnerable, as we can perceive that they have cracks or tears that are painted in white. The space in the image is relatively shallow, like that of a theatrical stage, and the scale of the inner tubes seems out of proportion, drawing the viewer's attention to the empty vessels. In fact, the tires seem like flat, cut-out forms and are reminiscent of a stage set. Each tire seems to occupy its own space, unaware of the other, reinforcing a sense of isolation between the two repeated images in the picture. A limited palette of muted colors consisting mostly of black and grayish blue allows the black color of the inner tubes to stand out, leading the eye through the composition. As with *Appropriated Memories*, the scene seems to be immersed in low light, and the smooth, clean surface of the painting gives the image a dignified feel that psychologically charges it. Here the light is dim, reflecting the idea of emptiness; the human figures are absent, perhaps dead. Rey's use of light and shadow is dramatic, and the setting of intense hues of blue and gray against darker shades of blue and black causes the colors to glow. It must be noted that the inner tubes depicted in *Balsas II* are not photographs, but paintings of photographs, which allows the manipulation of space by the artist and permits illogical relationships to coexist. The repeated image makes the inner tubes seem inversions of each other, suggesting that the scene is not unique and could be multiplied or repeated further, as even the water itself seems to frame the inner tubes, contributing to a multiplication of framing devices. By providing the inner tubes with such a sense of unreality, the artist has created a very specific mood of sadness and hopelessness.

Balsas V, from the same series, depicts a raft in a shape reminiscent of a coffin that sits at the center of the picture plane. Behind the homemade raft is a dark, shadowy, foreboding space of nothingness, emptiness, and desolation. The dark values in the background emphasize the idea of an ocean that stretches for many miles in the distance. Again, the mood of the piece is dark and sinister, as the artist has used a limited palette of dark tones that gives this particular vessel a ghostly look. As in all of the raft images in this series, the vessel is bathed in a spotlight. This halo effect separates the raft from the space behind. In *Balsas XII*, the viewer is presented with a small boat containing a single inner tube. While it seems less vulnerable than the vessels in the other two paintings, the somber mood and the absence of human figures conveys the idea of a boat that is also a coffin. Two other series on the *balsa* theme, *Constructions* (1996) and *Artifacts* (1998–1999), complete Rey's work and represent, in the words of the artist, "an intimate look at the objects selected by those fleeing their homeland, many of whom would not return or survive."[11] While *Artifacts* depicts objects found in the vessels such as rosaries, baby bottles, and maps, the *Constructions* were Rey's own small clay and wire representations of the vessels. The objects carried by the *balseros* and his own construction of these vessels allow Rey to personally grieve the death of a grandmother he never got to know and simultaneously participate in a communal mourning of all those who perished. These objects manifest the need of the artist to connect to a past he had hardly understood until this point in his artistic trajectory, and they are painted with the same veneration and solemnity that he had applied to the *Balsas* series.

The three series on *balsa*s and related objects constitute Alberto Rey's most political work, since the artist's depiction of these fragile vessels and objects confronts the viewer with an ocean holocaust whose proportions will never be documented. Unlike Cruz Azaceta and most of the artists and writers who have worked on this subject and given primacy to the human figure of the *balsero*, Rey's empty vessels and the objects left by those who perished suggest an absence in reference to the many deaths that have occurred in these dangerous crossings. Yet his link to the tragedy was also familial: his own grandmother had lost her life in the crossing in 1995, and his grandfather had arrived in 1997 from Cuba, also in a raft.[12] The entire series becomes a memorial that honors the community lost in these deathly crossings as the viewer, and most particularly the Cuban viewer, provides the context to Rey's act of memorializing by "understanding."

In 1998, Rey returned to Cuba for the first time in thirty-six years. As a consequence of his trip, Rey's work moved away from the Cuban story of identity as the artist decided to create colorful videos of Cuban coastal scenes. The solace of nature unperturbed by human greed and politics now possessed the dynamic of movement, signaling the experienced reality that was absent from his earlier work on identity. Yet, Alberto Rey's *balsa* depictions have become a stage in his artistic trajectory that could be considered a seed to his current meditation on the fragility of life.

At present he is involved with the depiction of salmonoids as part of his series *The Aesthetics of Death* (2006–): "As I looked more closely at the remains, I would search for details that would indicate what had led to their demise. I often saw these deserted or discarded bodies as metaphors for my own life. The majestic creatures that had, at one time, led noble battles in their attempts to survive and prosper. They now had become silent still-lives that were slowly being broken-down by the same elements that had supported them. There seemed to be a sad irony and elegance to the cycle."[13]

J. JOAQUIN FRAXEDAS'S *THE LONELY CROSSING OF JUAN CABRERA* (1993)

Born in Cuba and raised in Miami and Detroit, Joaquin Fraxedas came to the United States during the 1960s as a young boy. A lawyer by profession, he began to write fiction as a graduate student while he attended the University of Florida. Centered on a *balsero*'s story, his novel precedes by one year the mass exodus of August 1994, in which more than thirty thousand Cubans risked their lives in rafts and boats to cross the treacherous waters between Cuba and Florida. Fraxedas's focus on the *balsero* crisis has served to confront the generations that comprise the Cuban exodus in a way that had not been possible before. The writer captures this moment as his story demands an understanding of both the Cubans in Cuba and the Cuban American community in the United States.

Fraxedas's narrative is roughly contemporary to the visual work of Alberto Rey. A moving portrait of a collective tragedy, *The Lonely Crossing* is the fictional account of a treacherous raft journey from the island of Cuba to the Florida Keys. Depicting characters belonging to the various generations and migratory waves, Fraxedas seeks to reunite the ruptured part of his nation. In comparison to verifiable accounts such as that of Rafael Lima (quoted above), Juan Cabrera's meager transportation does not seem exceptional: "They brought the three deflated inner tubes . . . the nylon lines, the can-

vas tarpaulin, and the hand-operated Czechoslovakian air pump, along with a few personal items."[14]

From the start, Fraxedas's book pits humans against nature in a context quite reminiscent of Hemingway's sea adventures. Quotations from Cervantes and Homer set the poetic tone that frames this tragic saga: three people set sail on a raft, yet only one will reach the other side. Indeed, the future of Juan Cabrera's two companions seems bleak: Andrés was fifty-five-years old, had been a prisoner of Castro, and seems too weak to make the crossing. Raúl, a poor farmer, was overwhelmed by the trauma of the journey. Fraxedas effectively depicts the three men's harrowing experience on the open seas as they confront sharks and hurricanes. Even if the descriptions seem hyperbolic at times, the documentary force of the text is undeniable and mirrors real-life accounts. Not surprisingly, early in their tragic voyage both characters lose their lives. Only Juan is left and must make the crossing alone. During this perilous crossing, Juan Cabrera reflects on his past, and the reader learns about his life as a citizen under the revolution.

Two U.S. characters stand out in this tragic book: Vivián and Alberto. Vivián, a Cuban American who worked for the

Coast Guard, has been raised in both Cuban and U.S. cultures and can envision events from a more distanced perspective. She is also able to acknowledge flaws in her people, although she never forgets that she, too, is a member of her community. As a child of the first exiles, Vivián expresses a sense of lost identity and feelings of not quite belonging anywhere: "But for us . . . in our memories the flight has assumed the trappings of a paradisiacal expulsion . . . So we keep searching and waiting. For what? she thought."[15] Vivián's love-hate relationship with her own community is not atypical for her generation. She wants to be a source of pride for her people, while at the same time she recoils from the false promises and emotionalism of her parents' generation.

Alberto's story, on the other hand, enacts the plight of the first generation, as he typifies the lost idealism of the 1960s and the hopes of a quick return for the first generation of exiles. A veteran pilot of the failed Bay of Pigs invasion, Alberto earns his living as a flight instructor and devotes his spare time to spotting *balseros* off the Florida Keys. His job forces him to confront the daily tragedy of Cubans crossing the ocean in rafts such as that of Juan Cabrera. Vivián and Alberto's

metaphorical crossings become central in the development of the novel, for each embodies a different generation and thus has a different perspective of the consequences of 1959 for the Cuban nation. Through their psychological crossings, the horrors of Juan Cabrera's ocean adventure are echoed in the North American space. Together Juan Cabrera, Vivián, and Alberto encapsulate the generations and spaces that make up the fifty-plus years of the Cuban exile saga. These characters' questioning of their parts in the Cuban story helps readers of Cuban heritage make sense of their own roles as well.

In keeping with Fraxedas's desire to create mirror images of the dispersed communities he depicts in his story, Juan Cabrera becomes Vivián's chronological counterpart. Juan is raised under the revolution and disappointed by it. His life in Cuba has been a struggle from the beginning. Juan Cabrera's interest as a character lies in his sense of his own vulnerabilities. In fact, many times in the book Juan feels shame whenever he thinks about the things that he has done because of his own cowardice in expressing dissent. Eventually, and due to the help he receives from his exiled counterparts, Juan can understand what has happened and can better assess the complexities of being part of a displaced nation. Not unlike the visual representations of Alberto Rey, Fraxedas imagines the different fragments of his community and brings them together in his fiction. For this author, all Cubans (those in the United States and those in Cuba) have a sense of shared history. Affirmation of Fraxedas's ethnic community relies on this author's desire to present a good face to the dominant society. Yet, if the life-and-death struggle of Juan constitutes the main narrative strand in this text, Fraxedas's skillful depiction of the various communities and migratory waves comprising today's Cuba is what renders this novel a place in the imaginary trajectory of the *balsero* in the Cuban American narrative of exile. The problems depicted in his novel can be solved if there remains a viable ethnic community with which the individual can reconnect.

CRUZ AZACETA'S SWIMMERS (2010) AND PABLO MEDINA'S *BALSEROS* (2012)

At present, and in spite of the 1994 and 1995 migration accords, *balseros* have continued to risk their lives at sea. The *balsero* situation has been further aggravated by a major loophole in the accords known as the wet feet/dry feet policy: Cubans rescued at sea by the U.S. Coast Guard are in accordance with the agreements automatically returned to Cuba while those who make it to U.S. soil unassisted are allowed to apply for and usually receive political asylum. It is estimated that hundreds have died as a result of failed operations by *boteros* trying to deliver their illegal human cargo undetected by U.S. authorities.[16]

The most recent work of visual artist Luis Cruz Azaceta has concentrated less on the *balsero* and more on the absurdity of the Cuban condition. In 2010, a year that marked his fiftieth year in exile, Azaceta's art expressed this theme with a combination of sadness and irony. While the painter continues to deal with the *balsero* theme that he has explored for many years, his series *Swimming to Havana* (2008) and *Trajectories/Trayectorias* (2010) present the *balsero* from a distant and at times pragmatic perspective. *Tub: Hell Act* (2009), the central piece in *Trayectorias*, depicts a series of toylike figures of *balseros* in a bathtub bobbing aimlessly in the enclosed space. Another image, *Exile 50* (2009), from his *Swimming to Havana* series, portrays a small figure holding the island by a thread, like a kite or cloud, and presents the island of Cuba surrounded by fifty spikes that create a fence of enclosure, while *Swimming to Havana,* which bears the title of the entire series, depicts a labyrinth with a miniature *balsero* swimming inside with no exit available to him. In the words of Azaceta: "I think the idea of Cubans on the island wanting to leave and those of us in exile wanting to return creates the absurdity which is the ongoing state of suspension."[17] Azaceta's contemporary abstractions and figurations of the *balsero* convey asphyxia in an engulfing environment and the Cuban *balsero* trapped within a hopeless condition.

The same combination of sadness and absurdity is communicated in the latest novel of Cuban American writer Pablo Medina (b. 1949), who arrived in the United States in the 1960s and has published several novels and poetry collections. Published in 2012, *Cubop City Blues* is a collection of interrelated tales set in New York City. The central narrator is a blind storyteller who tells a series of stories to his dying parents, which makes up the bulk of this book. The tales are varied: some are magic and some are realistic and sorrowful, and even if all of them take place in the United States, Medina's Cuban heritage is evident in almost all of them.

Among these tales is the story of a *balsero* by the name of Johnny Luna, which Medina sets in 1995. After six months of carefully building his boat, which he names the *Ana Maria,* and after seven unsuccessful attempts at fleeing the country, Luna arrives at Haulover Beach, north of Miami, and finally sets out "to find the American Dream." Told in a tongue-in-cheek manner, the pathetic story of Johnny Luna is significant in tracing the evolution of the artistic depiction of the *balsero.* Medina opts for a farcical tone for his story, which involves confusion (Johnny and Obdulio, his *balsero* companion, land in a nudist camp in Haulover) and incarceration (the police do not understand who they are and why they were in the nudist camp, and decide to imprison the pair). However, this time the vessel is not a *balsa,* but rather a safe and secure boat that Luna had constructed surreptitiously in the back of a garage in his Havana neighborhood. When a reporter is sent to Haulover Beach to gather details of Johnny's crossing, Johnny is met with a surprise:

". . . the reporter explained to Johnny that crossing the Straits of Florida was a dangerous thing, and lots of people had lost their lives trying. Johnny said that that was because they didn't know what they were doing. The reporter said he understood, but they couldn't run a story on television about someone who had made the crossing on a sturdy boat he built himself. You are either trying to flee communism or off on a pleasure cruise, and believe me, nobody's interested in two guys on a pleasure cruise. This boat looks brand new."[18] The tragicomic story ends with the suggested suicide of the *balsero* as he walks into the ocean, crushed by the negative circumstances of his arrival. Although the consequences continue to be mortiferous for individuals such as Johnny Luna, there is much less compassion in the contemporary representations of the *balsero* story.

In her book *All My Relatives*, Bonnie TuSmith indicates that for ethnic artists community is a continuously evolving possibility that they strive to capture in their creative works. Adopting Thomas Bender's definition of community as "network of social relations marked by mutuality and emotional bonds," TuSmith observes that the notion of community calls attention to the positive values of close fellowship, social solidarity, idealism, and harmony.[19] For an ethnic artist, the idea of community can entail reuniting parts of a culture, asserting its identity, and mitigating the absence of culture by imagining in art and literature. Both Alberto Rey and Joaquin Fraxedas created works around the *balsa* at a time almost contemporary to the 1994 crisis, and thus their emotional impact is strongest. And if Fraxedas's idealistic rendition of the *balsero* wills an ideal community in the imagination, Alberto Rey's solemn renditions of empty *balsas* draw attention to the process of grieving as a questioning of identity. Located somewhere between the individual and the community, Rey positions himself as an observer whose only possible task is to memorialize these rafts as icons of confinement and freedom. At the same time, his "floating," empty *balsas* emphasize the artist's disconnection from family relationships and childhood memories.

Today the idea of community has become a source of tension for ethnic authors, since its utopian connotations are far from the reality to which these authors must conform.[20] Medina's and Azaceta's recent work on the subject take the narrative of displacement to a different point of understanding by explicitly suspecting the motivation of contemporary *balseros*. Medina's irreverence and Azaceta's ironic images of *balseros* provide a perspective on history that is as much about disenchantment as it is about truth. If the event of the crossing is contextualized in a farcical or ironic manner, then the tragedy is muted. Together, the images and narratives of these four artists not only represent stages in the development of each creator, but also provide an example of the constant reformulation of a pervasive icon of exile in the U.S. Cuban artistic production. Whether these depictions of *balsa*s and *balsero*s convey reverence and idealism or are jaded by historical distance and politics, U.S. Cuban artists have recoded the visual and narrative vocabulary of the *balsa*.

NOTES

1. Guillermo Cabrera Infante, *View of Dawn in the Tropics* (translation of *Vista del amanecer en el tropico*, 1974), trans. Suzanne Jill Levine, with the author (London: Faber & Faber, [1978]1990), 130.

2. Gracia, Jorge J. E. "Interview with Luis Cruz Azaceta, 2008." October 17, 2009. http://www.philosophy.buffalo.edu/capenchair/CAOC/Interviews/iAzaceta.htm. Accessed August 22, 2012.

3. The 1990s was a tragic decade for the *balseros*. For accounts contemporary to the crisis, see Liz Balmaseda, "Appalling, Outrageous—but not Surprising," *Miami Herald*, February 25, 1996, sec. A, p. 1.

4. Rafael Lima, "Tourists Don't Cry," *Miami Herald Tropic Magazine*, December 4, 1994, p. 8.

5. For interviews that discuss the trajectory and works of the artist see Andrea O'Reilly Herrera, *ReMembering Cuba* (Austin: University of Texas Press, 2001) and Jorge J. E. Gracia, "Landscapes of the Mind: An Interview with Alberto Rey" (2006), in *Identity, Memory, and Diaspora: Voices of Cuban-American Artists, Writers, and Philosophers*, eds. Jorge J. E. Gracia, Lynette M. F. Bosch, and Isabel Alvarez Borland (Albany: State University of New York Press, 2008), 91–103.

6. O'Reilly Herrera, 298.

7. Gracia, "Landscapes of the Mind," 98.

8. Letter from Alberto Rey to Isabel Alvarez Borland, September 2008. See also Isabel Alvarez Borland, "The Memories of Others: Ana Menéndez and Alberto Rey," *Review: Literature and Art of the Americas* 78, vol. 42, no. 1 (2009), 11–20.

9. Alberto Rey, 2008. Quoted from artist website: http://albertorey.com/appropriated-memories. Accessed August 22, 2012.

10. For a critical overview of Alberto Rey's works see Lynette Bosch, *Cuban-American Art in Miami: Exile, Identity and the Neo-Baroque* (U.K.: Lund Humphries, 2001), 138–146.

11. Quoted from artist's website.

12. From Oral Interview with Alberto Rey, conducted by Lynette M. F. Bosch in February 2012, in Fredonia, NY. Alberto Rey, "*Aesthetics of Death* Artist Statement," n.d., http://www.albertorey.com/paintings/aesthetics-of-death-artist-statement/. AccessedAugust 22, 2012.

13. Joaquín Fraxedas, *The Lonely Crossing of Juan Cabrera* (translation of *La travesía solitaria de Juan Cabrera*, 1993), trans. Raúl García Iglesias (New York: St. Martin's Press, 1993). All quotations belong to this edition.

14. Ibid., 124.

15. For complete coverage and details of the 1994 crisis, see Alfredo Antonio Fernández, *Adrift: The Cuban Raft People* (Houston: Arte Publico, 2000), and also Felix Masud-Piloto, *From Welcomed Exiles to Illegal Immigrants* (Lanham, Md.: Rowman & Littlefield, 1996)

16. Luis Cruz Azaceta, "Abstraction, Absurdity, and 'the Cuban Condition'" (interview) in *Cuban Art News*, November 12, 2010, http://www.cubanartnews.org/news/luis_cruz_azaceta_abstraction_absurdity_and_the_cuban_condition-997/816. Accessed August 22, 2012.

17. Pablo Medina, *Cubop City Blues* (New York: Grove Press, 2012), 222.

18. Bonnie TuSmith, *All My Relatives* (Ann Arbor: University of Michigan Press, 1993), 22–24.

19. See Cordelia Chavez Candelaria, "Difference and the Discourse of Community in Writing by and About Ethnic Others," in *An Other Tongue*, ed. Alfred Arteaga (Durham, N.C.: Duke University Press, 1994), 185–203.

4

Absent Presences and the Living Dead

Alberto Rey's Haunted Aesthetics

MARK DENACI

In the most general sense, Alberto Rey's seemingly eclectic artistic trajectory can be understood in terms of alternating levels of personal attachment and detachment from various people, places, and identifications: in Lynette Bosch's overview of Rey's career in this volume ("Alberto Rey: Intersections"), we first encounter Rey's developing attachment to the Cuban identity from which he had previously felt disconnected; we then learn of his subsequent sense of disillusionment with the realities of Cuba's present, and his detachment from themes directly related to Cuban identity in his post-2000 artwork; finally, we discover his renewed attachment to his home region of Western New York beginning with the *Trout Encounters* and *Biological Regionalism* series, complicated by his need to mourn the loss of previous personal attachments in *The Aesthetics of Death*.[1] This chapter will also concern itself with aspects of attachment and detachment in Rey's works; however, rather than concentrating mainly on how his biography relates to his imagery, as was discussed in previous chapters by Jorge J. E. Gracia ("The Construction of Identity in Art: Alberto Rey's Journey") and Isabel

Alvarez Borland ("Alberto Rey's *Balsas* series in the Cuban American Imagination"), it will instead consider the ways in which Rey's works operate formally and phenomenologically in relation to these themes. Coming from the perspective that works of art constitute more than the content of their represented images, I argue that both the material structure and the formal strategies of Rey's works contribute to the paradoxical and haunting play of absence and presence that has marked his oeuvre throughout his career. While many of the points I raise are applicable to his overall body of work, I focus on two series in particular, *Las Balsas* and *The Aesthetics of Death*, that I consider to foreground these material and formal relationships most explicitly. Of the material and formal issues I believe these works raise, I will begin with that of the status of painting itself.

In a historical moment when innovation in art is frequently seen as occurring in different types of new media, as well as installations and interactive approaches, painters are increasingly likely to face the question, implicitly or explicitly, of Why painting? Whether the question is a welcome one or not may differ consid-erably among artists, depending on how they understand their medium and their relationship to it. In the case of Alberto Rey, however, I believe that his work itself seems both to raise the question and to provide several compelling means of answering it. From fairly early on in his career, Rey's work has occupied a some-what ambiguous position in relation to its status as painting, particularly as figurative painting, sometimes seeming to resemble sculptural or even devotional objects as much as painted representations. In his most recent work, he has downplayed this ambiguity somewhat, although I will argue that vestiges of it remain, opening this work to some intriguing interpretive possibilities.

Of course, some readers may well wonder why the question of a painting's "status as painting" is a relevant or even interesting one. I would answer that the question of Why painting? has haunted the medium throughout much of the history of modernism and postmodernism, and certainly from at least the middle of the twentieth century, when influential critic Clement Greenberg argued that painting (among other traditional media) had lost its raison d'être in the modern era and would only survive as a serious art form if it could focus on what it had to offer that no other medium, such as photography, sculpture, or theater, could to the same extent.[2] Among other things, this position led to an implicit devaluation of figurative painting, as photography could always depict objects and figures more faithfully than painting or drawing (just as sculpture could better convey texture or mass). Greenberg's attempt to save painting from modernist irrelevance was seemingly short-lived, as first minimalism in the 1960s and various forms of postminimalism in the 1970s (including feminist, conceptualist, earth, and body art) seemed to push painting aside in what feminist critic Lucy Lippard famously referred to as "the dematerialization of the art object."[3] When painting came back into prominence in the late 1970s and early 1980s, initially under the guise of "neoexpressionism," it became the subject of hotly contested debates between those who saw it as a cause for celebration and those who saw it as an artistic regression (and symptom of political reaction).[4] While those debates have long since faded into history, painting remains a medium fraught with considerable historical baggage, and can rarely be approached "innocently" by any historically informed art critic. To some extent, all paintings come already weighted down (or perhaps carried aloft) by the question of Why painting?

As I have already claimed, though, much of Alberto Rey's work seems to engage directly with the question of its medium and how that might relate to the representational meanings the paintings may convey. Indeed, some of this engagement involves the works' particular status as objects, and, moreover, as objects of identification and desire. This approach is most readily apparent in such series as the *Icons* (1993–1995), the *Las Balsas* and *Balsas Artifacts* (1995–1999), the *Appropriated Memories* series (1996–1997), and the *Studio Retablos* series (1997–1999). While other essays in this volume have addressed the relationship between various iconographic elements of these series and Rey's biography,[5] I would like to focus on the relationships between their iconography and the form of their material support. To varying degrees of explicitness, each of these series presents itself as more than, or at least other than, simply paintings on canvas; rather, their images are painted on raised plaster supports that alternately bring to mind frescoes and altarpieces (including the small, devotional paintings for private use, to which the term *retablo* usually refers from the nineteenth century onward).[6] The images in the *Balsas* works, moreover, appear to "float" in wooden, boxlike containers. These aspects of three-dimensionality, of the painting's material support calling attention to itself instead of seemingly disappearing behind the image, suggest a quality of what art critic Michael Fried has famously termed *objecthood*. Significantly, Fried claimed objecthood as the central characteristic of the minimalist movement, which he viewed as a direct threat to the values of modernist painting as articulated by Greenberg. The effects of objecthood, he argued, were theatrical: we respond to objects bodily, in specific spaces, over specific durations of time, as opposed to appreciating them in the timeless, disembodied manner that he believed the best modernist art encouraged. Objecthood for Fried depended on a phenomenological "presence" (akin to "stage presence"), which he thought was far more readily available and ordinary than the transcendent, more virtual experience of "presentness." In the essay's final sentence, he memorably declared, "presentness is grace," implying that the more timeless experience he attributed

to modernist painting might partake in something equivalent to the sacred.[7]

Unlike so much of the subsequent postminimalist work that seemed to be attempting to embody the very phenomenological presence that Fried most feared, Rey's works seem to balance precariously on a razor-sharp borderline between object and image, presence and "presentness." Approaching a work such as *Balsas II* (fig. 9) for the first time, a viewer might not immediately recognize it as a painting: instead, it appears as a 30-inches-by-17-inches black, wooden box jutting out 7 inches from the wall, containing a 5-inches-by-10-inches contrasting beige panel (itself about 2 inches thick) that in turn contains a smaller (approximately 4 inches by 5 inches), darker, two-dimensional rectangle in which a painted image seems to emerge from the darkness. Before even getting close enough to make out the content of the image (which on further examination will reveal itself to be a pair of inner tubes, one of which is deflated and misshapen), a first-time viewer is likely to notice the Joseph Albers–like pattern of concentric rectangles, each alternating between dark and light. This alternating value contrast, moreover, continues into the small, painted image itself, where the blackness of its rectangular frame gives way to a grayish blue halo surrounding the pair of inner tubes composed entirely of lightly contrasting *grisaille.* Unlike a painting by Albers, however, this effect of concentricity is not produced through repetition of flat rectangles on a flat surface; instead, Rey creates it from a multitude of visual registers including the flat, the three-dimensional, the abstract, and the figurative. This seeming confusion of registers potentially creates a minor perceptual dilemma, as viewers may wonder whether they are looking at a sculpture, a painting, a found object incorporating what may initially appear to be an old photograph, or something else entirely. After all, the aspect of the work most recognizable as a painting makes up but a small fraction of its visible surface.

Of course, the distinction between "object" and "painting," which is strongly associated with the notion of "art for art's sake" (and what I will eventually be discussing in terms of "the aesthetic"), is a relatively recent phenomenon. Part of the reason Greenberg believed that modernist painting had to distinguish itself from other art forms was his contention that painting had lost its original functions in the modern era due to technological developments (such as the invention of photography) and the increasing secularization of Western culture. In earlier periods, a painting would have been seen less as an end in and of itself, and more like a functional object, of which one of the most important types was the altarpiece. Significantly, while altarpieces were normally painted on flat panels, they were often encased within elaborately shaped and decorated frames, blurring the distinction between painting and sculpture. Even in the modern era, certain religious painting practices have rejected the notion of art for art's sake; some relevant examples include the Orthodox tradition of painted icons, and the aforementioned Latin American tradition of home altarpieces called *retablos* and *ex votos.* In both traditions, the objects are not mere carriers of images to be contemplated aesthetically in an abstracted, Greenberg-and-Fried-approved manner, but rather to be used for ritual devotion; instead of mainly conveying an idea, an impression, or a memory, these works perform spiritual functions in the lives of their users. Rey has remarked on this this aspect of the traditional *retablo* in relation to his own work: "These folk paintings were visual prayers made for specific saints or religious figures. I was intrigued by how the artists managed to create a relationship between their everyday lives and a sense of spirituality through their art. I wanted to create my own series of work that brought this sense of spirituality into my everyday life."[8] While unquestionably demonstrating varying degrees of artistic skill, whether such devotional objects/images would be categorized as "art" from a modernist perspective is debatable to the extent that their "everyday life" function takes precedence over their aesthetic characteristics.

Unlike a devotional *retablo*, however, *Balsas II* seems rather clearly to be intended as a work of art: it has no recognizable extra-aesthetic function, and contains no directly recognizable religious imagery. In fact, as I pointed out in my description above, it initially impresses with its visually striking play of geometric abstraction. Nevertheless, it also insists on its own objecthood—the box frame in particular does not resemble a picture frame or even a sculptural form in any way, looking instead like a practical container of some sort that just happens to be attached, inexplicably, to a wall. To the extent that it might appear

sculptural, such an appearance most likely depends on a viewer's familiarity with the avant-garde modernist tradition of the readymade, in which ordinary objects are displayed (with or without modification) as works of art. And yet, the black box does not exactly look like an actual useful object, either: it is slightly too large to be a shoe-box, too small and shallow for other kinds of containers, and its deep black color does not suggest practical usefulness. Its dazzling contrast with the beige panel in its center also suggests aesthetic intent even before one notices the element of figurative painting on the panel. It seems to be a potentially useful object, but without any kind of clear use—a work of art disguising itself unconvincingly as something other than art.[9]

One possible "not quite art" object that it may resemble in some way is something I have already mentioned: the *retablo*. Like *Balsas II*, a *retablo* often contains a small, painted image surrounded by a somewhat boxlike frame.[10] Other than that very basic similarity, however, Rey's work of this period (including the *Studio Retablos*) does not overtly mimic the look or style of traditional *retablos*.[11] If *Balsas II* were meant in some way to function as (or merely to evoke) a *retablo*, it would appear to be a *retablo* translated into a starkly modernist idiom. More significantly, perhaps, it lacks the religious imagery central to any definition of a *retablo*.

Or does it? As mentioned previously, the represented inner tubes appear to be glowing, almost as if they are surrounded by some kind of halo. Could Rey be positing these simple inner tubes as objects of devotion? Up to this point, I have been treating the work somewhat phenomenologically, imagining an encounter with a viewer having no knowledge or expectation of the work and its potential subject matter. However, in the real world, relatively few viewers are likely to approach a work in such a "naive" manner, without any prior knowledge of the artist or his subjects. At least at this stage in his career, most people are likely to experience Rey's work in the context of a solo gallery exhibition, or perhaps through his website, in either event having some sense of the artist, his background, and his overall body of works. In most circumstances, viewers will see a work such as *Balsas II* in the context of a larger series, and many might be familiar with the connotations of the word *balsas* in a Cuban American context. Certainly, readers of this book are likely to have read about the series in one of the other chapters.[12] Such readers and viewers will understand that the objects depicted in the *Balsas* series are meant to be rafts used by Cuban immigrants to Florida in the early 1990s, and that Rey had tragically lost his grandmother to one such unspeakably harrowing journey. With the correct background knowledge, viewers most likely could not help but to see these rafts, including the aforementioned inner tubes, as symbols of human existence at its most extreme, both in terms of deprivation, suffering, and tragedy on the one hand, and of courage, resilience, and survival, on the other. In this sense, they are very much like those religious symbols that signify both suffering and its transcendence, and a halo seems more than appropriate for them.

At the same time, though, that the *Balsas* works take on this powerful spiritual resonance, Rey also resists presenting them as mere conveyors of a specific set of meanings. Had he simply wanted to make us respond emotionally to the experiences of Cuban *balseros*, he could have depicted those *balseros* during particularly dramatic moments in their journeys, rather than the modest *balsas* that accompanied them. Such an approach, however, would not convey the sense of loss—or its possibility—that these works arguably convey. In these works, we have no way of knowing whether or not the depicted raft's journey ended in tragedy or triumph—in fact, we get no information whatsoever about the people who used them, their stories, or their personalities, aside from the relatively few indexical marks they may have made on their homemade vessels. The object itself is all that we have left on which to project whatever emotions may be called up in us, emotions that will undoubtedly differ depending on our own personal backgrounds and histories. To what extent, then, might the insistent objecthood of these works have something to do with the particular way they function conceptually and emotionally? On one level, the works contain depictions of inanimate objects that almost certainly symbolize human beings, or aspects of human nature or spirit, that are completely absent from the objects themselves. On another level, the works themselves are physically much more than "depictions" of anything—as I have already pointed out, the figurative depictions occupy but a fraction of the works' material surfaces. What we have in front of us, then, is not merely a *depiction* of an object (a raft or pair of inner tubes) carrying symbolic meaning, but an actually existing object that seems to invite us to attach further symbolic meanings to it. Or perhaps what we are invited to attach to the work is not merely a set of meanings, but a sense of identification— we are invited to *become attached to* the object in a way that might not be possible with a disembodied image. From this perspective, the works do not just evoke the absent *balseros*, but make them somehow present within our own private yet solidly material worlds. Interestingly, to the extent that the rafts and inner tubes are significant as much for their absent contents as for their outer forms, they create a kind of *mise-en-abîme* in relation to the black "boxes" that contain them: essentially, the works become a series of concentrically embedded containers, each taking on a quasi-devotional function based on the oscillation between presences and absences.

This *mise-en-abîme* of framing, moreover, is complicated further by the presence of what appear to be handwritten markings in the upper-left corners of the beige panels. A closer look at these markings, which seem to be rarely acknowledged in most published descriptions of the works, reveals them to be consecutive sets of numbers such as 8.16, 8.21, and so on, stacked one on top of the other like lists of dates in a diary. According to Rey, that is exactly what they are, documenting the days he worked on the specific painting.[13] Beyond the *Balsas* and *Balsas Artifacts* works, these markings also appear on each work of the *Icons*, *Appropriated Memories*, and *Cuban Portraits* series, varying only in the numbers themselves and the length of the lists. Even before the purpose of the markings is known, they begin to subvert the apparent immediacy and self-evidence of the painted image by including *coded* meanings; once the codes are recognized as consecutive dates, moreover, they introduce an element of temporality that frustrates the timeless and disembodied effect of "presentness" so desired by Fried. On the most literal level, they indicate that the image was produced in stages, over an extended period of time; more figuratively, they suggest the indexical presence of a now-absent person—and not necessarily the artist—who could have made those marks.

In its continual play of presence and absence, materiality and representation, temporality and timelessness, the *Balsas* series brings to mind a rather famous and controversial episode in the history of twentieth-century aesthetics: Martin Heidegger's discussion of Vincent van Gogh's 1886 painting, *Pair of Shoes*. In his essay "The Origin of the Work of Art" (1933), Heidegger began to answer the vexing question of what art is by distinguishing it from what it certainly was *not*, which was either a "mere" thing or a useful piece of equipment. In trying to determine the characteristics most central to "equipment," he evoked a pair of peasant shoes as an example, and suggested van Gogh's painting as a means of visualizing them. After using the painting to describe in a somewhat sentimentally poetic fashion the characteristics of reliability he thought necessary to define "equipment," his entire argument took a sharp turn: while initially using the painting merely as an example, he ultimately argued that only by means of the painting could we fully understand the "truth" of the nature of equipment, leading to his central claim that the primary function of painting is to "perform the work of truth." Like the peasant shoes, which connect their wearers to the material "earth" while also moving them forward into the more conceptual "world," Heidegger considered painting to be something that connected the material and the immaterial (whether understood as conceptual, cultural, or spiritual).[14]

For several reasons, I would argue that any of Rey's *Balsas* paintings might have made even better examples for Heidegger than van Gogh's *Pair of Shoes*. It was never clear to me, in reading Heidegger's description of the latter painting, what the painting itself really conveyed that his written description of peasant shoes could not. Conversely, in the case of the *Balsas* series, I don't think I could possibly convey the artworks' emotional power, their ability to evoke the paradoxical possibility of a specific yet nonspecified presence, through description alone. Only in relation to these paintings can I imagine this particular type of evocation: if I were in the presence of actual *balsas*, they would certainly cause me to think about their users with great emotion, but their physical specificity might overpower their sense of standing for something or someone else. They would lack a sense of "as if" that opens the paintings up to so many possibilities. Perhaps the experience would be even more powerful than the one I have in the presence of the painting, but it would unquestionably be

a very *different* kind of experience. At the same time, the exaggerated materiality of these particular works—the way they jut almost forcefully into space rather than hanging politely against the wall—gives them a particularly pronounced presence, in Fried's sense of the term. They do not just convey potential meanings, but they also *embody* them. In Fried's terms, they combine presence with presentness, which may just come close to what Heidegger was trying to get at with his "earth" and "world" imagery. None of the works in the *Balsas* series is simply a self-contained object to be admired for its physical characteristics (the earth), as they each contain a representation evoking other people, places, and times (the world). On the other hand, none can be described adequately in terms of their representational content alone, as if they were simply *about* those (absent) people, places, and times, without also insisting on their presence as objects in our worlds of the here-and-now. As paintings, they are more than objects; yet, as objects, they are more than paintings—or, better, they call attention to the power of the objecthood of paintings in general.

The works that I have been discussing in terms of their direct relationship to devotional icons and altarpieces were all done in the 1990s. In the new millennium, Rey changed direction in his work, focusing almost exclusively on trout and their natural environments in two ongoing and related series, *Biological Realism* and *The Aesthetics of Death*. While these series might initially appear to abandon the phenomenological experimentation of his earlier works, careful consideration reveals a continuation of that engagement, albeit in a more subtle manner. This is particularly apparent in *The Aesthetics of Death*, beginning with the provocative title: it not only announces the works as meditations on life and death (already an ambitious project), but also participates in the long-running philosophical dialogue on the nature of aesthetics. Initially, the title seems like an odd fit for the works in question, relatively naturalistic representations of steelhead trout in varying states of decay; instead, one might have expected to see human corpses, perhaps, or skulls, gravesites, even weapons of war. Indeed, the juxtaposition of a universalizing title with such a specific and relatively commonplace subject matter almost seems counterintuitive. Yes, the fish are dead, and they are obviously painted, and thus objects of aesthetic contemplation; yet,

since the series is not called something like *The Aesthetics of Dead Trout*, the title encourages viewers to see the steelhead as broader metaphors, not merely for death in general, but for the *aesthetics* of death in general. But what exactly does that mean? It certainly seems to suggest an attempt to find beauty in death, but it may also imply some characteristic of aesthetics that relates to death.

That last observation leads to a further series of academic debates, as few terms are as widely contested in the history and criticism of art as *aesthetics*. As suggested by the term *anti-aesthetic*, most famously used by Hal Foster as the title of one of the earliest and most well-known anthologies of essays dealing with the topic of postmodernism in the early 1980s,[15] art critics and historians often associate the term *aesthetics* with the general strain of aesthetics popularly known as "art for art's sake," and more specifically the brand of formalism practiced by Greenberg, derived in turn from the eighteenth-century philosophy of Immanuel Kant. Coming from a perspective highly influenced by the Frankfurt School and certain strains of poststructuralism, the "anti-aesthetic" and "postmodernist" critics mainly objected to a conception of art as an autonomous sphere of human activity, detached from material, social, and political concerns.[16] Kant, on the other hand, had defined aesthetic judgment precisely as radically distinct from both individual gratification and social utility.[17] Although Kant's discussions of aesthetics did not specifically involve art—his examples were mainly natural objects, such as flowers—Greenberg's mid-twentieth-century definition of modernism in art emphasized not only the autonomy of art itself from individual and social interests, but also that of each individual artistic medium in relation to others. While he insisted that his framework was merely descriptive rather than prescriptive, its teleology was inescapable: to the extent that it was modernist, each medium tended to divest itself of all traits or characteristics not "proper" to it (that is, not belonging to some other medium). In the case of painting (his preferred medium), its "proper" characteristics were flatness, (two-dimensional) shape, and "opticality." Other traits formerly common to painting, such as narrative, three-dimensional illusionism, or even texture, were more "proper" to other media and therefore to be avoided in painting (or, at least, in "modernist" painting).[18]

If Greenberg's notoriously apolitical (and therefore, according to some, implicitly conservative or even reactionary) formalist aesthetics are the primary target of the critics associated with the *anti-aesthetic*, the latter term itself implies that more is at stake than formalism: in labeling their positions "anti-aesthetic," such critics would appear to disassociate themselves from virtually any conception of art as a special or separate sphere of activity (notwithstanding the immediate objection that an aesthetics of negation as implied by the term *anti-aesthetic* is in itself an aesthetic). In the wake of Foster's anthology and the dozens of similar projects that followed throughout the 1980s and beyond, more recent books with such titles as *Uncontrollable Beauty: Toward a New Aesthetics*; *Sticky Sublime*; *Art History, Aesthetics, Visual Studies*; and *Art History Versus Aesthetics* show signs of a renewed interest in aesthetics and its complex relationship with the history and criticism of art.[19]

Rey's title, *The Aesthetics of Death*, then, enters his series into a minefield of contested territory, all the more provocatively so because of some pointed allusions to Greenberg (which may or may not be intentional) in several of the paintings. In light of Greenberg's long and passionate promotion of nonfigurative abstraction, to claim a Greenbergian reference in such insistently figurative paintings may seem questionable. Yet, because of both the shape of the fish and the point of view from which they are depicted, the paintings literally foreground the very qualities that Greenberg emphasized in his formalist readings of abstract expressionist canvases: flatness, "allover" composition, and the reinforcement of the shape of the support. In spite of Rey's illusionistic technique, he uses it to depict not a three-dimensional space, but flat objects spread out against equally, even insistently, flat backgrounds. We view the lifeless fish as if from directly above, their flat bodies perfectly framed by their rectangular supports and pressed flush against the picture plane; this point of view contrasts with that presented in the *Balsas* series, which used foreshortening to depict the rafts and inner tubes as three-dimensional. Although, on the one hand, the trout clearly form figures against a background, on the other hand, their flatness in conjunction with the equally flattened stones and sandy areas making up their final resting places simultaneously resists the illusion of three-dimensionality. In *The Aesthetics of Death III*, the markings on the steelhead mimic both the shape and color of the flat stones, further deemphasizing the foreground-background contrast, while in *Aesthetics of Death IV*, the broken-up fish corpse wraps around the more loosely arranged stones to the point of becoming nearly indistinguishable from them. Similarly, in *The Aesthetics of Death I* and *II*, the fishes' tails blend in perfectly with the background colors, adding to the conflation of figure and ground. The stones in version *II*, moreover, make up the entirety of its background, extending beyond the frame in all directions. This hints at the "allover" form of composition that Greenberg recognized in both Jackson Pollock's drip paintings and the late works of Claude Monet, whereby the entire surface of the canvas becomes an evenly spread out foreground with little or no sense of contrasting background.[20]

The Aesthetics of Death VII (fig. 21), furthermore, seems to play with its allusions to Greenbergian flatness in particularly subtle ways. Initially, it appears to be somewhat of an exception to the rest of the series, with its half-submerged subject seeming to curl out of the water and into the surface sunlight; however, the tantalizing possibility of significant depth suggested by the broken surface of the water is quickly undercut as soon as one notices the fish's tail, which simply continues in its flat overall planarity underneath the transparent, watery layer, through which flat stones again mimic the shapes and colors of the fish. While never truly breaking with the illusion of three-dimensionality, therefore, Rey nonetheless also provides a study of largely two-dimensional planes (those of the flat fish, the flat layer of water, the flat stones, and the flat ground) in ambiguous relationships to one another.

In spite of these remarkably Greenbergian formal strategies, however, these paintings do not make any sort of uncritical return to a Greenbergian model of painting or a broader, Kantian aesthetics of autonomy. In fact, they contradict Greenberg's conception in at least two key ways (aside from their obvious figurative referentiality): one involves the nature of their framing support, and the other involves their complex intertextual relationships not only to other artworks by Rey, but also to various aspects of his biography and activities. In terms of their framing, while they are not as immediately object-like as the works of the *Balsas* series, they nevertheless share with Rey's various other series the characteristic of being painted on special plaster supports that Rey builds himself in his studio, rather than on canvas. In that sense, each painting is a singular, three-dimensional object that could not, for example, be reframed; they resemble nothing so much as portable frescoes, a format that inherently combines modernist autonomy with at least the evocation of a particular type of premodernist utility.

Rey's consistent references to relationships between art and everyday life offer hints at what I will shortly be arguing is an additional anti-Greenbergian (and anti-Kantian) aspect of *The Aesthetics of Death*. But my point here involves the objecthood of the works, their literal presence in the world as objects as opposed to images or representations. As I argued in the first half of this chapter, this aspect also characterized the *Balsas* series, which Rey has described as "minimal altarpieces."[21] Ironically, the physical "presence" of an altarpiece—its quality as an object of everyday life—is precisely what would disqualify it for Fried's resolutely idealist "grace." But this physical presence is exactly what Rey foregrounds through his structured supports. The art objects' qualities of physical presence, as well as their potential references to altarpieces, moreover, begin to call attention to the multiple paradoxes of Rey's title, *The Aesthetics of Death*. Unlike the *balseros* implicit in, yet absent from, the *Balsas* works, the steelhead are explicitly, visually present, but their very presence in painting implies their absence in the phenomenal world. This play of presence and absence, of course, may be said to be true of any representation, painted or not; however, by representing dead creatures rather than living ones, Rey seems to be engaging this representational ambivalence in a remarkably direct way: he brings the dead back to life, but only in that odd eternal life of the painted object. As uncanny as this zombielike aspect of representation may be, for example, in the genre of portraiture, these paintings actually reference the arguably even more uncanny representational form of the mounted trophy fish, forever hanging on the wall as a frozen monument to the fisher's skill, luck, and bravery— and possibly, ironically, to the life of the fish itself. Paradoxically, such trophies celebrate life and vitality by means of a dead body kept eternally alive as a flat and lifeless object.

When I claimed earlier that Rey's title suggested aspects of aesthetics that may relate to death, the type of oscillation between life and death brought into play by these fishing trophies is mainly what I has in mind. But such memorials are not normally considered to be works of art, and one might wonder whether their effects could be possible in art, in the absence of the actual, once-living bodies that characterize the mounted displays. As my earlier reference to portraiture might suggest, I do believe that most works of representational art engage in a similar phenomenological back-and-forth movement, though it may be less striking than in the case of the aforementioned trophies. Even in the case of nonfigurative abstraction, it is hard to escape the sense that something, whether an artist's emotional state or even a concept, is attempting to achieve immortality in the stillness of the work. On some level, this sense of immortality is one of the targets of the "anti-aesthetic" aesthetic, although the degree to which even the most contingent or ephemeral works or performances can escape at least some intimation of the deathly stillness of representation is open to debate. This play of life and death, presence and absence, in the work of art has been the subject of much psychoanalytically informed criticism. Paraphrasing Jacques Lacan, Steven Levine describes this characteristic succinctly: "Art neither succeeds in representing the presence of the object of desire under the guise of imitation nor does it simply fail to represent it and thereby yield only its absence. The affirmation of a negation, art represents the Thing's presence [. . .] in the very phenomenality of its absence, as its absence."[22] Again, while such descriptions may be applicable to all works of art, I would argue that *The Aesthetics of Death* series (and many, but by no means all of the works in the *Biological Realism* series) further heighten this aesthetic paradox through their oscillation between three-dimensional illusionism, formal intimations of flatness, and the three-dimensional objecthood of their altarpiece-like supports.

I suggested earlier that, in addition to their qualities of objecthood, *The Aesthetics of Death* paintings also resist a Greenbergian or Kantian conception through their lack of aesthetic autonomy. While the paintings' insistent flatness evoke the Greenbergian notion of a painting whose subject is mainly the formal properties of painting—art about art—Rey's artist's statement frames these works within a variety of contexts external to the formal properties of art:

> Over the past decade, I started to analyze why these lifeless forms affected me. With each body I documented, I tried to estimate their age, their genetic background and the life they led over the past few years. As I looked more closely at the remains, I would search for details that would indicate what had led to their demise. I often saw these deserted or discarded bodies as metaphors for my own life. The majestic creatures that had, at one time, led noble battles in their attempts to survive and prosper. They now had become silent still-lives that were slowly being broken down by the same elements that had supported them. There seemed to be a sad irony and elegance to the cycle.[23]

While Rey's references here to "silent still-lives" and even "elegance" may suggest a potential formalist reading of the steelheads' decaying bodies as abstract shapes in a carefully arranged composition, his emphasis on their previously lived existence, as well as their relevance as metaphors for his own life experience, considerably complicate such a reading. Certainly, Rey's experience of his own work does not even come close to meeting Kant's primary condition for purely aesthetic judgment: that is, disinterest on the part of the observer. For Kant, the actual existence in the world of an object—let alone the existence of something represented on or by such an object—should have absolutely no relevance to any judgment of its aesthetic merits.[24] For Rey, on the other hand, the fact that these corpses once lived is crucial: he identifies with the fish and relates them to his own life. Rey's interest in the life and death of steelhead trout, moreover, extends well beyond the subjective reflection suggested by the previously quoted statements: his website, in addition to detailing his artistic projects, also contains a link to the youth fly-fishing program in which Rey participates. Not only does Rey involve himself directly in the life cycles of the fish he represents, but this very involvement also connects him to his community and to the lives of its children.

The Aesthetics of Death series may also relate to a very different set of connections—or, perhaps, disconnections—between Rey and his world. In commenting on the closely related *Biological Realism* series, Rey explained that his turn to depicting the natural environment came in the wake of his disillusion following a recent visit to his native Cuba:

> In 1998, I returned to Cuba for the first time in 36 years. I experienced the real difference between "nostalgia" and "reality." Apart from the *Balsas* series, my work of the last fifteen years had dealt with a romantic vision of the past and the present. . . . After that trip to Cuba, I saw everything around me quite differently. . . . The new work would combine my interest in biology, the lost artistic notion of realism, and fish. . . . As most of our social and economic reliance had moved to an urban setting, the connection between nature and culture in contemporary society seemed to have been lost over the last few generations. This series would try to mend the lost connection by presenting paintings of fish and landscapes that were characteristic to a specific region.[25]

While Rey does not explicitly connect all of the dots here between his return to Cuba and the new direction he would take in his art, his comments invite us to speculate that the sense of lost connections to nature that he is concerned with in the *Biological Realism* series is related in some way to the loss of the Cuba that he had imagined for 36 years. Likewise, his focus here on realism, which would seem to extend to the grim realities explored in *The Aesthetics of Death* series, may be related to the replacement of his romantic vision of Cuba with that of a more sobering reality. Even in being excised from the literal, figurative subject matter of his recent work, Cuba, its memory, and its connection and disconnection to the artist seem to haunt these works in subtle and not so subtle ways.

While I claimed earlier that *The Aesthetics of Death* series seemed to evoke a formalist aesthetic in its flatness and careful orientation to the picture plane, the paintings nevertheless cannot be understood as self-contained exercises in form; instead, these works are also connected to a range of external contexts, from the impact of human society on nature to the artist's ambivalent relationship to his homeland, or the nineteenth-century American tradition of rugged marine-scapes and piscatorial imagery, to contemporary debates on the nature and status of painting. In the context of this series, I cannot help but think of these multiple, sometimes barely visible, connections as fishing lines. Fly-fishing, after all, can be understood to involve an aesthetics—indeed, an aesthetics of death—but its aesthetics of death is simultaneously an aesthetics of connection and engagement. Like the back-and-forth battle between a fisher and his or her prey, Rey's aesthetics oscillate between autonomy and involvement, absence and presence, death and life. And if *The Aesthetics of Death* presents death not as a definitive ending, but part of a cyclical pattern of life, these works should give much comfort to those who may be concerned about what sometimes appears to be the "death of aesthetics" in contemporary art critical discourse.

Returning to the question with which I began this chapter—Why painting?—Rey's works consistently seem to be attempting to address this question of their own necessity and ontological status. The answers they propose, however, are very different from those famously proposed by Greenberg in their insistent materiality and figurative referentiality; nonetheless, they refuse to reject Greenberg's modernist framework altogether, often foregrounding a seemingly disinterested aesthetics of abstraction. In fact, these works seem to cast doubt on our very ability to distinguish between materiality and referentiality, or engagement and disinterest. In this sense, while they can be seen as fulfilling Greenberg's desire to carve out a space for painting's continued relevance in the modern world, the solution they propose owes more to Heidegger's paradoxical play of "earth and world" than it does either to Greenberg's idealist self-referentiality or to "anti-aesthetic" sociopolitical instrumentalism. Why painting? Perhaps, Rey's works seem to reply, because only in painting can we simultaneously experience haunting presences in the midst of abstract design, objective materiality among the free play of aesthetic imagination, and powerful emotional attachment alongside coolly detached intellectual discernment.

The second half of this essay is adapted from an earlier essay, "Engaging Ambivalence: Alberto Rey's 'The Aesthetics of Death,'" originally published in the exhibition catalog *Alberto Rey: Life, Death, and Beauty* (Lexington, Va.: Staniar Gallery, Washington and Lee University, 2009).

NOTES

1. See chapter essays by Lynette M. F. Bosch, Jorge Gracia, and Isabel Alvarez Borland.

2. Clement Greenberg, "Modernist Painting," *Arts Yearbook* no. 4 (1961), reprinted in *The New Art: A Critical Anthology*, ed. Gregory Battcock (New York: E. P. Dutton, 1973), 66–77; esp. 66.

3. Lucy Lippard, *Six Years: The Dematerialization of the Art Object from 1966 to 1972* (Berkeley and Los Angeles: University of California Press, [1973]1997).

4. See, for example, Benjamin H. D. Buchloh, "Figures of Authority, Ciphers of Regression," Donald B. Kuspit, "Flak from the 'Radicals': The American Case Against Current German Painting," and Thomas Lawson, "Last Exit: Painting," in *Art After Modernism: Rethinking Representation*, ed. Brian Wallis (New York: Museum of Contemporary Art, 1984), 107–166.

5. See Bosch and Gracia chapters of this book.

6. See Gloria Fraser Giffords, *Mexican Folk Retablos*, rev. ed. (Albuquerque: University of New Mexico Press, 1992), and *The Art of Private Devotion: Retablo Painting of Mexico* (Austin: University of Texas Press, 1991).

7. Michael Fried, "Art and Objecthood," in *Minimal Art: A Critical Introduction*, ed. Gregory Battock (New York: E. P. Dutton & Co., 1968), 116–147.

8. Alberto Rey, "Madonnas of Western New York," n.d., www.albertorey.com/paintings/artist-statements-on-earlier-series/madonnas-of-western-new-york/.Accessed August 22, 2012.

9. The description here of usefulness without a clear use is purposely meant to evoke Immanuel Kant's notion of "finality without end," which he used to explain the particular paradox of aesthetic judgment wherein an object judged to be beautiful must appear to have been designed for some purpose, but that actual purpose cannot be acknowledged or considered in the judgment. See Immanuel Kant, *Critique of Judgement* (1790), trans. James Creed Meredith (New York: Oxford University Press, 1978), 61–62.

10. See Giffords, *Mexican Folk Retablos*, 2–15.

11. Earlier series, particularly the *Madonnas of Western New York* and the *Madonnas in Time*, make more explicit stylistic and iconographical references to Mexican *retablo* imagery without, however, emphasizing their objecthood to the same degree.

12. See Bosch, Gracia, and Alvarez Borland chapters of this book.

13. Alberto Rey, personal communication with author, summer 2006.

14. Martin Heidegger, "The Origin of the Work of Art" (1933), in *Poetry, Language, Thought*, trans. Albert Hofstadter (New York: HarperCollins, [1971]2001), 15–86.

15. *The Anti-Aesthetic: Essays on Postmodern Culture*, ed. Hal Foster (Seattle, Wash.: Bay Press, 1983).

16. As Foster explained, " 'Anti-aesthetic' also signals that the very notion of the aesthetic, its network of ideas, is in question here: the idea that aesthetic experience exists apart, without 'purpose,' all but beyond history, or that art can now effect a world at once (inter)subjective, concrete and universal—a symbolic totality." Foster, "Postmodernism: A Preface" in *Anti-Aesthetic*, ix–xiv; esp. xiii.

17. Kant, *Critique of Judgment*. See especially "Analytic of the Beautiful," 41–89.

18. While Greenberg's position developed over the course of several essays, it is most famously and succinctly argued in "Modernist Painting."

19. *Uncontrollable Beauty: Toward a New Aesthetics*, ed. Bill Beckley with David Shapiro (New York: Allworth Press, 1998); *Sticky Sublime*, ed. Bill Beckley (New York: Allworth Press, 2001*); Art History, Aesthetics, Visual Studies*, ed. Michael Ann Holly and Keith Moxey (New Haven and London: Yale University Press, 2002); *Art History Versus Aesthetics*, ed. James Elkins (New York and Abingdon, UK: Routledge, 2006).

20. See Clement Greenberg, "'American-Type' Painting" (1955), in *Modern Art and Modernism: A Critical Anthology*, ed. Francis Frascina and Charles Harrison (New York: Harper and Row, 1982), 93–103.

21. Alberto Rey, "Las Balsas (The Rafts)," n.d., http://www.albertorey.com/paintings/artist-statements-on-earlier-series/las-balsas-the-rafts/. Accessed August 22, 2012.

22. Steven Z. Levine, "Between Art History and Psychoanalysis: I/Eye-ing Monet with Freud and Lacan," in *The Subjects of Art History: Historical Objects in Contemporary Perspective*, ed. Mark A. Cheetham, Michael Ann Holly, and Keith Moxey (Cambridge, New York, and Melbourne: Cambridge University Press, 1998), 197–212; 204 (emphasis original).

23. Alberto Rey, "Aesthetics of Death Artist Statement," n.d., http://www.albertorey.com/paintings/aesthetics-of-death-artist-statement/. Accessed August 22, 2012.

24. "Now, where the question is whether something is beautiful, we do not want to know, whether we, or any one else, are, or even could be, concerned in the real existence of the thing, but rather what estimate we form of it on mere contemplation (intuition or reflection). . . . One must not be in the least prepossessed in favor of the real existence of the thing, but must preserve complete indifference in this respect, in order to play the part of judge in matters of taste." Kant, *Critique of Judgement*, 42.

25. Alberto Rey, "A Shift in Direction," n.d., http://www.albertorey.com/paintings/artist-statements-on-earlier-series/a-shift-in-direction/. Accessed August 22, 2012.

5

Trout as Form and Symbol

LYNETTE M. F. BOSCH

For the past 15 years, I have lived in Western New York and have worked on several series of paintings that investigated Cuban and American culture. Many years ago, I began reading about local history and began researching local entomology, biological cycles of regional salmonids (trout) and the role of local rivers on culture. . . . As I acquired more information about the region, I found myself being seduced by the angling art of Henry Inman, Thomas Doughty, Winslow Homer and Thomas Cole: the fish still lives of Gustave Courbet, William Chase and Emil Carlsen: the landscape work of Matin Johnson Heade, José María Velasco and the early work of Alexis Rockman.

—Alberto Rey, Artist Statement,

In the city of Fort Lauderdale, Florida, there is found the International Game Fish Association Fishing Hall of Fame & Museum.[1] The Hall of Fame & Museum's interactive displays and its extensive research library—focused on the history and practice of fishing—are unique in their current and global perspectives. The Museum's mission emphasizes: conserva-tion, the promotion of responsible and ethical fishing practices, and record keep-ing.[2] The Museum has a research library and collection, as well as interactive and informative displays. Both historical and community oriented, the Museum is the contemporary manifestation and summa-tion of American traditions of fishing and angling. In keeping with these traditions, the International Game Fish Association (IGFA) Fishing Hall of Fame fosters communal gathering for fish *aficionados* in a tradition of fellowship and exchange of information that predates the American Revolution.

The first American institutional gathering of fisherfolk and, possibly, the first such organization was "The Schuylkill Fishing Company," of Pennsylvania (or "State in Schuylkill"). This "Company" was founded as an exclusive angling club established in 1732, near Philadelphia.[3] The club was established under a treaty with the chiefs of the Lenni-Lenape (Delaware) tribe, and its original name was "Colony in Schuylkill." In 1782, after the American Revolution, it changed its name to "State in Shuylkill." Its clubhouse, called the "Castle," was located on the Schuylkill River Falls close to the town of Fairmount. Pollution from sewage forced the "Castle" to move in 1937, for the second time, as, in 1822, the Fairmount Falls Dam project ruined trout fishing in that part of the river. In 1844, the club was incorporated as the "Schuylkill Fishing Company." Fish House Punch[4] was the reputed beverage of choice for club members and was imbibed on every celebratory occasion. May 1 was the official

opening day of fishing season, according to the Club's rules. No less than General Lafayette was a member of the "Company." He was welcomed into the club, when he visited the "Castle" on July 21, 1825. Presently, the club is based on the estate of William B. Chamberlain on the Delaware River, near Andalusia, Pennsylvania.

Traditions of fishing and art were linked to the "Company" early in its history, and in 1830, a print was issued that represented the "Castle of the State in Schuylkill."[5] Between 1834 and 1907, members of the club could have looked at, collected, and even hand-colored Currier and Ives prints of trout and other fish favored by anglers.[6] Thus was the artistic representation of fish and fishing linked to the communal gatherings of anglers and fishermen by the use of images by the practitioners of an activity that formed one aspect of the American national identity—linked to fishing and angling. When these American traditions began, in the colonies, the local populations of Native Americans were displaced, and the subsistence fishing practices of these original peoples were discarded in favor of fishing as a sport of luxury. The populations of fish began to suffer from undue harvesting of their numbers, even as increasing populations and industrialization brought pollution to the environments. Sports fishing and the denaturing of the environment went hand in hand, yet as America seemed to be endlessly bountiful, the depredation of its natural resources was not clear for decades. Fishing for food or sport or both became part of public and private life in the United States.

The Fishing Hall of Fame is a public museum while the "Schuylkill Fishing Company" is an exclusive private club. Between these is the middle ground represented by the Orvis company, founded in 1856 to promote sporting traditions for all interested in the American manifestations of fishing and hunting as activity and sport, and to sell the equipment and merchandise necessary for these activities. Alberto Rey is a certified Orvis fly-fishing guide and, as such, he stands at the center of the many environmental and preservationist activities in which Orvis is involved. As an organization, Orvis is also part of the American national consciousness and of the visual traditions that record the presence of Orvis in American culture. Because clubs, stores, societies of all kinds, and the collections of books and images that chronicle their activities and interests have been a part of the history of these individuals, organizations, and institutions, such records have become embedded in the mainstream of American identity and our visual culture.

It is within these parameters, contemporary and historical, of piscatorial conviviality and gathering and dissemination of information, foundational and contemporary, that American visual and literary traditions about fishing and angling developed. From the time of the Colonies to the current state of our rivers and streams, and to global concerns about the fate of fish, the present comments on the past in a continuum of ongoing interaction with our natural landscape and its flora and fauna. As a result of a demand for images reflecting the concerns, experience, knowledge, and activities of American hunters and fishermen and -women, there developed an American tradition of landscape and wildlife painting that was an extension of parallel, older European artistic traditions. European landscape painting, still life painting, and paintings of individual animals, hunters, and fishers depicted engaged in their activities had been an artistic topos since late Antiquity and the Middle Ages.

Renaissance and Baroque artistic traditions incorporated such scenes into the artistic mainstream, including works by artists such as Rembrandt van Rijn (1606–1669), Nicolas Poussin (1594–1665), and Claude Lorraine (1600–1682). Based on the styles and imagery created by these artists, eighteenth- and nineteenth-century European artists, such as Thomas Gainsborough (1727–1788), John Constable (1776–1837), and J. M. W. Turner (1775–1851), in England, as well as Theodore Rousseau (1812–1867), Jean-François Millet (1814–1875), Camille Corot (1796–1875), and Gustave Courbet (1819–1877), in France, developed the models for the styles and types of landscape painting that would inspire and instruct American landscape artists.

Paintings of fishing, fishing parties, and images of individual and groups of fish became part of the larger genre of American landscape painting, as early as the eighteenth century, with such images increasing in the nineteenth century. By the twentieth century, such works constituted an increasing category of artistic practice that continues in the twenty-first century, as a center of artistic creativity. It is within these traditions that Alberto Rey's piscatorial and landscape paintings are situated. Such paintings became markers of American national identity and entered the mainstream consciousness as documents of the life of the United States, its land, its wildlife, and its people. Thus, for Rey, whose work as an artist has been focused on the definition and depiction of identity, the turn to the representation of landscape, fishing, and fish is part of the continuum of his artistic interests.

Even more specifically, Rey's paintings on these topics are explorations of his American identity, whereas his earlier work explored his Cuban identity. As a hyphenated American, Rey's life echoes that of earlier American painters of landscape and wildlife, who came from immigrant and recently arrived families. Thus, this aspect of Rey's work as an artist places him within a larger current of American artists, who, like him, sought to understand their national identity by representing the topography, flora, and fauna of the United States. To better understand Rey's place within this American tradition, its development is outlined below, with an emphasis on the significance of his contribution to this genre.

Fishing in the waters of the rivers, streams, and creeks of the United States was an activity that signaled that born-Americans and new immigrants were established members of the American community. The rivers that were sites of fishing activity were also thoroughfares that provided transportation, the flow of goods, communication, and centralized locales for the development of towns and cities. The tributaries of American rivers connected bodies of land and water to each other, and these waterways became sites where different social classes interacted in ever-changing mobility, as the flux of migrations and settlement spread across the country. The artists who depicted and recorded the development of life in eighteenth- and nineteenth-century America produced a series of images that are artistic and historical, and which can be interpreted from a variety of perspectives. They simultaneously convey an Edenic vision of the United States, even as they are a record of the vanishing wilderness they extolled. In these paintings, seeming depositories of the conviviality of culture and nature, the reality recorded, however idealistically, is the displacement of nature by human culture. Despite the problematization of these paintings—the result of hindsight knowledge and the contemporary realities of nature under siege—the original intent of these paintings is evident in their content. The idyllic scenes of American places, people,

and occupations recorded in these works documents how America was and how it changed through the last three centuries, since these images began to be produced. Even now, they are testimony to the manner in which early Americans saw their surroundings and understood their role within the natural landscape they inhabited. In these pristine landscapes, the anglers are almost without exception men and white. These were not landscapes of difference or inclusion, and the message these paintings represent is one of European, male culture brought to the new venue of the United States, where it reproduced itself in a new environment. These eighteenth- and nineteenth-century paintings continue to be a source of information about early America; they are also a source of inspiration for contemporary artists, who pursue the same subjects even as they reflect on current approaches and concerns for their parallel images. Rey is fully aware of this visual history and its connection to high and popular American culture, and he is an informed contributor to this ongoing history of art.

Rey fully participates in the different aspects of this cultural continuum. As an American exploring his identity, Rey understands that such explorations have been mediated by these types of paintings. Rey is conversant with the history of the clubs, societies, associations, and museums that chronicle this aspect of American life. For Rey and for his works on the subject of fish and fishing, these artistic currents, as well as the institutions that support these activities and their history, provide a context for his multiple identities as artist, angler, and American citizen. As an Orvis guide and as a fisherman, Rey's engagement with fish and fishing is at the core of his personal identity. As an artist who addresses his life experience through visual expression, the fish with which he has become acquainted and which have become part of his life have also become part of his work and his identity as a member of the community of those who are concerned with maintaining and preserving the flora and fauna of the waters of the world.

Rey's paintings of fish and fishing explore a full range of visual and thematic concerns: paintings of fish, alone or in schools; paintings of landscapes, seen from a distance or close up; portraits of some of the people Rey has met while traveling to fish; views of the banks of rivers, streams, and creeks in which Rey has fished; and detailed portraits of different species of fish, with an emphasis on trout. Rey paints fish alive, hunted, dead, and rotting, taking the spectator through the entire life-cycle of the fish that have been the main subjects of his work since the year 2000. For each of the types of representations in which Rey explores fish and their world, there are painterly and sculptural traditions, the teleological origins of which can be discerned in sixteenth-century scientific realism as practiced by artists such as Joris Hoefnagel (1542–1601). But the traditions that are pertinent for understanding the context of Alberto Rey's work are those of American, English, European, and Latin American eighteenth- and nineteenth-century landscape and wildlife painting, which continue to inspire Rey and other contemporary artists working with similar subjects. This essay will also contextualize Rey within his peer group of contemporary artists, such as Alexis Rockman, Walton Ford, and James Prosek.

The act of fishing is complex, with many dimensions and implications that are part of the interaction between those who fish and the fish they pursue. Fishing raises practical issues (How do you best fish, and with what?), ethical issues (Is it right to kill fish for sport instead of for food?), religious and spiritual issues (Can fishing bring one closer to God?), social issues (Can fishing make an individual a better person?), conservation issues (With the diminution of species, should there be fishing at all?), scientific issues (What does the state of fish tell us?), preservation issues (How do we restore and ensure endangered populations of fish?), and issues of self-preservation (What becomes of humans in a world where fish are poisoned into extinction, along with other animals?). These issues outlined here have been the topoi of literary and pictorial discussion and concern ever since Sir Izaak Walton published *The Compleat Angler* in 1653.[7] The remainder of this essay will trace the history of this branch of American painting and its critical reception.

In 2002, William H. Gerdts outlined the development of the American representational history of fishing and its accompanying literary, philosophical, and religious associations.[8] Gerdts began his overview by noting that the first representation of fishing in the United States was made, in 1585, by John White, the artist attached to Sir Walter Raleigh's colony on Roanoke Island. White's painting represented Native Americans fishing on North Carolina's Outer Banks. This image depicted fishing as a food-gathering act. Later, as Gerdts discussed, American illustrations of fishing emphasized the sport of fishing, its conviviality, and its availability, with interwoven allusions to specific societal and environmental ideologies that included religious associations for the act of fishing.

By the late eighteenth century, paintings such as William Winstanley's *View on the North River Evening* (1792–1793), now in the collection of the Ladies Association, Mount Vernon, Virginia, exemplified an accepted genre that juxtaposed the interaction between nature and urbanization in an idyllic setting. From such images, Gerdts traced the emerging development of paintings about fishing as an American genre, the origins of which can be traced to between 1801 and 1804. Such early works featured single anglers fishing on riverbanks, groups of anglers fishing together, and scenic views of the banks of rivers and streams, with the occasional specific portraits of individual anglers. Among the paintings that encouraged the growth of this category of painting was Francis Guy's *View of the Presbyterian Church and All the Buildings as they Appear from the Meadow* (1804), now in the Maryland Historical Society, Baltimore, where fishing is a part of the scenic view, incorporated into town life and endowed with spiritual associations through its proximity to the depicted church. Thus, the pictorial vocabulary of idealized town and landscapes juxtaposed with the activity of fishing associated with American spirituality became consistent themes in this developing category of American imagery.

These initial images of fishing received a boost, as Gerdts pointed out, with the US publication, in 1847, of Sir Izaak Walton's *The Compleat Angler*. The sudden availability of this manual spurred many American artists, who were also avid fishermen and anglers, to begin to create works that recorded the activity of fishing, its participants, and its locales. One early famous, but now lost, painting inspired by *The Compleat Angler* was De Witt Clinton Boutelle's, *The Young Waltonians* (1853), which was sold at the Americas Art Union in New York on December 1853. Boutelle's title was a tribute to the author of the famous book. Boutelle went on to create many such paintings, in a style that can be characterized as academic realism—with a romanticizing

edge. Boutelle characterized fishing as a convivial engagement, enacted in tranquil landscapes evocative of peace and plenty. The fish are either not visible or appear as a small part of the expected ensemble of nature, man, and occupation. Nonetheless, their implied or actual presence is crucial for the depicted scenes, as it is the fish that are the catalyst for the representations of those who seek them and the landscapes depictions of the places where they are sought.

These early landscape/fishing paintings are part of the American tradition that Alberto Rey studied when he began to paint *Trout Encounters*, and to a degree they are a prototype for his representations of the fish, rivers, streams, and creeks that emerge in his work. Thus, although Rey's style is a contemporary and unsentimental rendition of landscape painting, these early paintings are nonetheless part of the artistic continuum that inspired Rey when he began *Trout Encounters* and continued with his parallel series, *Biological Regionalism* and *The Aesthetics of Death*. Despite the differences in style, approach, and intention, both Rey and the nineteenth-century landscape and fishing painters share a desire to record the specificity of the landscapes within which humans inhabit when fishing, as well as the actual appearance of the fish they seek.

Among the artists discussed by Gerdts, and who inspired Rey, is Thomas Doughty (1793–1856), an artist who was active in Philadelphia, Boston, and New York. Doughty was one of the founders of American landscape painting, a precursor to the Hudson River School, and an artist who emphasized fishing as one of the activities that grounded the national identity. Between 1816 and 1822, Doughty created a series of paintings that defined the genre of piscatorial art. His images presented fishing as a sport in which multiple fishermen engaged, their camaraderie being a significant part of the ethos of these paintings. One can envision such paintings decorating the homes and clubs of the members of "The Schuylkill Fishing Company," who in enthusiastic bursts of fellowship and conviviality would have raised cups of Fish House Punch, as they extolled the pleasures of fishing. One can also imagine such paintings as being part of the historical collections of the Fishing Hall of Fame and Museum in Fort Lauderdale.

While Doughty's realistic, yet idealized and romantic, depictions of landscapes are the better-known part of his production, Doughty also created lithographs of individual trout that were intended to accurately portray the individuality of specific species of trout in a manner that can be described as scientifically realistic. One such example of this genre, *Trout of Silver Lake and Brook Trout*, is now in the Cabinet of Natural History and American Rural Sports, which is part of the Amon-Carter Museum's collection in Fort Worth, Indiana. Doughty's lithograph is rectangular, reflecting the contours of the trout. The lithograph's background is plain white, and the fish is represented in great detail. In so illustrating the trout of Silver Lake, Doughty was following an older and English representational tradition that focused on the accurate rendition of the colors, shapes, and morphological details of individual species.

This older English tradition, followed by American artists, was evident in the work of British artists such as Stephen Elmer (1799–1879), John Russell (1745–1806), and A. Rowland Knight (1879–1921).[9] Each of these artists represented fish, with an emphasis on trout, focusing on the specific depiction of them in a highly realistic manner. Such a portrayal emphasized the individual traits of each type of trout. These English artists mentioned above created works that emphasized the trout's experience and perspective—before, during, and after being fished out of the waters they inhabited.

Doughty participated in bringing this tradition to America, where he and other American artists, such as Thomas Inman (1820–1876), Emil Carlsen (1853–1932), and William Merritt Chase (1849–1916) created portraits of the trout species that inhabited American waters. The desire to portray the local and national fauna of the United States is also found in the birds of John James Audubon (1785–1851), who was the counterpart of Thomas Doughty. Hence, Doughty's portraits of trout belong to a larger effort on the part of American artists to map their country's wilderness and record its flora and fauna. Rey's current work is in a continuum with the work, effort, and intention of these artists. Doughty spent the last years of his life in Owego, New York, not that far from Fredonia, where Rey lives and works. In Owego, Doughty focused on painting the wildlife and landscape of the Susquehanna River, in a manner similar to that which Rey now employs to study individual bodies of water and the trout that live there.

Doughty's close contemporary, John James Audubon, most famous for his paintings and prints of the birds of America, was born in Les Cayes, on the island of Saint-Domingue (now Haiti). Audubon is a parallel to Rey in that he was a hyphenated American of multiple identities. In 1791, Audubon's father had him brought to France, where Audubon became immersed in French culture. At the age of eighteen, in 1803, Audubon sailed for the United States, where he became a French American and one of the country's leading artists.

Audubon traveled incessantly throughout the United States, in order to find and portray all of the species of birds that belonged to his acquired country. Although not born in the United States, Audubon's work has become a signifier of America and of its once-bountiful bird population. Audubon's scientifically accurate renditions of birds posed against flat, monochrome backgrounds are akin to Rey's minute presentation of the details of the species of trout that he paints, and Rey's constant travels are an echo of those of Audubon and of all the American landscape and wildlife painters, who were constantly on the move in the United States, Europe, and Latin America, seeking to expand their pictorial vocabulary and their cultural knowledge. Rey's work directly connects contemporary spectators to this visual past that is part of the American artistic heritage, and his life is a parallel to that of the founders of the traditions within which he works.

As these artists and their contemporaries portrayed and preserved the appearance of the fish, birds, animals, vegetation, and landscapes that defined the United States, they also developed images that would become an intrinsic part of the national identity. The luministic landscapes of Frederic Church (1826–1900), Thomas Cole (1801–1848), John Frederick Kensett (1816–1872), and Sanford Robinson (1823–1880) brought to the idyllic presentation of the United States as a country of boundless plenty, a dimension of spirituality that was the direct product of the emphasis on the sublime found their work. America was God's land, and in merging the spiritual with nature and God, through their adopted representational style, the land and its creatures became glorified and endowed with an inherent metaphysical existence that defined the American

spirit. The uplifting beauty of their works connected to the explicit abundance of this landscape and its endless vistas. Thus, these American painters founded the idea that American nature was infinite, continuously productive, and divinely manifest of God's blessing on the actions of Americans. The implicit and explicit presentation of bounty seemed to suggest that the resources so presented could be exploited because they were renewable and inexhaustible. That they were not is the reality of our lives, and this reality is inscribed in the art being created by contemporary painters of landscape and wildlife. While the premises on which American landscape and wildlife painting were developed proved to be wrong, the manner in which these artists presented the United States became an intrinsic part of our national identity. Their work continues to be inspirational to contemporary artists, even when these artists have a different message to convey about our natural resources.

The artists who so defined American national identity by focusing their creative energy on representations of fishing and fish include: Alvar Fisher (1792–1863), Thomas Cole (1801–1848), Robert S. Duncanson (1821–1872), William L. Sonntag

(1822–1900), Henry Inman (1801–1846), William James Hubard (1807–1862), Charles Lanman (1819–1895), Asher B. Durand (1796–1886), Samuel Coleman (1832–1920), Jerome Thompson (1814–1886), George Caleb Bingham (1811–1879), Walter Brackett (1823–1919), and Winslow Homer (1836–1910). Among these, it is Walter Brackett and Winslow Homer whose bodies of work are the closer precedent for Alberto Rey's contemporary investigation of the ongoing engagement with fishing that is part of the American national identity. These two artists are especially significant in relation to Rey because they depicted scenes of fishing from the perspective of the fish, even as they also separately studied the landscape environments in which fish live.

Rey's interest in presenting fishing from the perspective of the fish and his deliberate placement of the point of view as immersed within the waters in which fish live is parallel to Brackett's *The Rise, The Leap, The Last Struggle*, and *Landed*, a lost series, known through reproductions, that initially places the spectator on the level of the trout and ends with the trout on the bank, seen from a bird's-eye view. This type of image immersion in the experience of the fish is also found in the work of Samuel Marsden Brookes (1816–1892), Gordon Trumbull (1841–1903), Samuel Kilbourne (1836–1881), and J. L. Petrie (active 1890s), who, along with Winslow Homer, created the standards and forms of the genre of painting watery nature in all of its manifestations. Thus, Rey's contemporary paintings find their roots in the foundational work of the painters who were active in the Catskills and the Adirondacks, and who lived and worked in New York State, New Jersey, Pennsylvania, Massachusetts, and Connecticut. As an artist who lives and works in Western New York State, Rey belongs to a national tradition of artists who portray their country and whose artistic expression of their knowledge and experience of it has caused them to participate in the creation of a record of the times and lives they lived and live.

On a more material plane, the images of conviviality wherein different types of men fished alongside each other enabled and promoted a path into the mainstream of American life. Many among the generation of artists who painted in the late eighteenth and nineteenth centuries were either the children of recently arrived immigrants or were born elsewhere and came to this country with their parents.

For all, fishing, hunting, and exploring were a natural extension of their desire to discover what was to them and their families a new country of which they became a part. Thus, Rey's engagement with fishing is a contemporary example of a tradition that affirmed and confirmed an American identity that dates from the establishment of a national ethos. His paintings of his penetration into the American waters he has fished is a process of assimilation parallel to that followed by the early immigrants who made their home in this country.

One example of a first-generation artist who followed such a path to total assimilation was Henry Inman (1801–1846), who was born in Utica, New York. Inman's father, William, was born in Somersetshire, England, and came to the United States in 1792, when he settled his family in Whitestown, New York. After receiving his initial training in New York, Inman moved frequently, living in Philadelphia and Mount Holly, New Jersey, and traveled in England to expand his visual repertoire. Inman was a portraitist as well as a landscape painter, and he actively developed the genre of painting that featured fishing as part of a national occupation.

Others, such as Martin Johnson Heade (1819–1904), who was born in Lumberville, Pennsylvania, belonged to more established American families. Heade came from a family of prosperous farmers, who recognized his talent and apprenticed him with Edward Hicks (1780–1849), the American folk artist. Heade traveled to Europe and throughout the United States, and even to Brazil, where he painted landscapes, hummingbirds, and orchids. His American work focused on landscapes and the sports of fishing and hunting, and he was an experienced hunter and fisher. In his later years, Heade settled in Florida in Jacksonville and St. Augustine, where he continued to paint landscapes and the activities he pursued.

The artists who belonged to the group among whom Inman, Doughty, and Heade can be counted focused on representing the locales of fishing found in the areas where they were born and lived—the Catskills, the Adirondacks, the Hudson, and the Delaware—and on preserving the landscapes familiar to them as they themselves hunted and fished. Because the creation of an American national identity was part of their self-definition as artists, and as the next generation of their families born in the United States, their paintings are a repository of collective visualization of an essential America defined through the depiction of its landscapes and occupations.

But Rey is not exclusively American, and his mixed heritage as a Cuban with European roots has caused him to study European traditions of landscape painting, and especially of landscapes where hunting and fishing coexist. It can be said that the first book about fishing and hunting linked to artistic illustration was the fifteenth-century fishing and hunting manual made for the Emperor Maximilian I (1459–1519).[10] Later books on hunting and fishing, as well as the developing European imagery based on these activities, can be ontologically connected to Maximilian's illustrated how-to manual. Thus, Sir Izaak Walton's *The Compleat Angler* (1653) is also part of this continuum that extends through to today's *Field and Stream Magazine*. Rey's paintings thus connect us to a complex web of history, literature, individuals, the history of art, religion, and the manner in which our contemporary lives echo our past history. To move from Rey to Maximilian I takes only a moment and a realization of how culture, as an associative connec-

tor, collapses time, as then and now come together in changing interconnections of evocative artistic imagery.

The European and Latin American sources of inspiration for Rey are primarily represented by his interest in French painter Gustave Courbet (1819–1877) and the Mexican painter José María Velasco Gómez (1840–1912). In his three ongoing series, *Trout Encounters*, *Biological Regionalism*, and *The Aesthetics of Death*, Rey has incorporated aspects of the work of these artists, who in their own time drew upon and contributed to the formation of the national identities of their respective countries. Quintessentially French in his presentation of contemporary life in his surroundings, Courbet selected subjects and themes within the genres of landscape and still-life painting that were connected thematically and compositionally to the nineteenth-century exploration of modern life in France in which the Impressionists and Realists collaborated. Courbet's sources were seventeenth-century still-life paintings and landscapes produced by artists such as Willem Claeszoon Heda (1594–1682), who specialized in lush still-lifes with fruit, plants, animals, insects, and fish, and to the landscape paintings of Peter Paul Rubens (1577–1640), Rembrandt van Rijn (1606–1669), and Jacob Isaakszoon van Ruisdael (1628–1682). In turn, American landscape painters knew Courbet and the artists who inspired Courbet. Hence, Rey, in absorbing the lessons of the American painters, followed their teachers back in time to those who, in turn, inspired and taught them about art and nature, from Doughty, to Courbet, to Rembrandt, and back down through the chain of imagery that came to the Americas—North and South—with the Europeans who conquered and became part of these territories.

Beyond the European influence, Rey also studied the work of José Velasco Gómez, whose Mexican landscapes are directly and deliberately intended to define Mexican identity. Rey's Hispanic identity and his search for correspondences in art that could resonate with his self-identification as a Latin American responded to Velasco's sharply linear artistic style and to the strong, bright colors that define his palette. Rey's stay in Mexico, when his parents brought him out of Cuba, is another link between him and the country Velasco painted. Thus, Rey's current style is a personalized blend of the American, the European, and the Hispanic.

One more extra-American current can be identified to belong within the constellation of inspirational sources Rey has used, and that is Cuban nineteenth-century landscape painting, exemplified by the landcapes of Leopoldo Romañach y Guillen (1862–1951), who was a professor of color theory at the Academia San Alejandro in Marianao, Havana. Nineteenth-century Cuban painters worked in styles that paralleled the academic romanticism found in American nineteenth-century landscape painting and, in a manner similar to that of the American painters, sought to create a national identity by rendering Cuba's landscape in an idealized manner based on the traditions of Rembrandt, Rubens, and Ruisdael. Thus, Rey's current work should be understood within this stream of national and international cultural expression, similarly linked by a desire on the part of artists to give pictorial form and life to the world they identify as defining their cultural and personal identity. Rey belongs to this continuum and consciously encompasses within his network of associations a variety of artistic idioms that, while being international, are solidly grounded in the life he lives in his home in Western New York State and from which he travels to connect to the places from which his inspiration has come. Thus, for Rey, the definition of identity and the demarcation of home involves movement that enables comparison and a wider perspective that informs the local about the global.

The American artists named above, who were responsible for establishing paintings of fishing, hunting, and landscapes as new American genres, were as peripatetic a group as Rey is as an individual. Although very much a part of their American locales, Heade, Doughty, Inman, and their contemporaries traveled and moved constantly. Their more famous contemporaries—Thomas Cole, Frederic Church, and George Caleb Bingham—also traveled extensively in the United States, Latin America, and Europe. These painters, who had lives of constant motion, who visited or lived in other countries, and who explored the world through their work, remain the models for Rey, whose life has followed a path similar to that of the artists who have directly inspired him. Among the group of mobile predecessors most important to Rey is Winslow Homer (1836–1910), whose paintings and watercolors of the American landscapes he explored and whose representation of trout and other

fish from within their watery habitat or rendered from a close up have formed inspirational models for Rey.

There is another aspect of the early American landscape painters that resonates with Rey's life. As with Rey, the eighteenth- and nineteenth-century painters were either born in foreign countries, or they were the children or grandchildren of recent immigrants. These American painters explored their country as a way of defining their own American identity, and their consistent travel, some to other countries, resonates with Rey's own movements from Cuba to Mexico, to the various parts of the United States, and to his continuing travel to other countries. These painters of the American past and Rey are linked by their employment of the forms of the fish they painted, as symbols of the places and people they explored and met, as they made their way around the world in a journey of identification and discovery of environments that were new to them. Yet, these new worlds were familiar because they were linked through the transcendent medium of nature and through the occupations of fishing and hunting, which are as universal as they are specific. Culturally adept and able to move in different social and national groups, these early American artists were comfortable with diversity and moved easily from one culture to another. Rey is their contemporary kin, as his multiple identities enable him to move and adapt to a variety of cultural contexts and diverse populations while he pursues the fish he paints.

For Rey, the work of these artists became a source of inspiration, but also a medium whereby he could connect to the artistic traditions of the United States as he explored the American side of his identity, incorporated into his personal interest in fishing. Thus, the genre that became a signifier of America as a country and a measure of American identity in the eighteenth and nineteenth centuries performed the same transformative process for Rey. Rey's desire to connect to his American identity through his paintings of the flora, fauna, and landscapes found in Western New York State are an echo and parallel of the artistic mission and vision of earlier American artists. In following their lead, Rey was able to ground himself in the essence of his home's territory. As with the early painters of these traditions, who imbued their work with the presence of a spiritual dimension, Rey's images also allude indirectly to the ability of nature to connect us to an existence and consciousness beyond the material.

For some of these artists, who were also fishers and anglers, the fish they sought became a symbol of their national identity and of its welcoming abundance, evocative of Christ's miracles of the loaves and fishes and of the occupation of many of the Apostles, who were fishers before they were called to follow Christ. The fish as symbol of Christianity appears in the Roman catacombs and on bumper stickers visible on cars that travel on our roads today. Fishing has been a holy activity since Christ was said to have walked on the waters of the Sea of Galilee teeming with fish and to have asked his followers to believe and do the same. Thus, the American identity formed by and through images of fishing was also a profoundly religious and spiritual identity linked to the origins of the Gospels. Preachers and ministers fished and used fishing as an allegory of salvation.

The visual history of landscape, fishing, and hunting is one aspect of American identity that Rey has explored in his work. Another part of this exploration consists of Rey's familiarity with the debates that accompanied the depiction of these themes. Fishing and angling in early America also had an ethical, religious, and spiritual dimension that became topics of discussion in the eighteenth and nineteenth centuries. In a chapter in this book, John Orlock describes the major literary works that were developed simultaneously with the art of angling.

In his essay on the pictorial development of fishing and angling, Gerdts briefly outlined the main areas of debate about the process and experience of fishing (see esp. pp. 185–88). In his consideration of the development of American landscape painting, Gerdts began his discussion with Georg W. Bethune, a minister in the Dutch Reformed Church, in Philadelphia, who addressed "The Literary Society of Yale College" with a talk titled "A Plea for Study," where he maintained that angling fosters "quiet habits," "a fondness for retirement," and "love of nature," and leads to "a long life."[11] Bethune was a spokesperson for conscientious fishing, and in his "Bibliographical Preface" he wrote that "an angler, kind reader, is not a fisherman, who plies his calling for a livelihood, careless in what way he gets his scaly rewards."

Bethune raised an important discussion in his considerations of fishing, as he separated angling as an occupational pastime from fishing as a means to earn a living. In essence, Bethune considered that fishing was for the common mercenary, while angling was the higher form of fishing for the more noble sectors of society, who performed it as an activity that would elevate the mind and heart. Bethune is implicitly but not directly drawing class distinctions—the angler does not live from his practice and is free to pursue it as an exercise of the mind and soul because he can afford to take the time for an activity that is neither about needing to eat nor earning a living. Thus, in Bethune's words we can see that fishing may have brought different classes to the same waters, but that distinctions such as Bethune's distinguished significantly between the classes of people who pulled fish from the same waters.

Gerdts also discussed Henry Ward Beecher's "The Morals of Fishing," in which Beecher explored the pros and cons of fishing for food as opposed to fishing for sport.[12] Beecher and others held the position that although fishing was a pleasurable activity, the actual catch should be limited to reasonable consumption as food. For Beecher, the "collateral enjoyments" of fishing were communion with nature and a similar spiritual uplift comparable to that described by Bethune. Beecher's position makes it clear that there were anglers who frowned on wasteful catches of fish that could not be consumed, but were pursued simply for sport.

When to fish, as Gerdts pointed out, was also important, as there were debates about whether it was appropriate to fish on Sundays.[13] Some preachers and ministers forbade fishing on the Lord's day, while other encouraged it for its salubrious effects on the soul, pointing out that in the "Gospel of John—Simon Peter saith unto them—I go a fishing." The Rev. Joseph Seccombe (1706–1760), parish minister for Kinston, New Hampshire, whose pseudonym was "Fluvialis Piscator," approved of angling any day.[14] So did Roger Wolcott (1679–1767), who wrote extensively about the advantages found in enjoying fishing.[15]

But, against these proponents of actual fishing, as opposed to angling without the focused purpose of actually catching fish, were writers such as Elijah Fitch (1746–1788), who considered it sinful to kill fish for sport altogether, as he wrote in his poem "The Beauties of Religion" (1789).[16] Samuel Low (1765–1800) also

considered it barbarous to kill fish.[17] Thus the ethical and moral debates about fishing in the eighteenth and nineteenth centuries focused on a variety of topics that were not just about how to fish, but also about why and to what end one fished.

At the time when these considerations of fishing (and hunting) were unfolding, the enormous abundance of wildlife and forests in the United States was already diminishing from careless use—the Buffalo of the plains being one example—yet still plentiful enough that the idea of conserving fish or of considering species extinction was unknown. Certainly, vanishing species of animals had already been experienced by this time, as exploration introduced foreign species dangerous to the local flora and fauna. It should be noted that "The Schuylkill Fishing Company" was forced to move twice: once when a dam disturbed the river, and again when the trout died from pollution. Hence, already in the late nineteenth and early twentieth centuries, the idyllic plenty of an earlier time was giving way to the new realities that went hand-in-hand with the destructive aspects of industrialization.

The outstanding example of a vanished species is, of course, the dodo bird,

artists for whom these topics are important for their work.

Among twentieth-century and contemporary artists, whose work emphasizes fish and fishing, are: Alexis Rockman (1962–), Walton Ford (1960–), Ogden Minton Pleissner (1905–1983), Emile Alberto Gruppe (1896–1978), Neil Welliver (1929–2005), and James Prosek (1974–). Within this group, Rey's closest contemporaries are Alexis Rockman and Walton Ford, although his career coincides with that of Neil Welliver and to a lesser degree with that of Emile Gruppe. While these artists are a tiny percentage of twentieth-century and contemporary artists who worked with similar subjects, they are illustrative of trends in landscape painting and in the painting of America's flora and fauna. As such, these artists are a representative peer group for Rey, and his work can be analyzed in comparison with theirs, so that his personal contribution can be assessed.

Emile Albert Gruppe was born in Rochester, New York, into a Dutch family that eventually became American.[18] His father, Charles Paul Gruppe, was also a painter, who painted with the Hague school of artists and also worked as an international dealer. Gruppe grew up in the Netherlands until 1913, when his father settled the family in the United States shortly before World War I began. After serving in the U.S. Navy, Gruppe settled in Gloucester, Massachusetts, where he became part of the Cape Ann group. Gruppe worked in an eclectic style that combined aspects of Rembrandt, Cézanne, and Impressionism into a realistic style that was tinged with romanticism. As with Pleissner and the earlier American landscape painters, Gruppe's presentation of nature was idyllic. Gruppe's style is the next evolutionary step that links the nineteenth century to the twentieth, being more modern in the dress, architecture, and material culture of his images, yet still tinged with the academic romanticism of earlier art.

One of the twentieth-century artists who forms a bridge between older and modern artistic traditions of landscape painting is Ogden Minton Pleissner.[19] Pleissner was born in Brooklyn, New York, and grew up making frequent visits to Wyoming, where he learned to hunt and fish. He studied art at the Art Students League of New York and taught at Pratt Institute. During World War II, he was a correspondent for *Life Magazine*, and he traveled extensively, linking his work as an artist to his interest in fishing and hunting. A significant number of Pleissner's works are in the Shelburne Museum in Shelburne, Vermont. Pleissner's style was realistic and idealized in a twentieth-century version of the academic romanticism of the eighteenth- and nineteenth-century painters. His landscape representations are panoramic and frequently include the depiction of sportsmen. While Pleissner's work is as idealized as was that of the Hudson River School, he is a painter of modernity, as is evident in the topical references found in his work that point to the aftermath of Impressionism, Expressionism, Cubism, and Abstraction. Pleissner's world is the world we know from our childhoods and recent history, and his tonal compositions are rendered in a sharp plein air style free of the chiaroscuro tenebrism of earlier American artists and of artists of Gruppe's generation. Yet, in Pleissner's time, America was still bountiful, and his paintings emphasize communion with a pristine nature that seems eternally renewing.

Neil Welliver, who died recently in 2005, belongs to a more current group of landscape artists whose repertoire extends to the representation of fish, with an emphasis on trout.[20] Welliver was born in Millville, Pennsylvania, and studied at Philadelphia College, then Yale University. He taught at Cooper Union and at the University of Pennsylvania. Welliver began as an abstract painter and then moved to realism as he changed his thematic subjects to include natural landscapes and their flora and fauna. Welliver's style remained somewhat abstract, yet idealized, and his paintings are representations of nature as available and abundant. Although by 2005 the environment was already in crisis, this unfolding threat to the rivers, streams, and panoramic views Welliver specialized in painting is not evident in his work. Welliver's images emphasize the beauty of nature rendered into beautiful art, mediated by strong lines, colors, and shapes that leave the spectator suspended between the actual and the imagined sublimity of communion with nature. The continuing idyllic and idealized rendering of the American landscape by the artists who chronicled it changed as the next generation of landscape and flora and fauna painters grew up in the aftermath of the realization that nature was not endlessly renewable.

Alexis Rockman, who belongs to the group of contemporary artists that has turned away from previous traditions of painting nature, was born in 1962 and concentrates on the representation of the natural world in an unnatural manner.[21] Rockman studied at the School of Visual Arts in New York City and received his MA from the Rhode Island School of Design. Rockman specializes in paintings that are the direct heirs of Thomas Cole and Martin Johnson Heade in compositional structure and thematic echo, except that Rockman's landscapes, plants, animals, and fish seem to have undergone an apprenticeship with Salvador Dalí and Hieronymus Bosch instead of with seventeenth-century realism. Rockman's hyperrealistic and hallucinogenic landscapes include myriad creatures, some recognizable as actual animals.

Rockman's landscapes render nature adulterated, mechanized, subverted, and reconceptualized into a formalistic style that derives elements from cartoon and comic book art, advertising, and video games while retaining a connection to American folk artists such as Grant Wood (1891–1942). Rockman's message is clear: nature's integrity has been destroyed, and what we now have are frogs with three legs, rabbits who box in an eerie night light, and farms where food is manufac-tured instead of raised and grown. Rockman is an overt social commentator, who represents mutant animals and desecrated natural environments in a confrontational form and style that does not allow the spectator to escape from his purgatorial paradises created by technology instead of nature.

Walton Ford was born in 1960 in Larchmont, New York, and is another member of the younger generation for whom nature is a symbol of societal disjunction and dystopia.[22] Ford's BFA is from Rhode Island School of Design, and he currently lives in Great Barrington, Massachusetts. His style has elements of Pieter Breughel, Arcimboldo, Karl Bodmer, and George Catlin, all painters of nature and landscapes. However, Ford is more directly the heir of John James Audubon, who provides the inspiration for his depictions of flora and fauna painted in a hard-edged style that takes Audubon's clarity to a level of sharp delineation that transforms nature into a commentary on art. His work is large-scale, even monumental, and it conveys an intricate network of iconographic, metaphorical, and symbolic visual languages that demand and defy interpretation. As with Rockman, Ford is a voice of conscience who anthropomorphizes birds, animals, and fish into ironic scenarios that comment on human foolishness and self-destruction.

Rockman and Ford represent one current visual vocabulary for representing nature; James Prosek pursues another approach.[23] Prosek was born in 1975 in Stamford, Connecticut, and graduated from Yale University. In 1996, Prosek published *Trout: An Illustrated History*, followed by *Joe and Me: An Education in Fishing and Friendship* (1997), and in 2005, he published *Trout of the World*. All three books combined, along with Prosek's other books, provide illustrated guides to and histories of trout as a global species, and are testimony to Prosek's involvement with fishing and with contemporary concerns about the state of the environment and the preservation of the fish that are a significant part of his work. In 2004, he cofounded World Trout, an organization that promotes awareness, information, and preservation of endangered trout species. Prosek works in painting, drawing, watercolor, and taxidermy. His style is clear, linear, and detailed, and ranges from small-scale to monumental works. He places highly realized renderings of individual fish or animals against white or monochrome backgrounds that evoke the hand-colored prints of Currier and Ives, as well as the naturalistic renderings of Thomas Doughty and other American and English artists who employed scientific naturalism to portray the essential nature of the species they depicted. Although Prosek's work does demonstrate a wry, ironic, and wittily abstruse spirit, he is not overtly political, and in his work, the fish and animals he paints are presented in a straightforward manner. Thus, Prosek's art is not an illustration of his social and political stance; they are works of art intended to be received as such, which could be linked to his ideological stance but are not overtly connected in their form and content to his political positions.

Each of the artists discussed above chose to make the representation of nature one of their main subjects of research and study. In moving from the eighteenth to the twenty-first century in this very brief and indexical summary of artistic styles, thematic choices, and underlying intentions, the trajectory traced begins with the representation of America—the beautiful and bountiful—and ends with an artistic agenda that forces us to understand that the old America is gone and replaced with hybrid creatures who interact with each other in dislocated scenarios that predict additional social and planetary dissolution. Thus, the message promoted by some contemporary nature and landscape artists is one that is intentionally ironic, tongue-in-cheek, and inescapably nihilistic, as their paintings leave the spectator in a Dantian mood of abandoning hope for the Earth upon entry into the world of their imaginations. Fiercely effective, the styles of Rockman, Prosek, and Ford do not allow us to escape the consequences of our actions, and in trapping our gaze, they confront us with their message.

Rey's ongoing series *Trout Encounters*, *Biological Regionalism*, and *The Aesthetics of Death* form part of the debate about fish and landscape as form and symbol that is part of the history of art that dates back to the Renaissance and was continued by the painters of subsequent centuries, even into our contemporary world. Rockman, Ford, and Prosek also reference the same artists who inspired American eighteenth- to twentieth-century nature artists, but the visual outcome and message given is very different. Despite these differences of approach and intention, today's nature artists are connected, through twentieth-century artists such as Pleissner and Welliver, to earlier tra-

ditions that go back to Renaissance and Baroque art. Rey and his contemporaries are heirs of traditions of changing modernity that mark the passage of time, who inscribe the past into their vision of the present to prod us into imagining a future that is rapidly becoming a present reality. What will our world be like if nature, as we know it, is destroyed? Who will we be without the flora and fauna on which we rely? Would we exist in a final spasm of cannibalistic destruction until the last human is forced to eat of his or her own flesh to survive—as did the protagonist of Stephen King's short story, "Survivor Type," in which surgeon, Richard Pine, marooned on a deserted island, slowly consumes himself? Or will we actively participate in preventing such an end for our last descendant? Rey's paintings are a quiet form of meditative activism, and one that is rooted in the communal existence that links all species. Rey neither preaches nor forces confrontation—he simply suspends the existence of the natural world before us so that we can contemplate the implications of his representations for ourselves and for future generations.

Rey's focus on fish and on nature has attracted scholarly and critical attention, since he intentionally changed his work in this direction. In 2001, James Prosek wrote on the evident spiritual and symbolic dimension that is part of the pictorial essence of Rey's paintings of fish and their environments.[24] He addressed the range of symbolic possibilities by pointing out that fish are a universal symbol of peace, order, strength, and perseverance (Zen traditions); an auspicious symbol of abundance (Chinese tradition); part of the Passover meal (Jewish tradition); the sign of Christ (all Christian traditions); and in alternative religious practices, Pisces is the astrological symbol for duality. It was also Prosek who indicated that the steelhead trout found in Western New York State bodies of water are not indigenous, but are native to California. They are a transplanted species that flourished in their new home. Hence, Prosek drew the parallel between the transplanted steelheads and Rey's Cuban origins and his American life, thereby emphasizing the role that identity plays, as a subtheme, in *Trout Encounters.*

In 2005, Suzanne Proulx pointed out that the steelhead trout "have a life preoccupation with finding home" that parallels Rey's search for a permanent home and a cohesive identity.[25] Proulx also emphasized the iconic aspect of the images of single fish depicted within rect-angular frames, reminiscent of fish trophies hung above fireplaces to record a catch. Yet, Proulx referenced these iconic trophies not within the world of sports but within the matrix of Catholic culture close to Rey's Cuban identity and original culture.

In the same catalog for which Proulx wrote her essay, Lynette M. F. Bosch emphasized that "The act of fishing evokes diverse associations, which run the gamut from mundane activity to spiritual practice. At its most essential, fishing represents the acquisition of food necessary for survival. As such, fishing constitutes an elemental reality that reflects one of nature's fundamental principles of consumption and survival, since fish are prey as well as predators. . . . For the fish, the contest is always a battle for life. For the one fishing, the meaning of the engagement varies and it is precisely this metaphysical space that is explored in Rey's paintings, wherein we plunge simultaneously into the world of the fish and into the minds of those who pierce below the surface of the waters fish inhabit." Movement of any kind disrupts the water, and so the fisher of trout must be prepared to withstand the tiny torments of bugs, itches, and twitches that are part of the human condition. In trout fishing, absorbing discomfort in order to reach the goal results in a process akin to that of Zen meditation, where physical discomfort is transmuted into spiritual gain.[26]

In 2008, Rey's next two series, *Biological Regionalism* and *The Aesthetics of Death*, were exhibited at the Staniar Gallery at Washington and Lee University. Dinah Ryan, Johanna Drucker, and Mark Denaci wrote the essays for the accompanying catalog.[27] Ryan's essay, titled "Drifting Sideways and Up," described how Rey's exhibition was coordinated with a scientific exploration of the fauna found in the pools alongside St. Mary's Creek, located in the area where the gallery is situated. Ryan wrote, "Alberto Rey is a painter, a fisherman, a preacher, a fly fishing guide, a man with deep connections to family and several communities. Faced with recent 'family deaths and serious illnesses,'" he has been intrigued by the thought of reintroducing piscatorial art ". . . into a contemporary aesthetic . . . while creating a venue to investigate our own mortality. . . ." A thread that runs through all of Alberto Rey's work, particularly his *Biological Regionalism* and *Aesthetics of Death* series, is the attempt to see a place, a family, or a community as a piece within a whole and to see the relation of these constituents. Thus, Ryan brought together the manner in which Rey employs the subject of fish to encompass his personal experience and knowledge, connected to universal themes of life and death and communal existence.

Johanna Drucker took a more overtly political stance in her contribution to this catalog.[28] As Drucker wrote, "This is the late era of globally networked ecosystems, all painfully sensitive to the least degree of climatic transformations caused in the massive systems of exploitative use (even as these are denied and trivialized in too many official circles). . . . The history of organic life is filled with mutations, migrations, and peculiar residual backwaters where species continue unaware of the very improbability of their survival." Drucker situated Rey's paintings of fish within the contemporary debates on ecological and species crash that has been brought about by careless industrialization.

From the perspective of contemporary art and critical theory, Mark Denaci's essay for this exhibition predominantly discusses how Alberto Rey responds and reacts to the description of "modernism" in art forwarded by the critic Clement Greenberg.[29] Denaci simultaneously engages with and resists Greenberg's conception of painting while moving in a thoughtfully paradoxical direction. As Denaci wrote, "While I claimed earlier that the 'Aesthetics of Death' series evokes a formalist aesthetic in its flatness and careful orientation to the picture plane (all Greenbergian principles), the paintings nevertheless cannot be understood as self-contained experiments in form. Instead, Rey's paintings reference a series of social issues, such as: the impact of human society on nature; the artist's ambivalent relationship to his homeland; the 19th-century American tradition of paintings of rugged land and ocean areas; and contemporary debates on the nature and status of painting. In this context, I cannot help but think of these multiple, sometimes barely visible connections as fishing lines. Fly-fishing, after all, involves an aesthetic—indeed, an aesthetics of death—but its aesthetics of death is simultaneously one of connection and engagement. Like a back-and-forth battle between fisher and prey, Rey's aesthetics oscillate between autonomy and involvement, absence and presence, death and life."

In 2010, Rey's work was discussed by Gerald Mead, who wrote the essay for the exhibition "Alberto Rey: Biological Regionalism: Ellicott Creek, Amherst, New York, USA."[30] Mead's assessment of Rey's work likened his intentions and path to those of the English painter J. M. W. Turner (1775–1851), the American Mark Rothko (1903–1970), and, most significantly for the exhibition at the Burchfield Penney, to those of Charles Burchfield (1893–1967), whose family provided the base for the collection that has become the Burchfield Penney Art Center at the Buffalo State College campus of the State University of New York. Meade perceived in Rey's art the engagement with form, color, and light of Turner; the spirituality of Rothko; and the abiding interest in the representation of nature that characterizes Burchfield's watercolors, drawings, and paintings. Mead also indicated how Rey expanded his pictorial repertoire to include video in the installation that sought to bring the spectator to the locale of Ellicott Creek in order to enable a connection between the experience of art in a museum and the world of nature that inspired the art the spectator sees.

It is now 2013, as this book is being written, and Rey is preparing for the Burchfield Penney exhibition that will open in Spring 2014, and his work on *Trout Encounters, Biological Regionalism,* and *The Aesthetics of Death* has developed thematically and challengingly for the artist and the spectator. A few observations can be made about the form, content, and atmospheric impact of Rey's images—in paint or video. Throughout these series, there is a dearth of direct human participation in the imagery Rey has developed, although there are occasional representations of the people Rey has met on his travels. Despite the occasional human presence in this work, the lack of human presence in Rey's images is most striking when studying his paintings as a group, which allows viewers to perceive this lack as a thematic movement within the body of work.

For Rey, it is all about the fish. The intense focus on the fish that Rey depicts means that the spectator is immediately engaged with Rey's subject, whether the individual work represents a group of fish or a single fish underwater. Images of single fish, depicted as though they lay on a bank, are represented in a style evocative of sculptural renditions, as though these fish were carved and painted wall trophies from a very successful fishing trip.

Yet, resonant as they are with this aspect of display of a catch, Rey's fish take on independent life from such associations, as they exist on their own terms as individual representatives of their species. The manner in which Rey delineates their contours, and carefully marks their colors and the texture of their scales, fins, gills, and eyes, tells the connoisseur which type of fish is present, such details are so minutely rendered. Rey has painted steelhead trout, rainbow trout, brown trout, brook trout, bull trout, cutthroat trout, king salmon, and sea run trout. His repertoire also includes char, Dolly Varden trout, stripers, brook trout, grayling, small mouth bass, largemouth bass, and tarpon. For each type of fish, he has also made studies of their surroundings and environments.

Although Rey's fish are sensitively rendered, he does not sentimentalize the animals. There is a deliberate objective distance that Rey adopts as he steps back to enable the spectator to personally interpret the images he forwards. Rey doesn't control the emotional response by engaging in narrative in a direct or obvious way. His style is realistic, with a touch of hyperrealism that never tilts into surrealism. The represented fish appear as equals to the spectator; hence, the artist enables or mediates but does not define the encounter. Thus, Rey's paintings are not people-centric and he does not anthropomorphize his subjects. In this, he is very different from his contemporaries, such as Walton Ford, Alexis Rockman, and James Prosek, as these artists either humanize their animals, birds, and fish, or they develop scenarios that are centered on obtaining specific responses from the spectator.

Rey avoids the challenging and, sometimes, confrontational aspects evident in the work of these artists and in the work of other contemporary artists—one thinks, for instance, of Damien Hirst's (b. 1965) *The Physical Impossibility of Death in the Mind of Someone Living*, part of his *Death* series, which is intended to shock and even disgust by placing an actual dead animal in front of the spectator as a work of art. Hirst's nihilistic message is the opposite of Rey's intention, as Rey wants to remind us, even in his *Aesthetics of Death* series, that we are all in the same cycle of life and death. Where Hirst exploits the animals he uses in his series, much as industrialization has exploited nature, Rey's objective presentation enables spectators to forge a link with the natural cycles of life and death and to place themselves within these cycles in a manner that is meditative and profoundly spiritual.

Rey is aware that nature is fragile and ephemeral, as is life. There is embedded in his fish a sense that they may be the last of their kind, that he is making a record of what may one day be what existed in the past. Yet, Rey makes it clear that the fish that are here are very much alive and engaged in their natural cycle of life, reproduction, and death. While we may be living in a world that feels as though we were participating in the Last Days of Pompeii, we are all far from being extinct, much as Rey's fish continue to exist, engaged in their lives with their cycles of reproduction and death. Thus, Rey's work can be interpreted as a subtle form of activism and an indirect expression of spirituality and kinship with the natural world. The possibility of extinction for the species he paints—fish and human—is only one part of natural life and existence. The cycle is our cycle, and, in rendering his fish as he does, Rey makes us aware that we share their mortality and that our actions matter, as do their lives.

In Rey's images, the more frequent–than-not erasure of intrusive human presence achieves an expression of innate identity for the natural landscape and for its denizens. Increasingly, the spiritual aspect discerned in Rey's work has become more important, and the connections between transcendent states and the contemplation of the iconic image of the fish have become more emphatic. The fish, usually trout, depicted by Rey are the counterparts of the Zen concept of *suchness* or the Sanskrit "Tathata," translated as *thusness* or *suchness*. The intrinsic meaning of this concept for Buddhists refers to the existentialist awareness of true reality that is beyond the mirage of material existence and which can only be perceived when form and symbol are understood to be only signifiers of true existence, but not the actuality of experience.

The fish represented by Rey are a manifestation of *suchness* because they are not self-conscious or self-aware. Because they live in the moment, they are a manifestation of the essential being to which we all belong. The integrity of being of each fish, depicted by Rey, in its essential nature as both the form and the symbol that represents their *suchness* enables us to understand how each depicted fish is itself and part of the whole. In the absorption of the details of the fish, which are simultaneously real, yet rendered as ideals, Rey lets the fish be fish as he enables the spectator to connect to the existence beyond Rey's

representation of what is perceived by sight in art, yet exists as truth in nature.

Rey's images let the fish be fish on their own terms, and the artist and the spectator cannot make them anything other than that—their "Tathata." They are both nature and art, with each sphere respected by the artist, who accepts the innate and intrinsic manifestation of what it is that is fish and what it is to be fish even as he connects to our restless consciousness that seeks to make fish be something more and something less than fish. Rey's work prevents us from erasing the existence of the suchness of his subjects by his rendering in a style that is realistic but that always reminds us that this is not the real, but a painted effigy of what is real.

In effect, Rey issues the invitation to the encounter with reality that is the real subject of his paintings. And he refuses to mediate that encounter, because it exists across a gap of experience that indicates the void separating humans from their natural, metaphysical, and united nature. Rey's work is painfully aware of the solipsistic alienation that separates human beings from each other and from their place in existence. His paintings, videos, and installations are thus meditations on achieving connection, presented in a matrix of awareness, perception, and realization designed to bring us to the moment when we say—being is this—in a moment of essential awareness of existence. Thus does Rey seek to bring us to a moment of enlightenment when we can value the life of the fish he represents in a manner that takes us into a moment of absolute connection.

It is Zen *suchness* that Rey offers in his objective, yet aware, observant, yet removed, present but absent, rendition of existence in the world of trout. In Rey's work, one of the fish that became linked to American identity is revealed as itself being an indexical marker of the changing life of the country to which Rey was brought and which now defines his existence and ours. As a sign of its land, its environment, and its people, Rey's fish are a moment of *suchness* that has become the culminating expression of Rey's search for identity and his quest for home.

Among the contemporary painters of fish and wildlife, Rey's *The Aesthetics of Death* series is an important contribution to fish and wildlife painting. Rey began this series during a time in his life that permanently changed its patterns. Within a few close years, his sister died, his father-in-law died, and his wife, Janeil, was twice diagnosed with cancer. At this juncture, Rey's life was divided into the time before these events and the time after, as they represented a rupture in the continuity of his life that was equivalent to his parents' exile from Cuba. While Rey was too young to have memories of that break between a former and a subsequent life, as a result of this series of conflated events, each of these traumas created a resonance with the experiences of his parents and of other exiles who had experienced similar dislocations. As Rey processed the reality and the understanding of life after these traumatic events, he located his newly gained knowledge and understanding of what trauma can do to change the course of existence in his renditions of the dead and rotting fish that are the subjects for *The Aesthetics of Death.*

It would have been easy and simple for Rey to have represented dead fish as negative images of the end of life, overwhelmed by dissolution and decay. But Rey chose to give form to a harder lesson—the acceptance of change gained through the intimate knowledge and observation of the dead. Zen practice again becomes the parallel for Rey's artistic intention, as part of Buddhist practice is the observation of the decay of corpses. Instruction in this aspect of Zen meditation is intended to produce a state of equanimity in the students, who set themselves death as their subject of study. In the colors, forms, and actual and implied smells of death, there is also a connection to life as the corpses of the dead are the homes for new life. Thus, the record of the end is also the event of a new beginning.

At the end of the meditation on death, the Zen students are meant to understand that it is all one and to cease from fearing their personal end. Rey's goal was to give form to the beauty of death to evoke a similar response in the spectator. Death is our constant companion, and its feared moment is the end of the human cycle, but it is not the final stage of our material existence. We become transformed by death in the same way that Rey's fish are consumed by waves of color and forms of change that transpose them into petrified moments in the process toward the final transformation into new forms.

Rey's "The Aesthetics of Death" is original in intention and in presentations, as his monumental paintings extend to the edges of our sightline, defining our perspective on the world. Their message is universal and defined by the imagery he employs to bring us to a moment of enlightenment about our death. Indeed, the trout die—as individuals and, perhaps, as a species. We may all be destroyed. Yet, this destruction is natural and should be accepted as part of the cycle of what is. Eternal *suchness* is the true meaning of *The Aesthetics of Death*, and the message of this series is acceptance and the knowledge that in the acceptance of change and of endings is a renewal and an ease of life that is the only actualized joy of existence. In creating this series, Rey has shown himself to be a painter of a spiritual depth that is the product of a lifetime of being, seeing, recording, and communicating. *The Aesthetics of Death* series is, for now, his most compelling presentation of the initial recognition of unity in life that was the catalyst for *Trout Encounters* and which propelled him into *Biological Regionalism*.

As was mentioned at the beginning of this chapter, John Orlock's essay, which follows this chapter, addresses the literary tradition that has traced the development of the pragmatic and the philosophical aspects of fishing, and especially fly-fishing, from Classical antiquity to the present. This literature has been important for Alberto Rey, even though his work is not directly illustrative of the literature Rey has read as he has developed his skills as an angler and a fisher. The importance of this work for Rey fits within the larger context of fishing as a cultural activity and as a marker of identity as well as a meditative state. The act of fishing is multidimensional and crosses from a food-gathering process to an occupation, to sports, to, as Mark Denaci points out in his essay, an aesthetic engagement on many levels, which for Rey is a crucial part of his identity as an artist.

Orlock's essay traces what writers have said about fishing, how philosophers have analyzed fishing, and how the different types of literature about fishing have created a culture of fishing and of writing about fishing that doesn't require a reader to fish in order to understand the process, its importance, and its cultural contribution. The chapters of this book have addressed Rey's work and its context directly, beginning with the imagery, intention, context, and content of Rey's work. Orlock's essay is more concerned with the intellectual and cultural foundation on which Rey built the visual exploration of his experience and knowledge about fishing. In a parallel manner to Rey, who began to work in painting, moved to sculpture, then incorporated video in created environmental installations, Orlock moves from printed text to film in his consideration of the literature on fishing. Hence, while Orlock writes as a writer about those who have written about fishing and what it means to fish, his territory is simultaneously tangential and ancillary to Rey's process. Thus, Orlock's chapter concludes with Rey's assessment of what the literature about fishing that Orlock discusses has meant for him, thereby bringing the artist, who is the subject of this book, into direct connection with the territory Orlock has mapped out.

NOTES

1. IGFA Fishing Hall of Fame & Museum: http://www.igfa.org/Museum/Visit-the-Museum.aspx). Accessed August 22, 2012.

2. Mission statement: "The International Game Fish Association is a not-for-profit organization committed to the conservation of game fish and the promotion of responsible, ethical angling practices through science, education, rule making and record keeping."

3. For the early history of the club, see W. Milnor, *An Authentic Historical*

Memoir of the Schuylkill Fishing Company of the State in Schuylkill: From Its Establishment on that Romantic Stream, New Philadelphia, in the Year 1732, to the Present Time, (Philadelphia, Pa.: J. Dobson, 1830).

4. Fish House Punch was composed of one cup of sugar, three and half cups of water, one and a half cups of fresh lemon juice, one (750 ml) bottle of Jamaican amber rum, twelve ounces of Cognac, two ounces of peach brandy, and was served on a block of ice and garnished with lemon slices.

5. See Montclair Art Museum, *Piscatorial Pictorials: A Private Collection*. January 14–February 25, 1973 (Montclair, N.J.: Montclair Art Museum Press, 1973), fig. 20. A print of the "Castle" of the State in Schuylkill, by Swett P. K. & Co. Philadelphia, 1830.

6. Bryan F. Le Beau, *Currier & Ives: America Imagined* (Washington, D.C.: Smithsonian Press, 2001); Christopher W. Lane, with D. H. Cresswell and C. Cades, *A Guide to Collecting Currier & Ives* (Philadelphia, Pa.: Philadelphia Print Shop, 2001); Alexandra Bonfante-Warren, *Currier & Ives: Portraits of a Nation* (New York: Metro Books, 1998).

7. Izaak Walton, *The Compleat Angler*, ed. Charles Cotton (Tyler, Tex.: Arcturus Press, 2010).

8. William H. Gerdts, "The Art of Fishing in the United States," in *Winslow Homer: Artist and Angler*, ed. Patricia Junker and Sarah Burns (London: Thames & Hudson, 2005), 185–226.

9. See, Tom Quinn, *Angling in Art* (London: The Sportsman's Press, 1991), passim.

10. See Michael Mayr, *Das Fischereibuch Kaiser Maximilians I, Wagner's: Innsbruck*, 1901; Paul Van Dyke, "The Literary Activity of the Emperor Maximilian I," *American Historical Review* 11 (October 1905): 16–28; A Fisherman's Library: Honoring the Gift of Angling Books from Robert A. De Vilbiss '33, Chapin Library, Williams College, September–November, 1995, 2).

11. Gerdts, *The Art of Fishing*, 185–186.

12. Ibid., 186–187.

13. Ibid., 185–187.

14. Ibid., 186.

15. Ibid., 187.

16. Ibid., 187.

17. Ibid., 187.

18. Emil A. Gruppe, *Gruppe on Painting: Direct Techiniques in Oil* (New

York: Watson-Guptill), 1976; Emil A. Gruppe, *Brushwork for the Oil Painter* (New York: Watson-Guptill, 1977); and *Gruppe on Color: Using Expressive Color to Paint Nature* (New York: Watson-Guptill, 1979).

19. For a leading collection of Pleissner's works, see: http://shelburnemuseum.org/. Accessed on August 22, 2012.

20. Neil Welliver, *Neil Welliver Prints: 1973–1995* (Rockport, Me.: Down East Books, 1976); Robert Doty and John B. Myers, *Neil Welliver: Paintings, 1966–1980* (University Press of New England, 1982); and Mark Strand and Michael Culver, *Neil Welliver: Paintings, 1983–2001* (Ogunquit Museum, 2001).

21. Stephen Jay Gould, Jonathan Cary, and David Quammen, *Alexis Rockman* (Monacelli Press, 2004); Joanna Marsh, Kevin J. Avery, and Thomas Lovejoy, *Alexis Rockman: A Fable for Tomorrow* (D Giles Ltd, 2011); Alexis Rockman, *Alexis Rockman: Manifest Destiny*, ed. Robert Kennedy, Arnold Lehman, Maurice Berger, Sheri Pasquarella (Gorney Bravin + Lee: Brooklyn Museum, 2005); and Douglas Blau, *Alexis Rockman* (Gorney Art Publ., 1992).

22. Bill Buford, *Walton Ford: Pancha Trantra* (Taschen, 2007); Steven Katz and Dodie Kazanjian, *Walton Ford: Tigers of Wrath, Horses of Instruction* (Harry N. Abrams, 2002); Walton Ford, *Paintings by Walton Ford* (Bowdoin College Museum of Art, 2000).

23. James Prosek, *Trout: An Illustrated History* (Knopf, 1996); James Prosek, *A Good Day's Fishing* (Simon & Schuster Books for Young Readers, 2004); James Prosek, Peter Matthiessen, Robert M. Peck, and Christopher Riopelle, *James Prosek: Ocean Fishes: Paintings of Saltwater Fish* (Rizzoli, 2012); James Prosek, *Trout of the World* (Stewart, Tabori and Chang, 2003); James Prosek, *The Complete Angler: A Connecticut Yankee Follows in the Footsteps of Walton* (Harper, 1999); James Prosek, *Early Love and Brook Trout: With Watercolor Paintings by the Author* (Lyons Press, 2000); James Prosek, *Joe and Me: An Education in Fly-Fishing and Friendship* (William Morrow, 1997); James Prosek, *Fly-Fishing the 41st: Around the World on the 41st Parallel* (Harper, 2003).

24. James Prosek, "What Is a Fish and Why Paint Them?" in *Trout Encounters*, Adams Art Gallery, Dunkirk, New

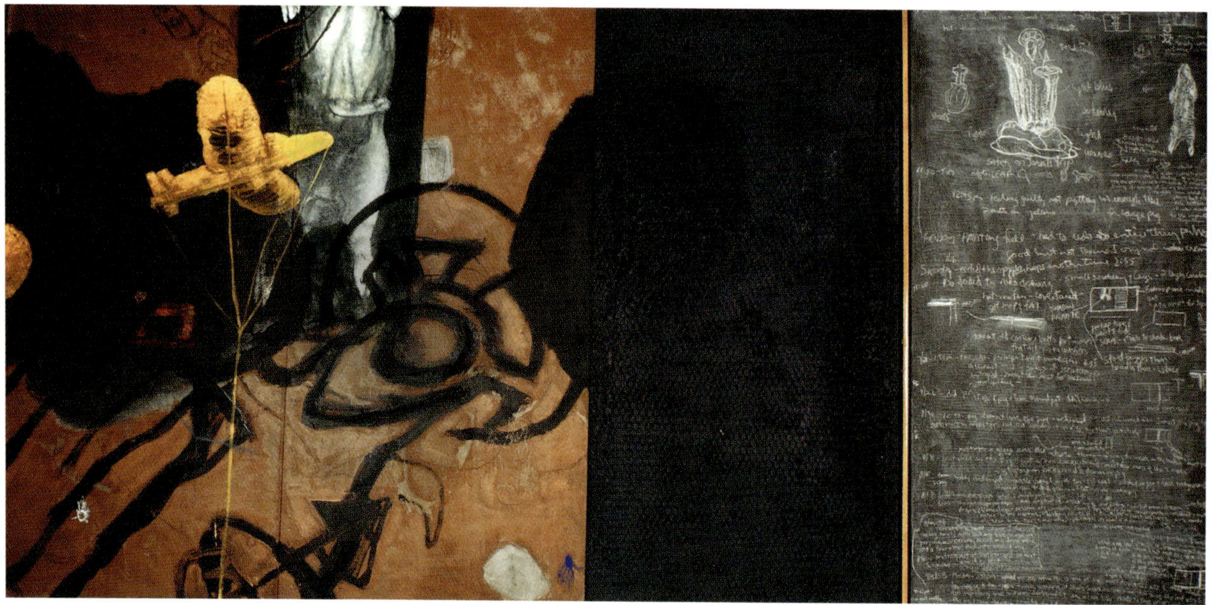

Fig. 2. *Transitions* (*Autogeographical Series*), 1988. Oil paint, tar, dry pigment, acrylic paint, chalk, graphite, wire, 96" × 192". Castellani Art Museum, Niagara University, NY.

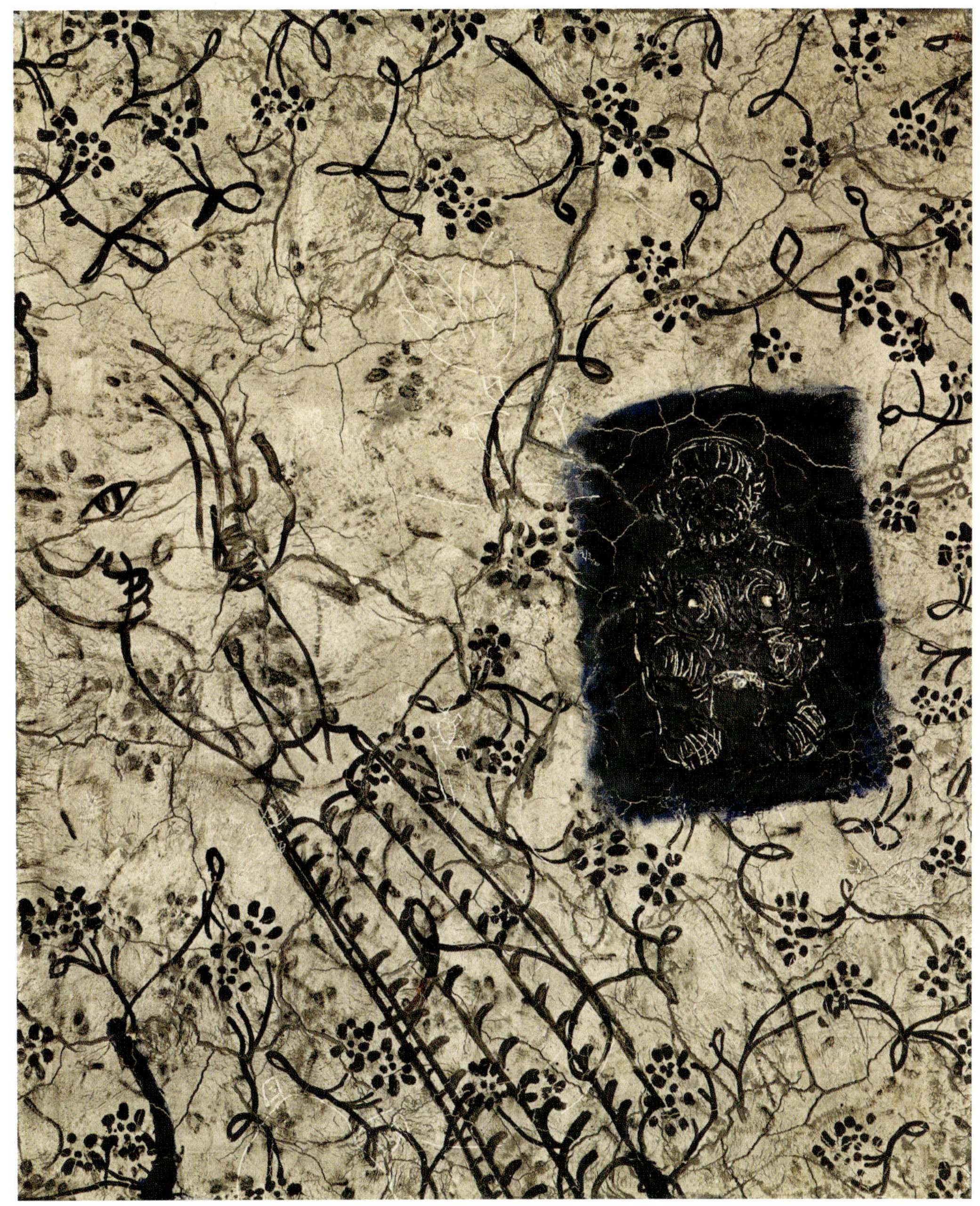

Fig. 3. *Black Lace Series: Fertility,* 1989. Oil paint and ink on flour compound, 40" × 48". Artist's collection.

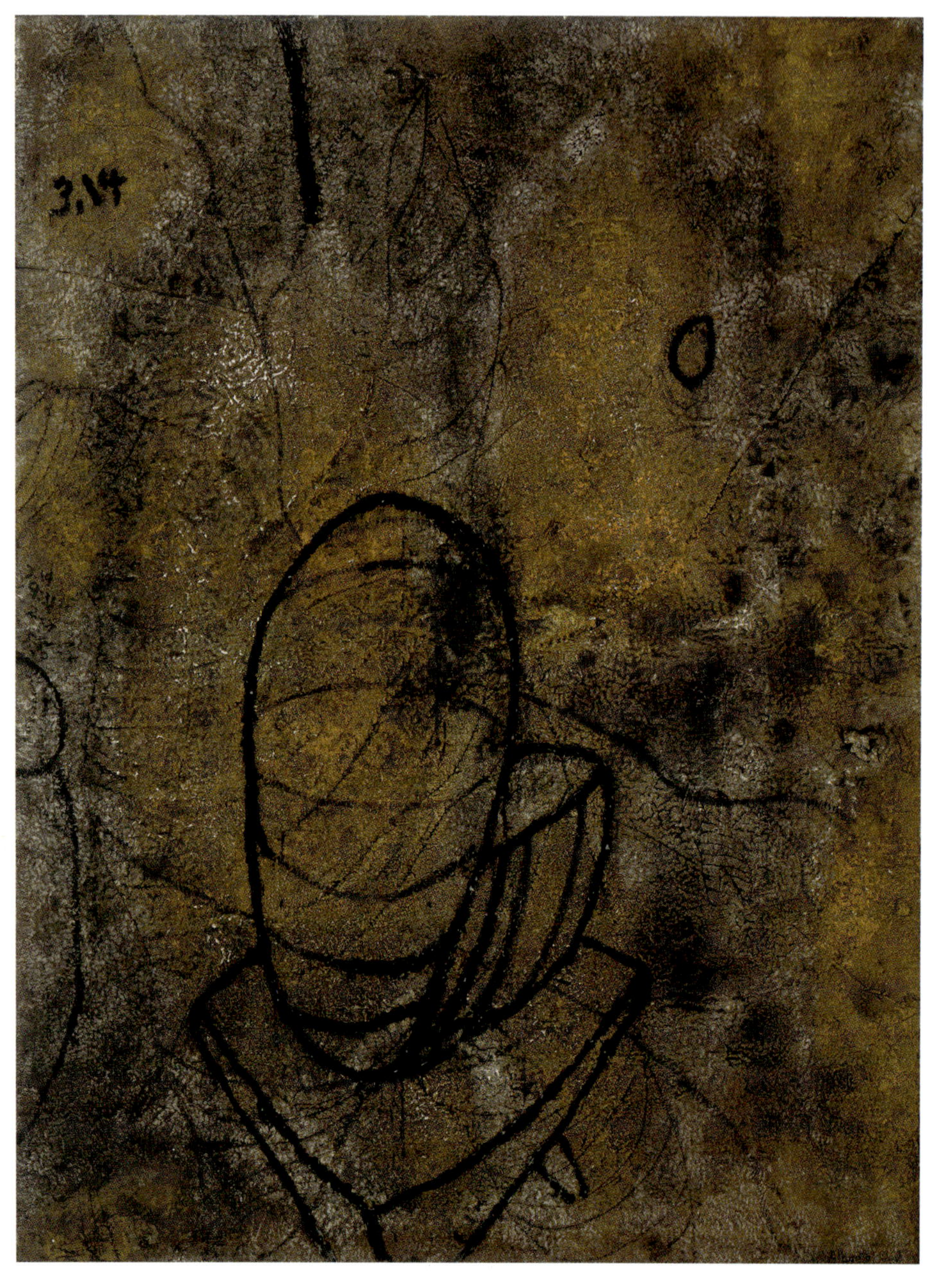

Fig. 4. *Post-Nuptial Gold: Time* (*Binary Forms Series*), 1991. Ink, oil paint, flour compound, and rabbit skin glue on canvas, 96" × 72". Albright Knox Art Gallery, Buffalo, NY.

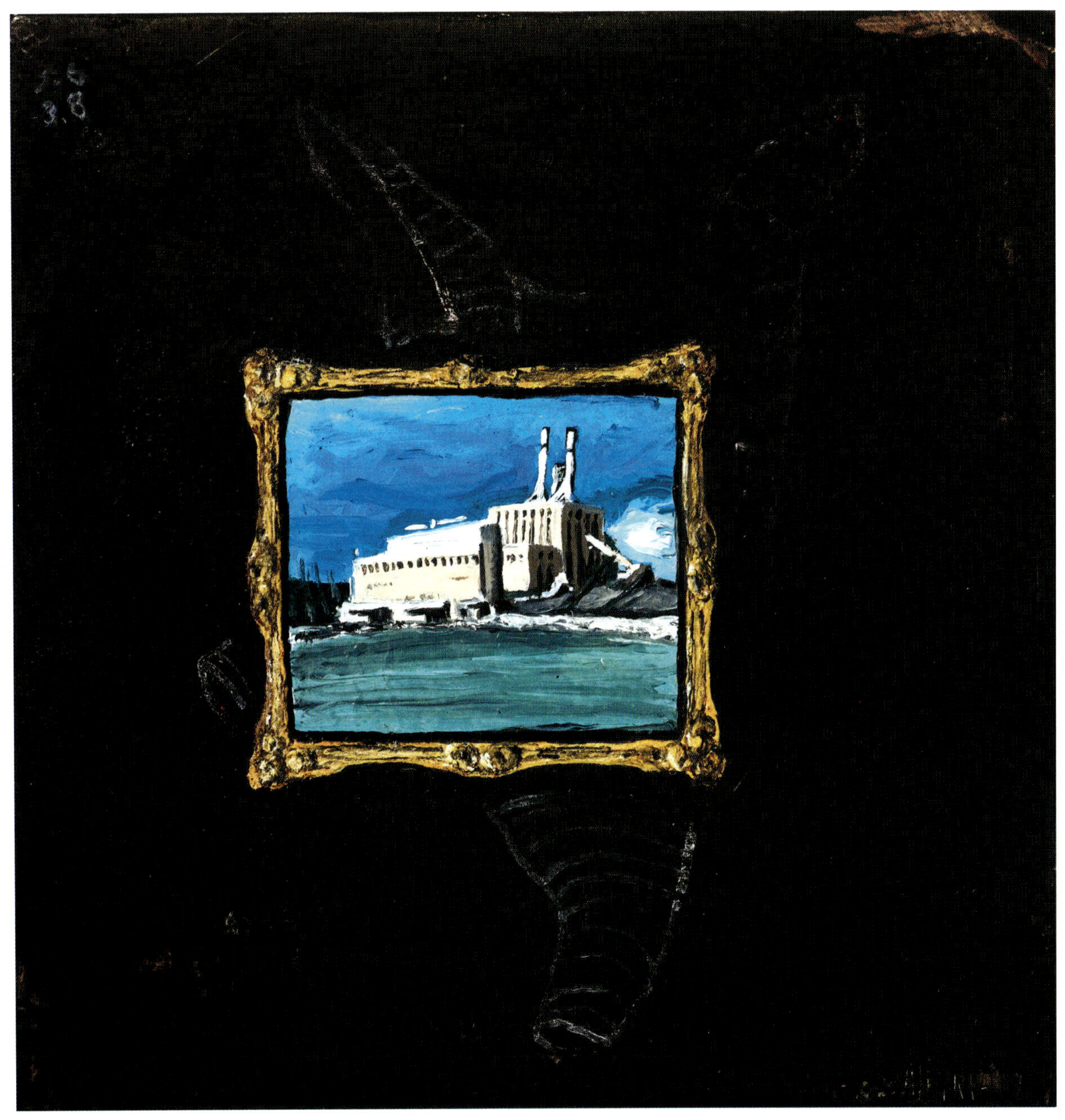

Fig. 5. *Madonnas of Western New York: Niagara Mohawk, Dunkirk, New York*, 1992. Oil on wood, 6" × 6" × 3". Artist's collection.

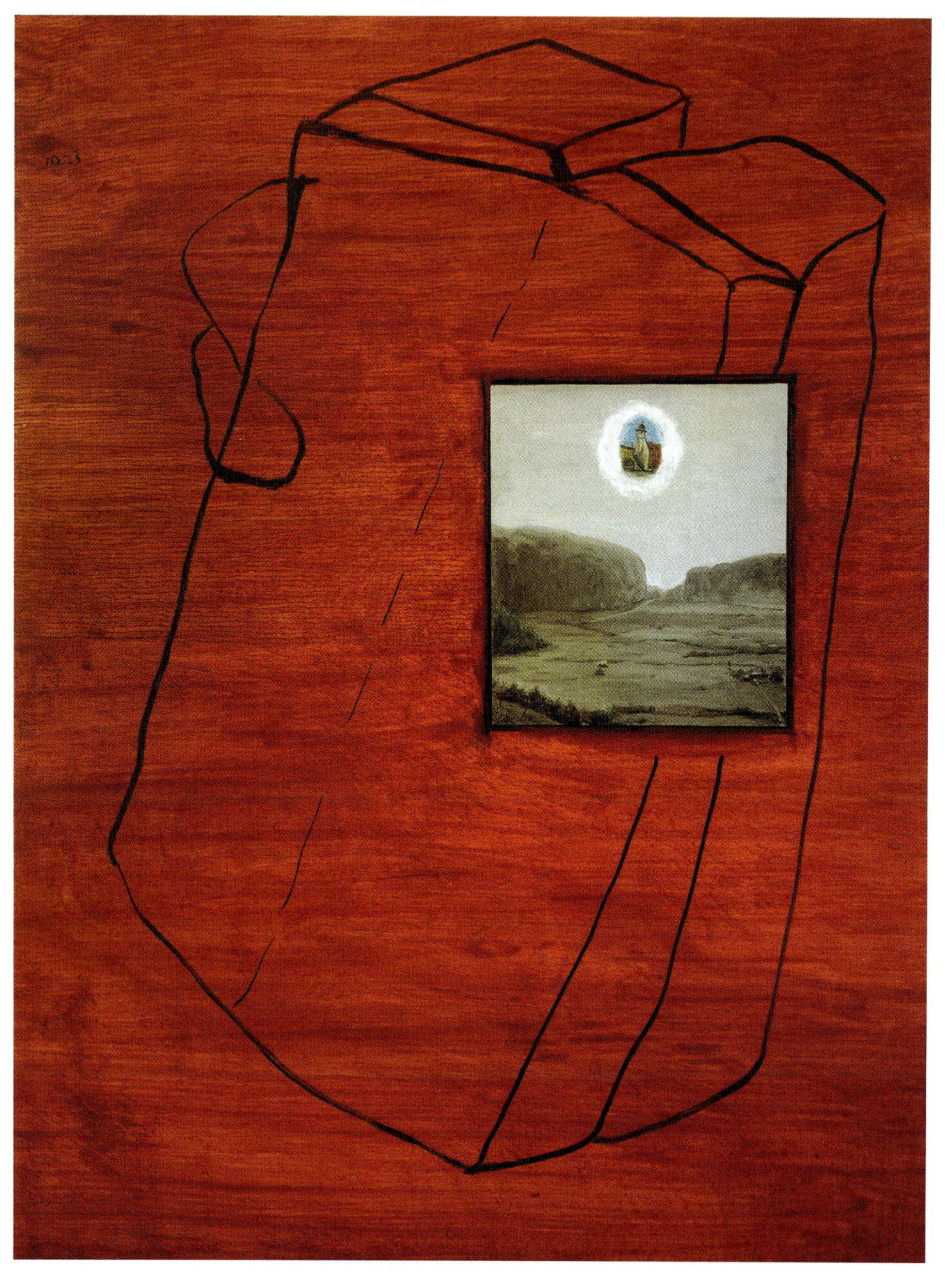

Fig. 6. *Madonnas in Time: Viñales, Cuba/Punxsutawney Phil*, 1993. Oil on wood, 30" × 36" × 4". Tampa Museum of Art, Tampa, FL.

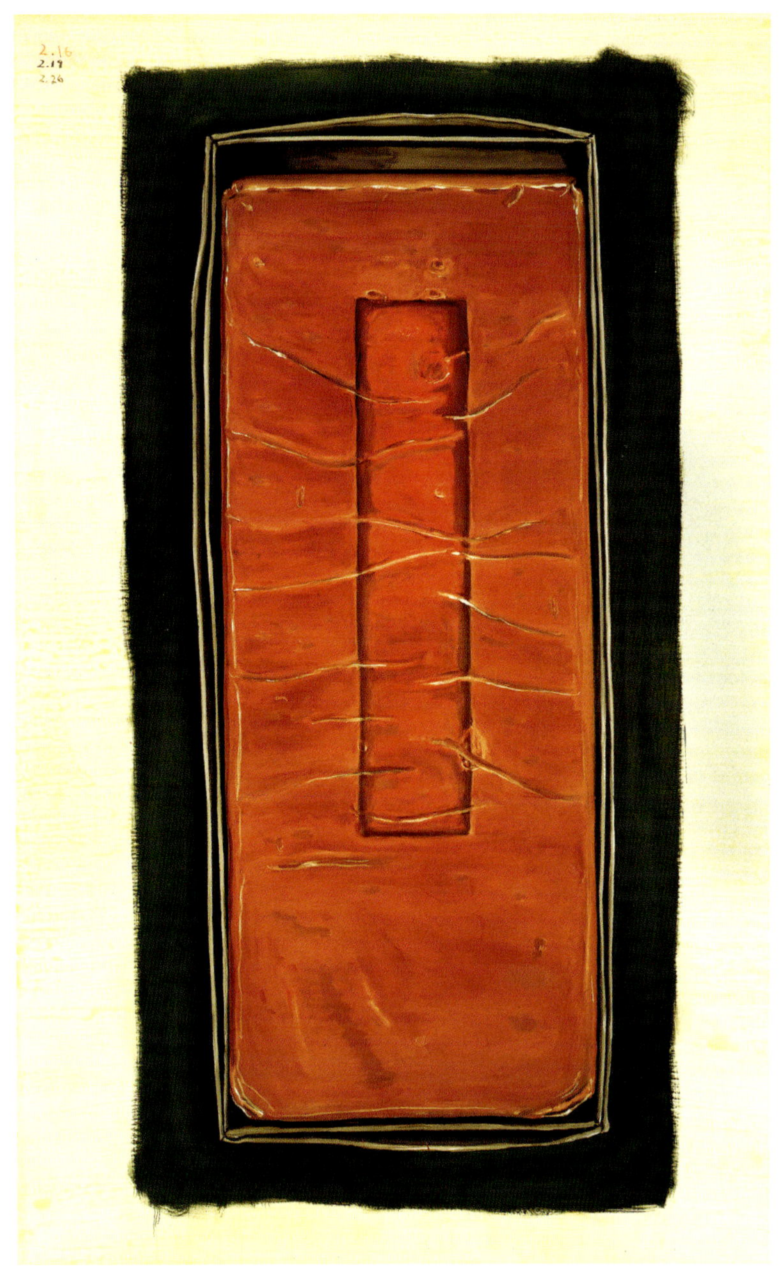

Fig. 7. *Icon Series: Ancel Guava Paste*, 1994. Oil on plaster, 96" × 48" × 4". Museum of Art, Fort Lauderdale, FL.

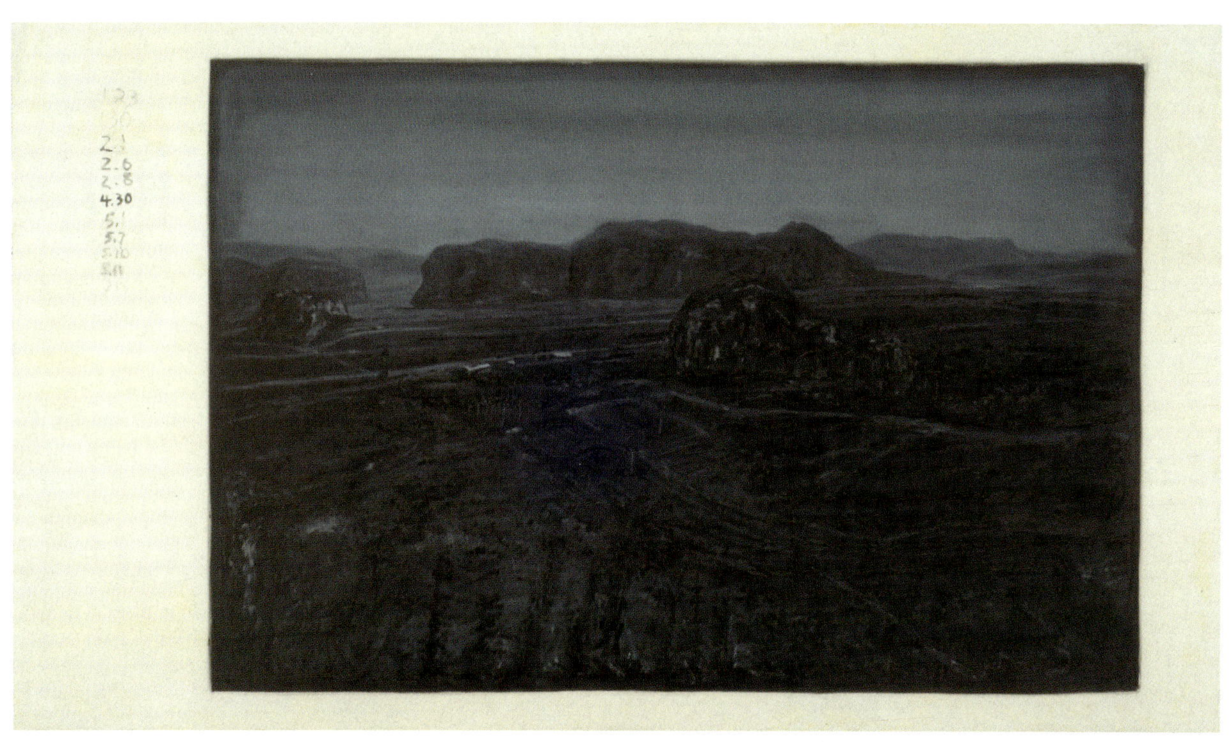

Fig. 8. *Appropriated Memories: Viñales, Cuba*, 1995. Oil on plaster, 48" × 84" × 4". Burchfield Penney Art Center, Buffalo, NY.

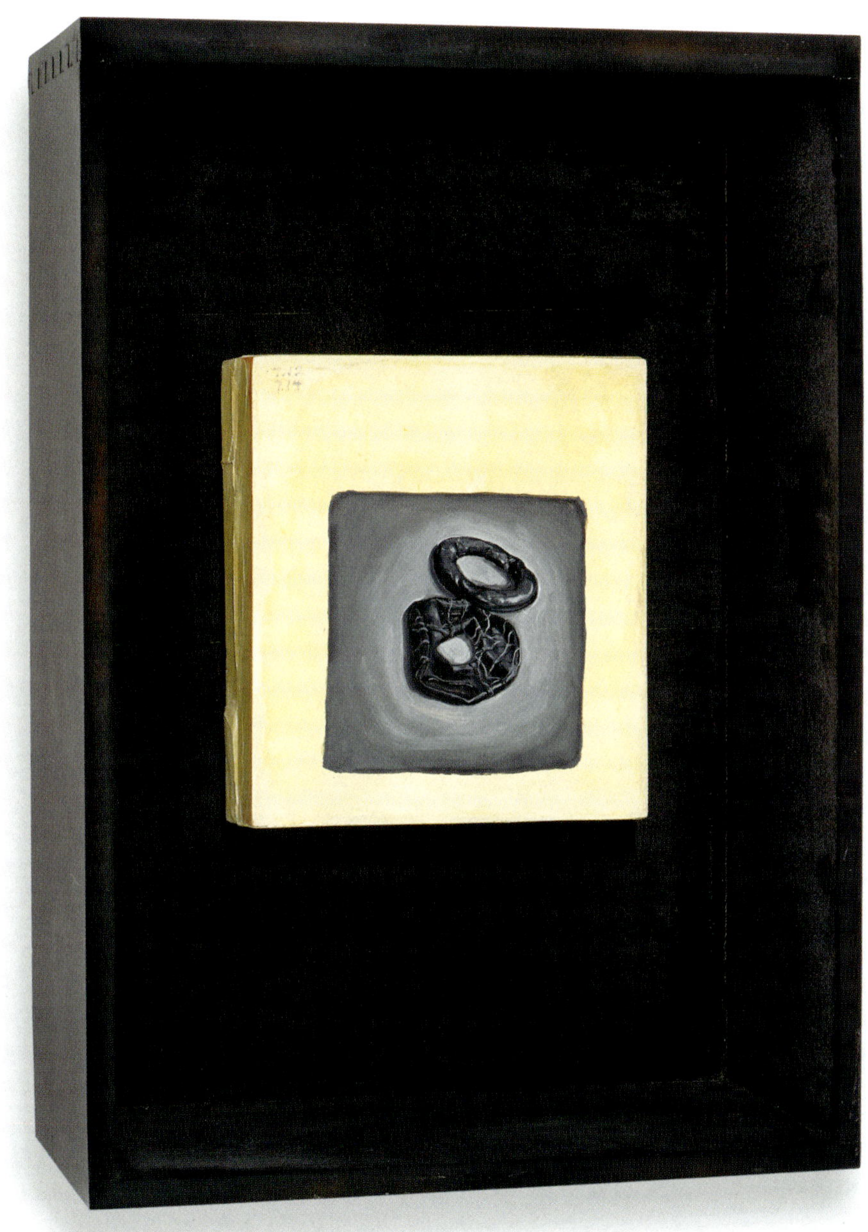

Fig. 9. Detail of *Las Balsas (The Rafts): II*, 1995. Oil on plaster, outside box 19.5" × 14" × 11.5" / inside painting 9" × 18" × 2.5". Artist's collection.

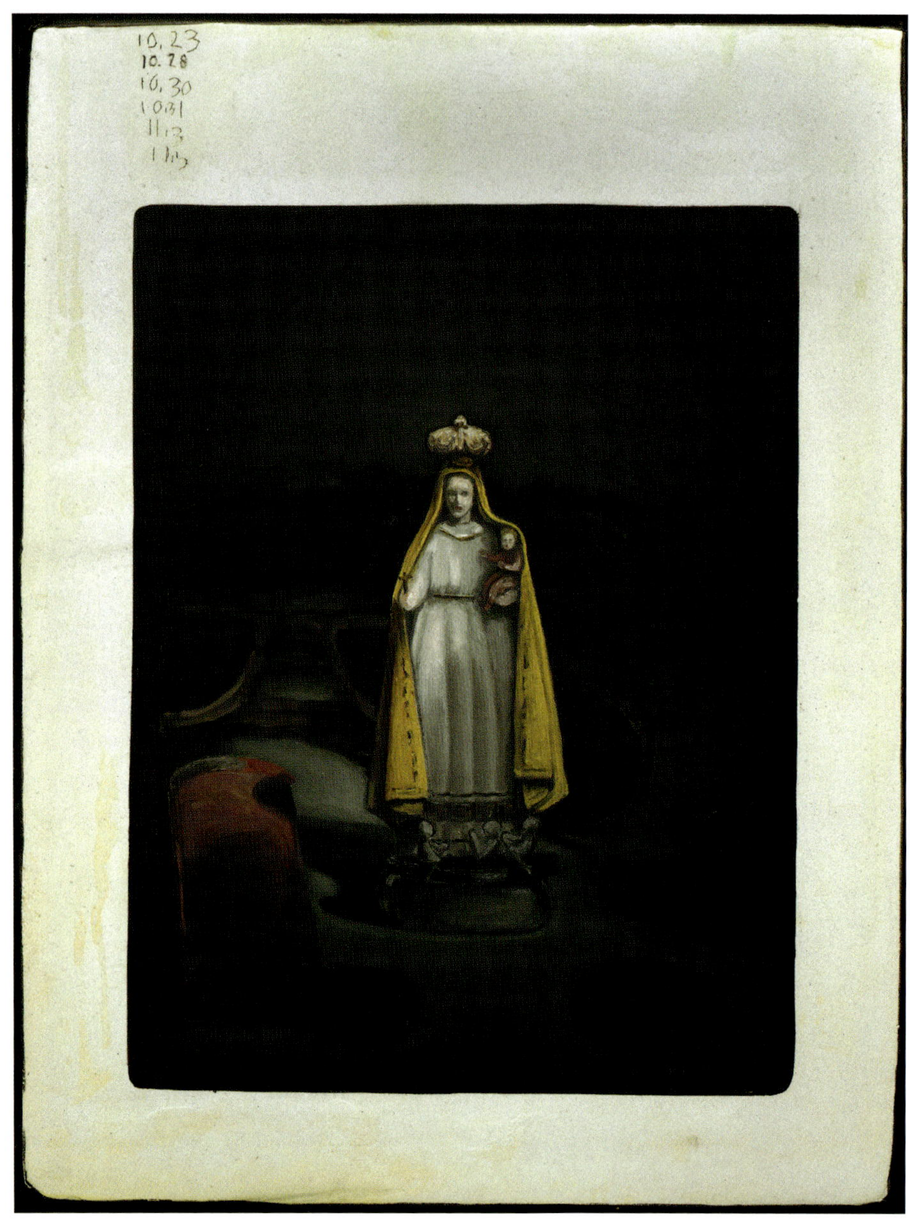

Fig. 10. *Las Balsas (The Rafts) Artifacts: Caridad de Cobre*, 1997. Oil on plaster, 15.5" × 12" × 14". Private collection.

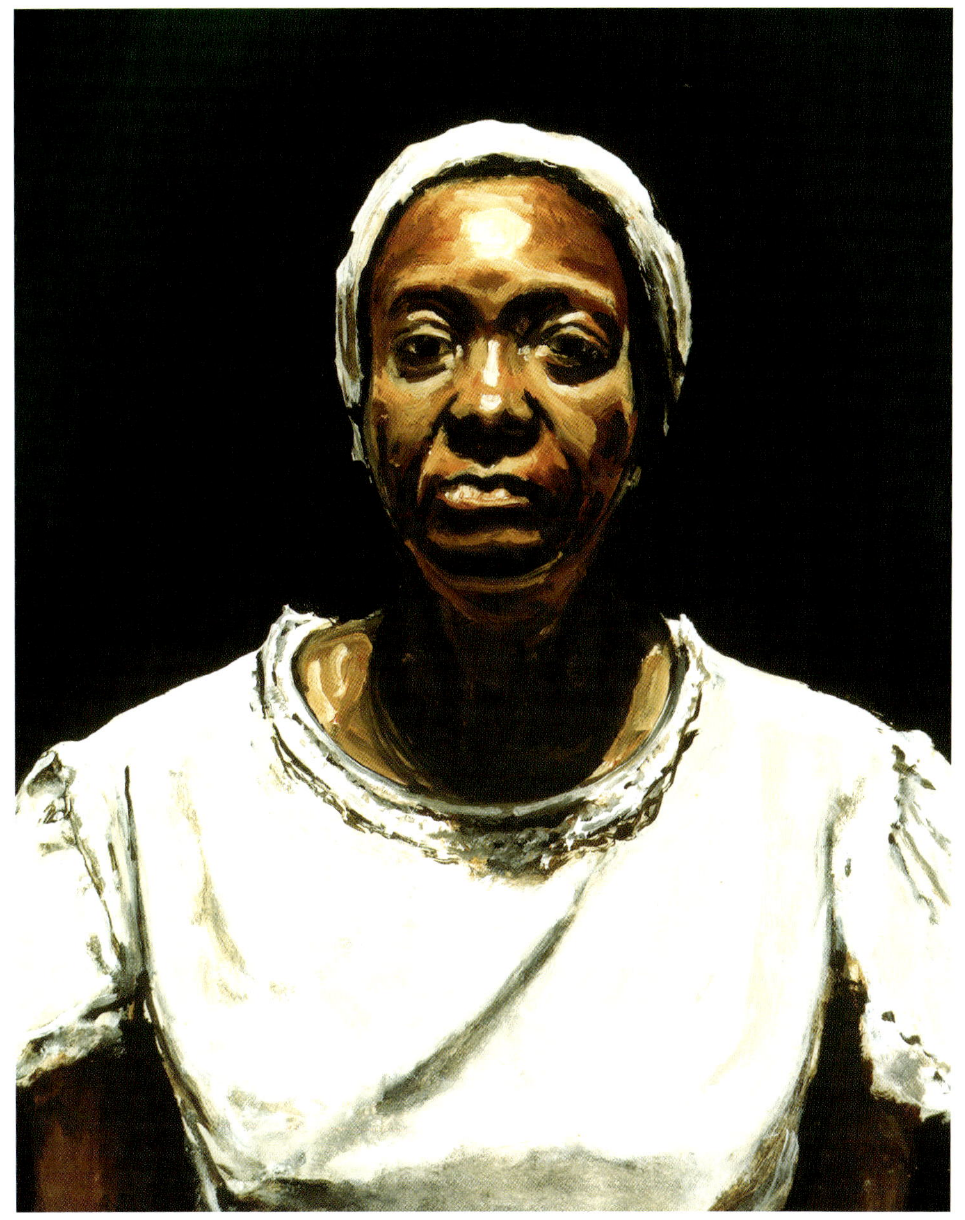

Fig. 11. Detail of *Cuban Portrait Series: Hilda, Agramonte, Cuba*, 1998. Oil on plaster, 15.5" × 12" × 2". Artist's collection.

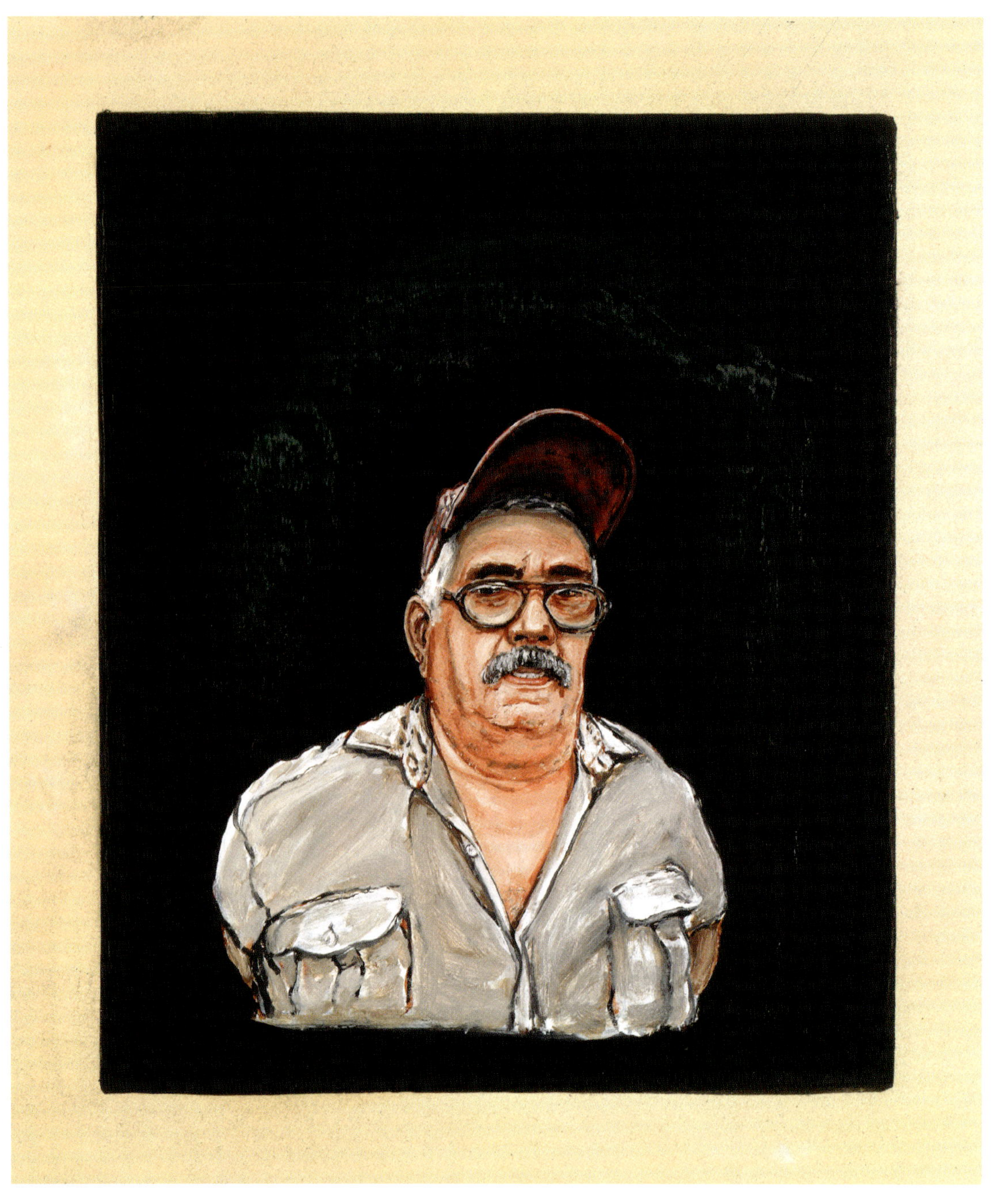

Fig. 12. *Cuban Portrait Series: Alberto, Agramonte, Cuba,* 1999. Oil on plaster, 15.5" × 12" × 2". Artist's collection.

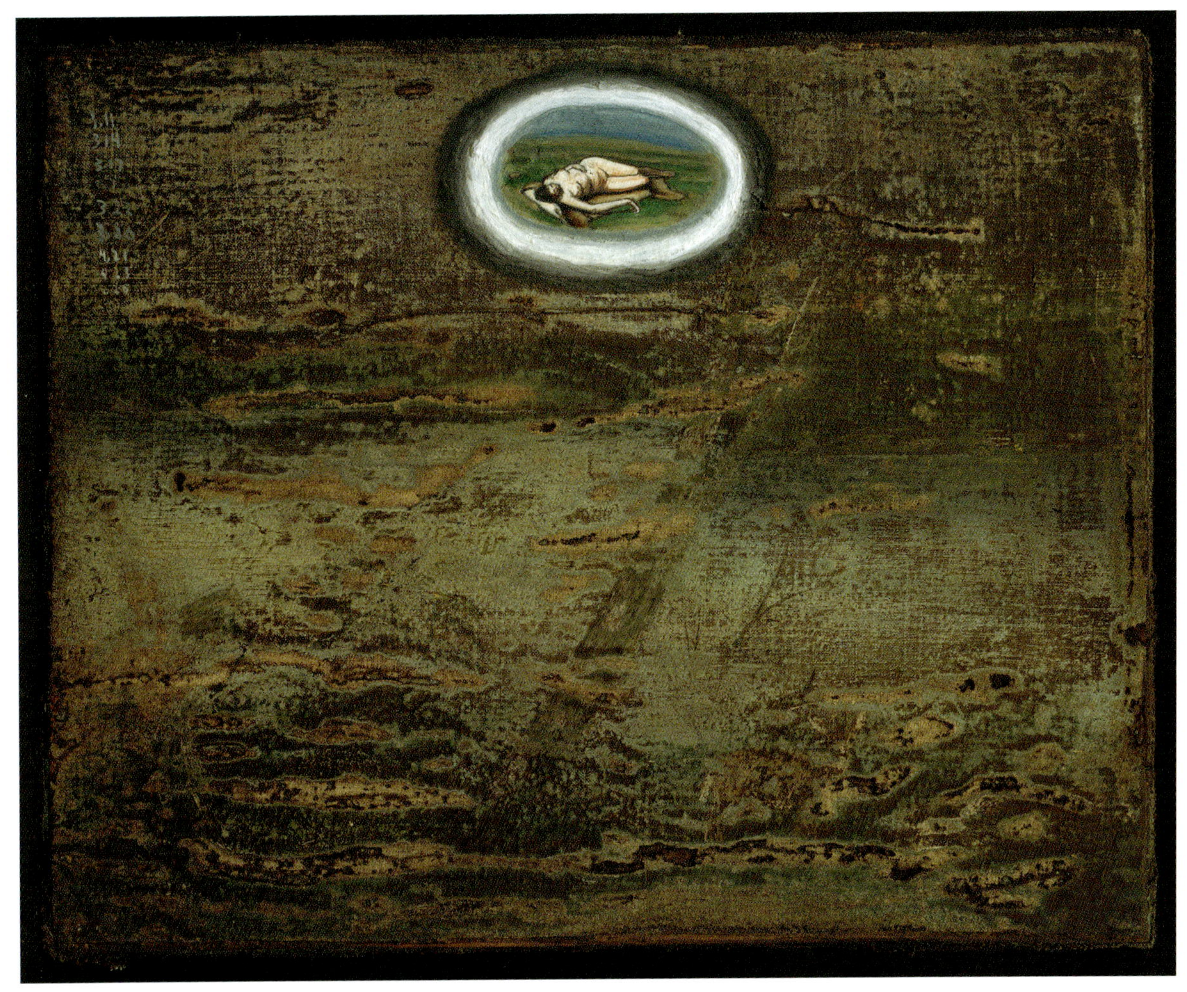

Fig. 13. *Studio Retablos: Mexican Figure*, 1999. Oil on canvas, 14.5" × 17". Artist's collection.

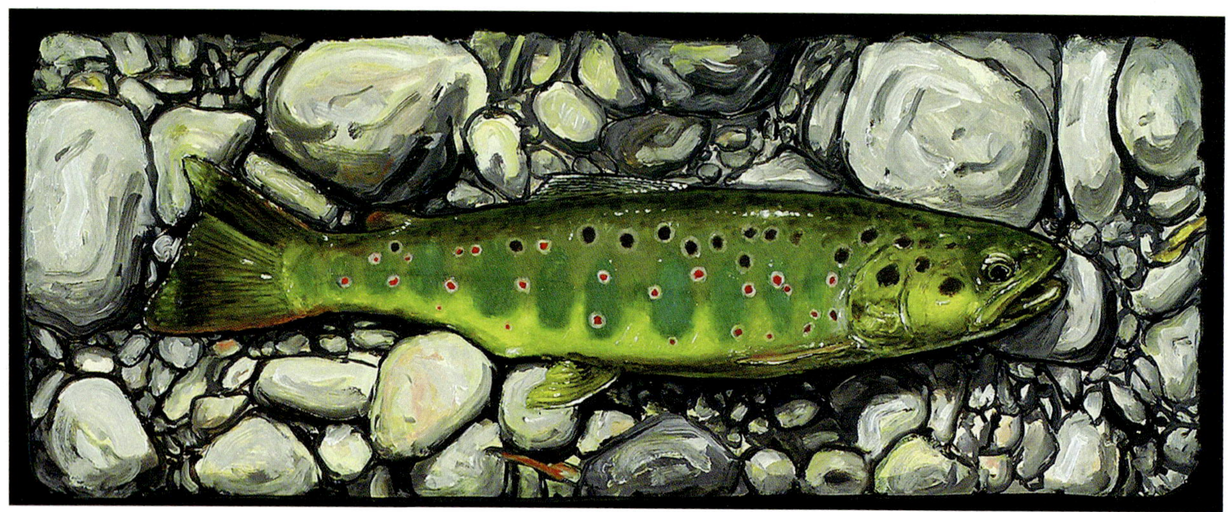

Fig. 14. *Trout Encounters: Brown Trout, Hosmer Creek, Sardinia, NY*, 2003. Oil on plaster, 15.5" × 33". Private collection.

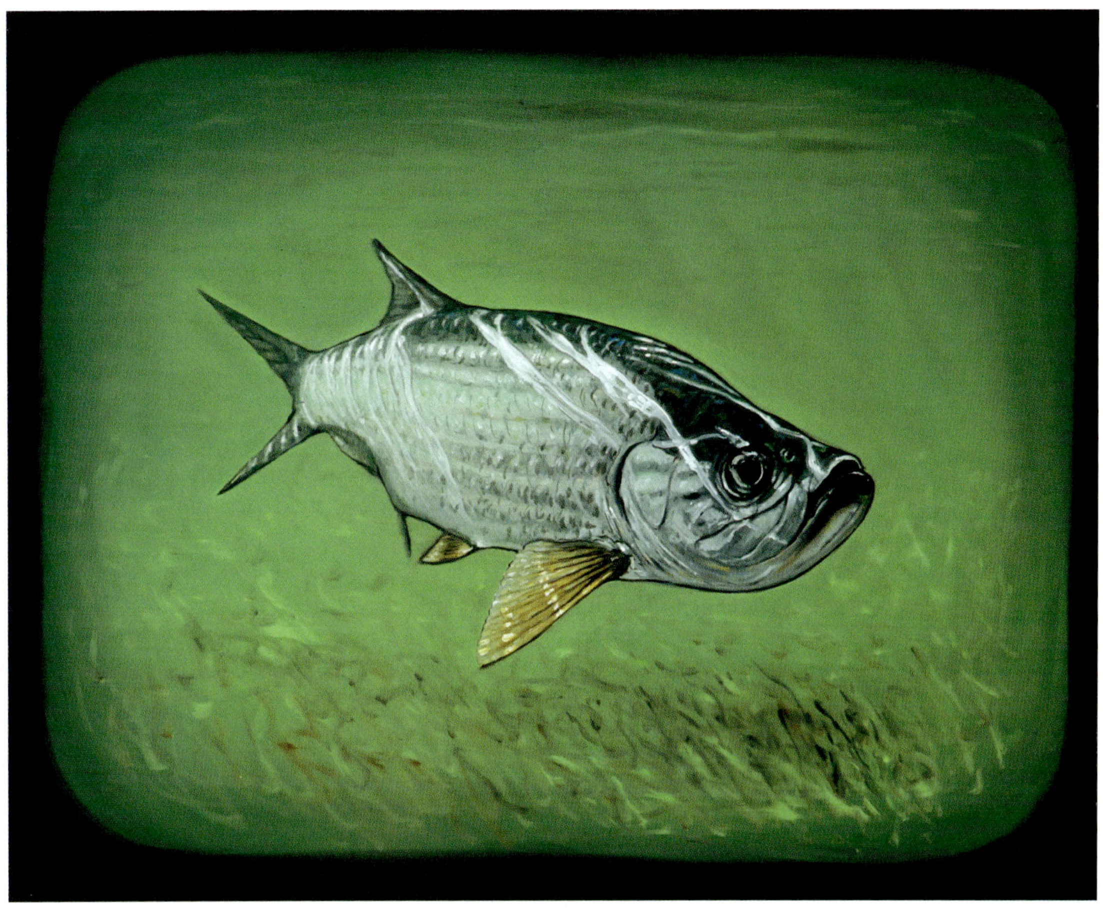

Fig. 15. *Biological Regionalism: Tarpon, Jardines de la Reina (The Queen's Gardens), Cuba*, 2004. Oil on plaster, 33" × 48". Private collection.

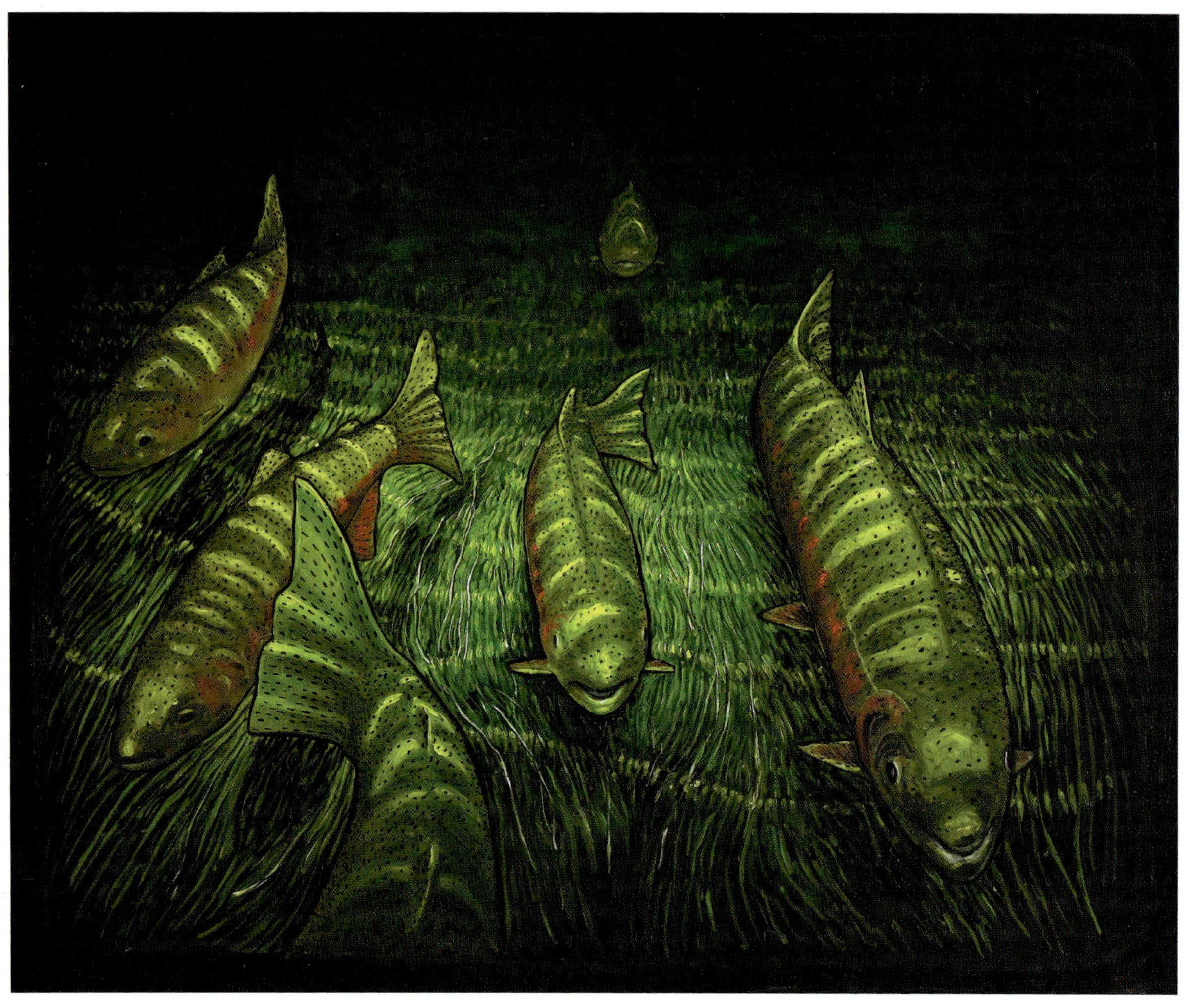

Fig. 16. *Biological Regionalism: Rainbow Trout, Big Horn River, Montana, USA*, 2005. Oil on plaster, 48" × 52". Artist's collection.

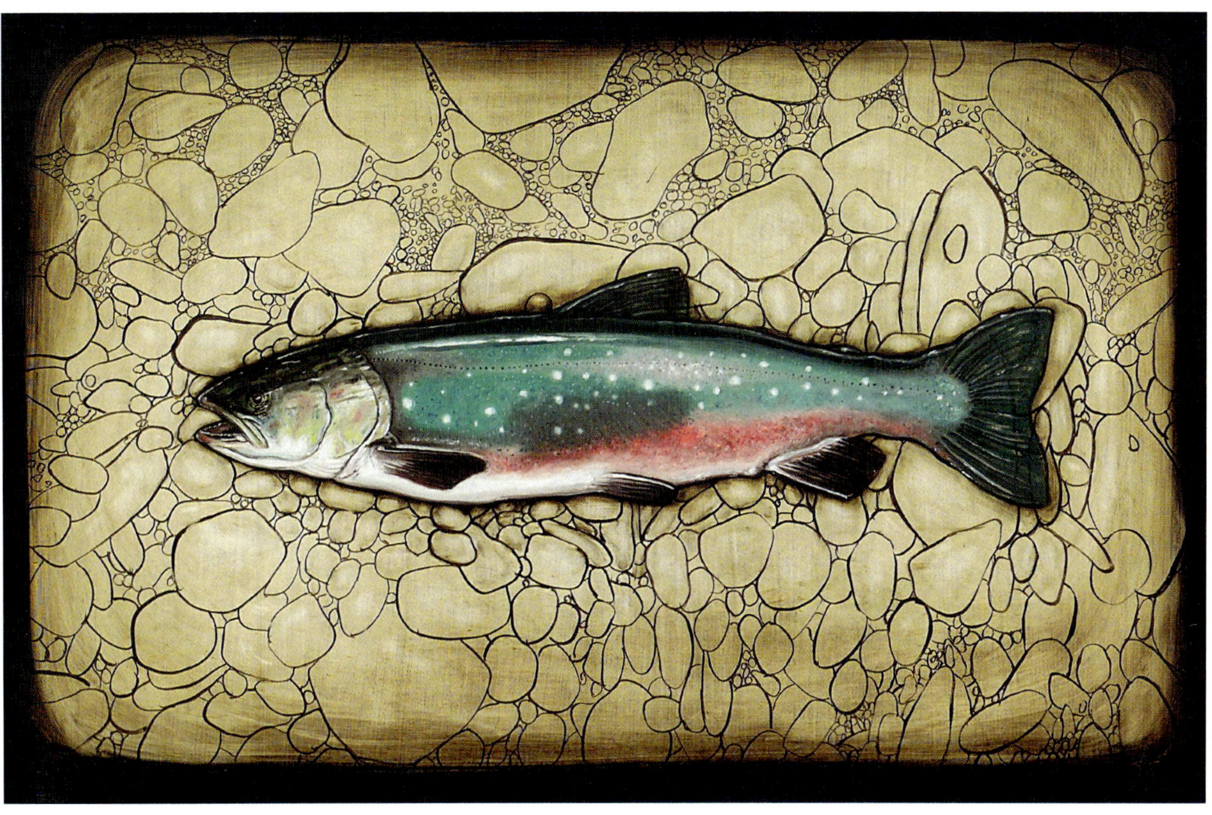

Fig. 17. *Biological Regionalism: Arctic Char, Hrútafjarðará River, Iceland*, 2008. Oil on plaster, 33" × 48". Private collection.

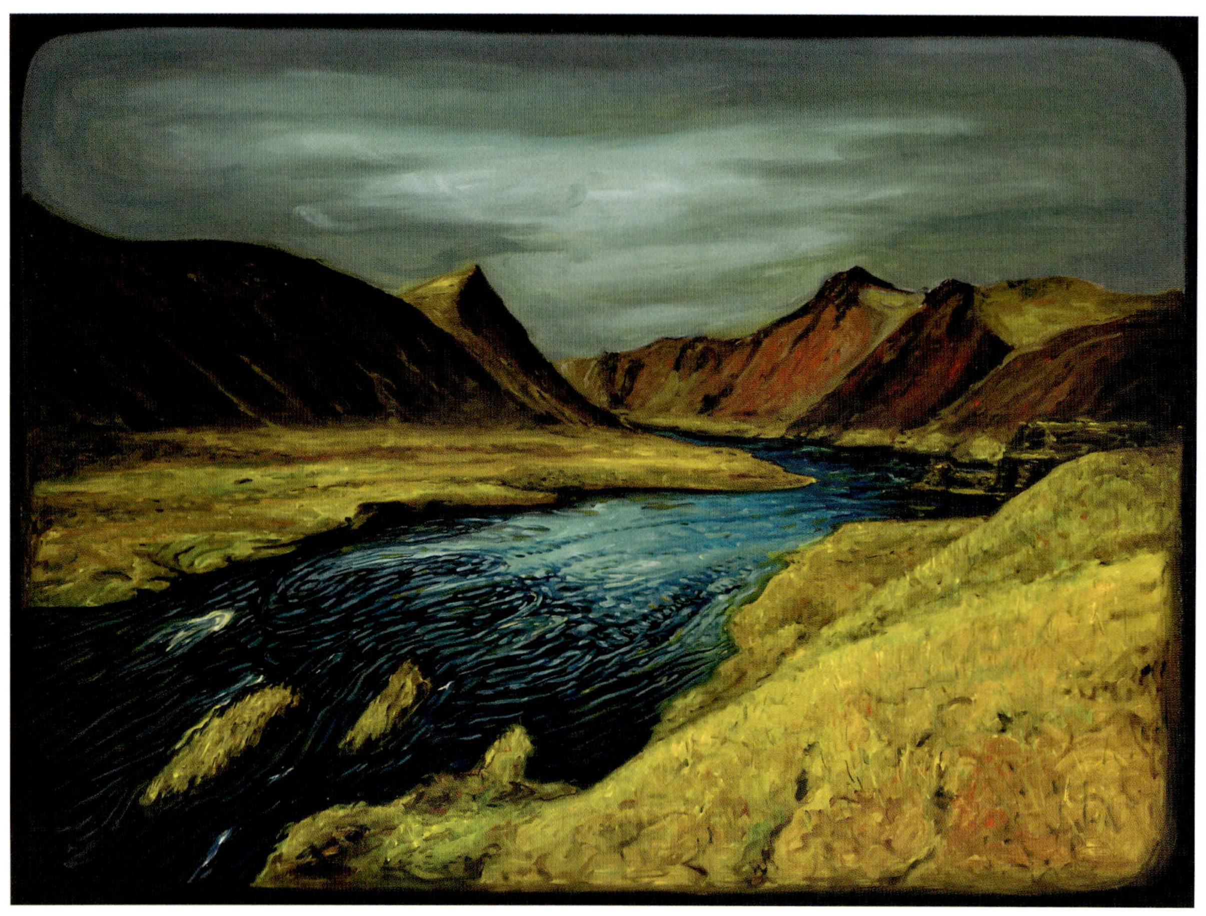

Fig. 18. *Biological Regionalism: Breiðdalsá River, Iceland*, 2009. Oil on plaster, 48" × 63". Artist's collection.

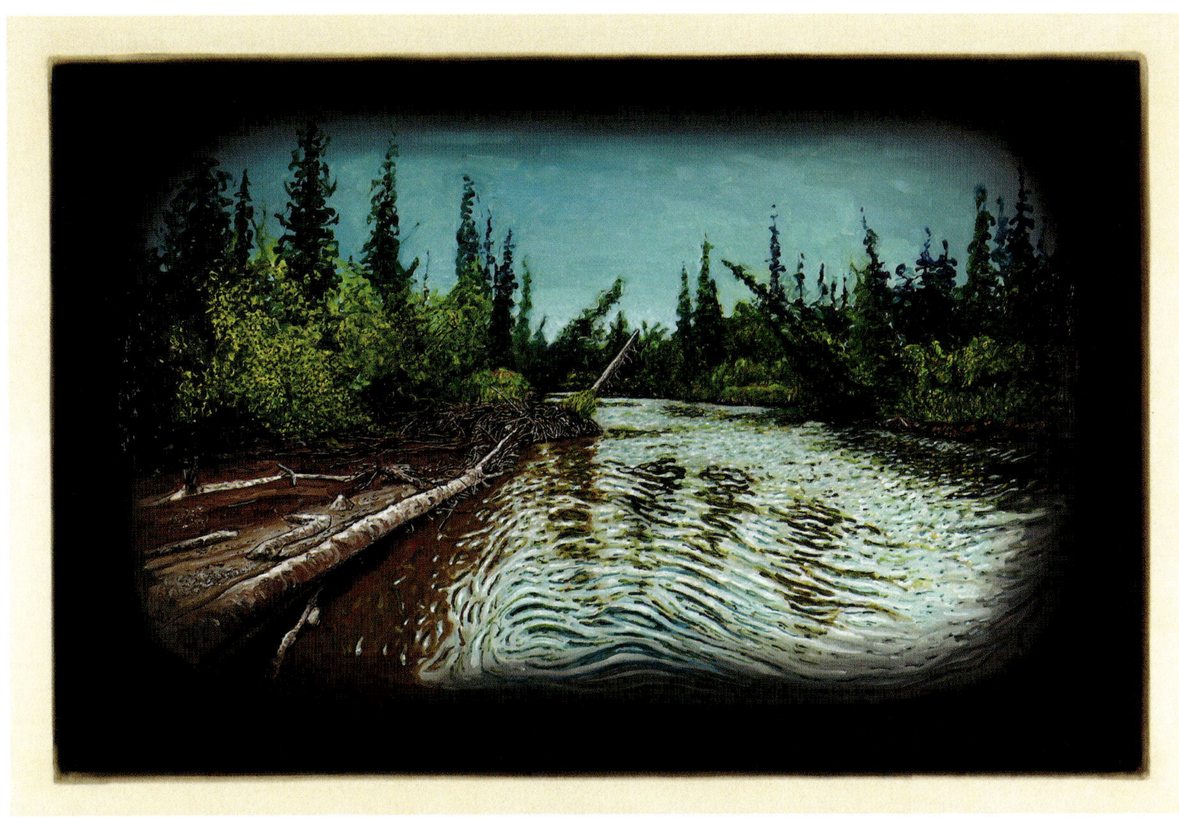

Fig. 19. *Biological Regionalism: Aniak River Tributary, Aniak, Alaska, USA*, 2006. Oil on plaster, 42" × 63". Artist's collection.

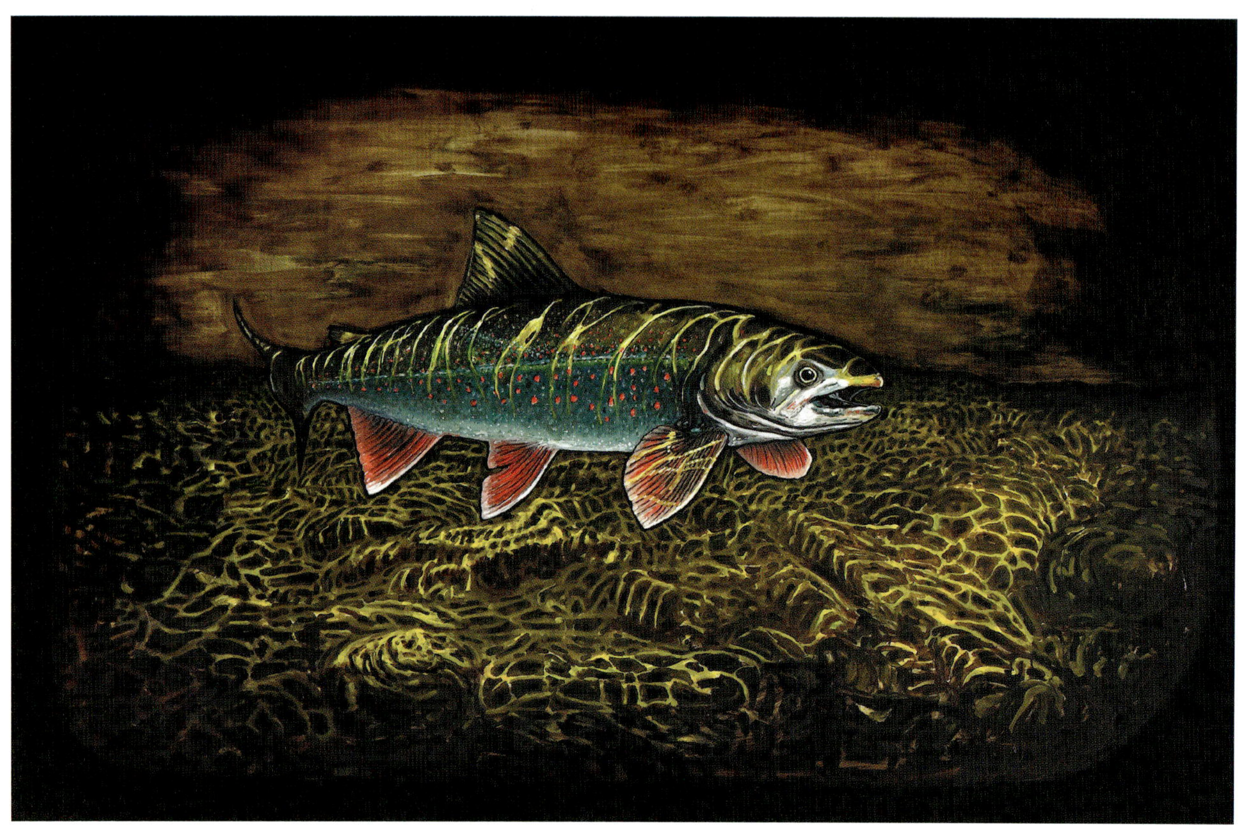

Fig. 20. *Biological Regionalism: Dolly Varden, Aniak River, Alaska, USA*, 2007. Oil on plaster, 42" × 63". Private collection.

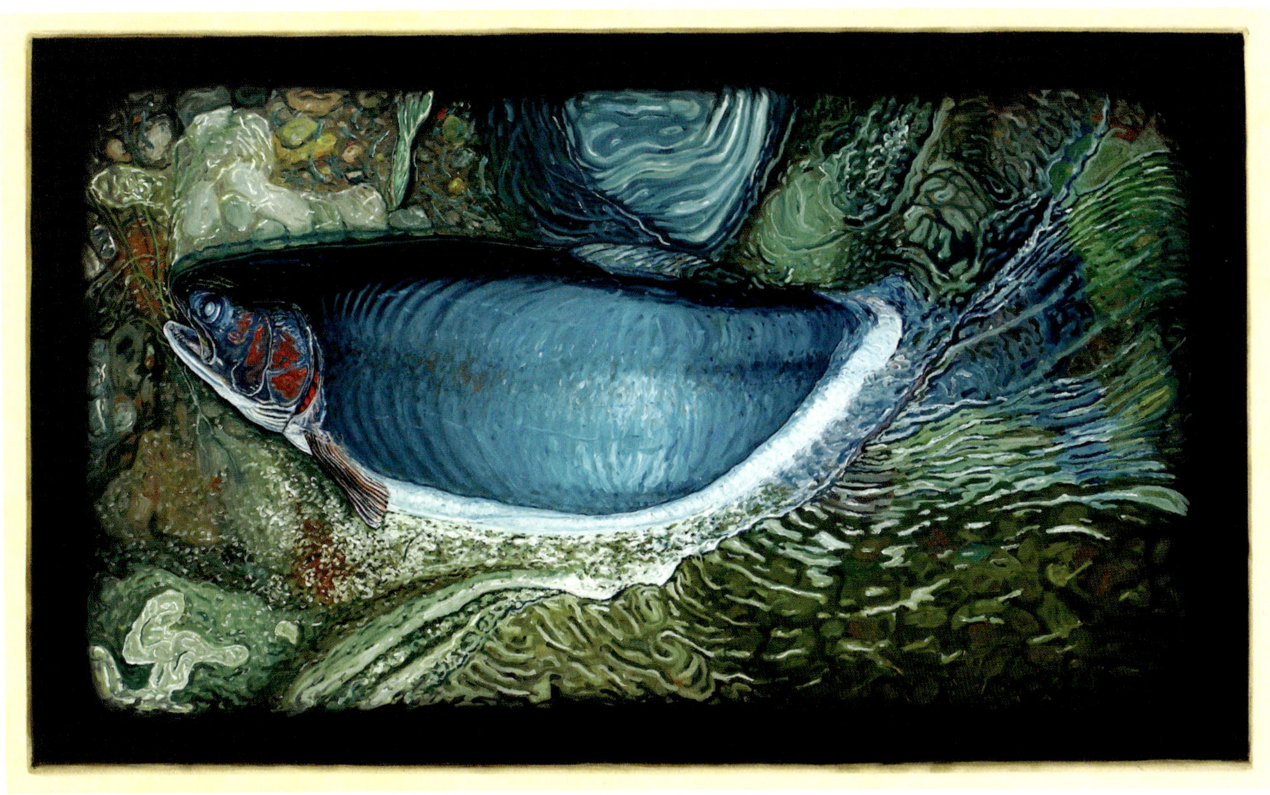

Fig. 21. *Aesthetics of Death VII*, 2008. Oil on plaster, 72" × 120". Burchfield Penney Art Center, Buffalo, NY.

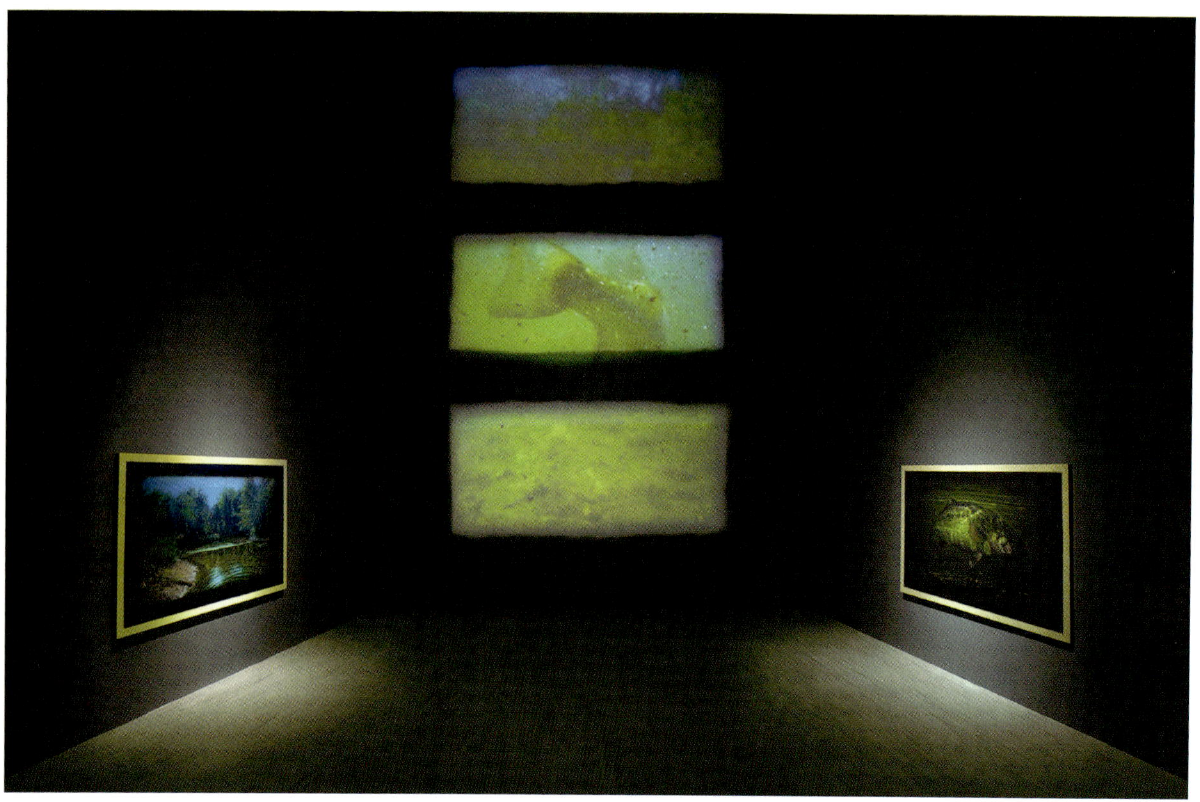

Fig. 22. *Biological Regionalism: Ellicott Creek, Amherst, New York, USA*, 2010. Installation image of Lightwell Gallery, University of Buffalo, Buffalo, NY. Artist's collection. (Photo Credit: Biff Hendrich.)

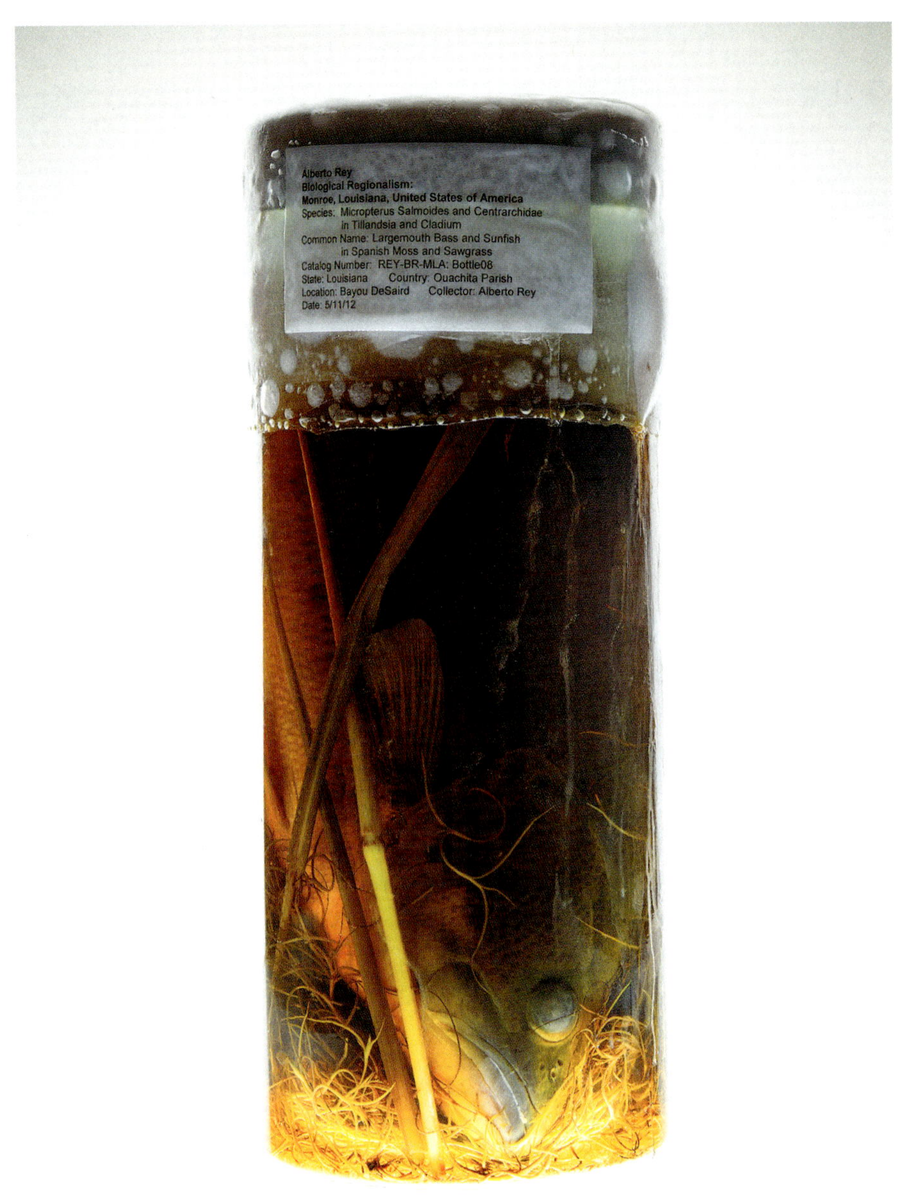

Fig. 23. *Biological Regionalism: Largemouth Bass, Sunfish, Spanish Moss and Sawgrass, Monroe, Louisiana, USA*, 2012. Mixed media, 13" × 4.75". Masur Art Museum, Monroe, LA.

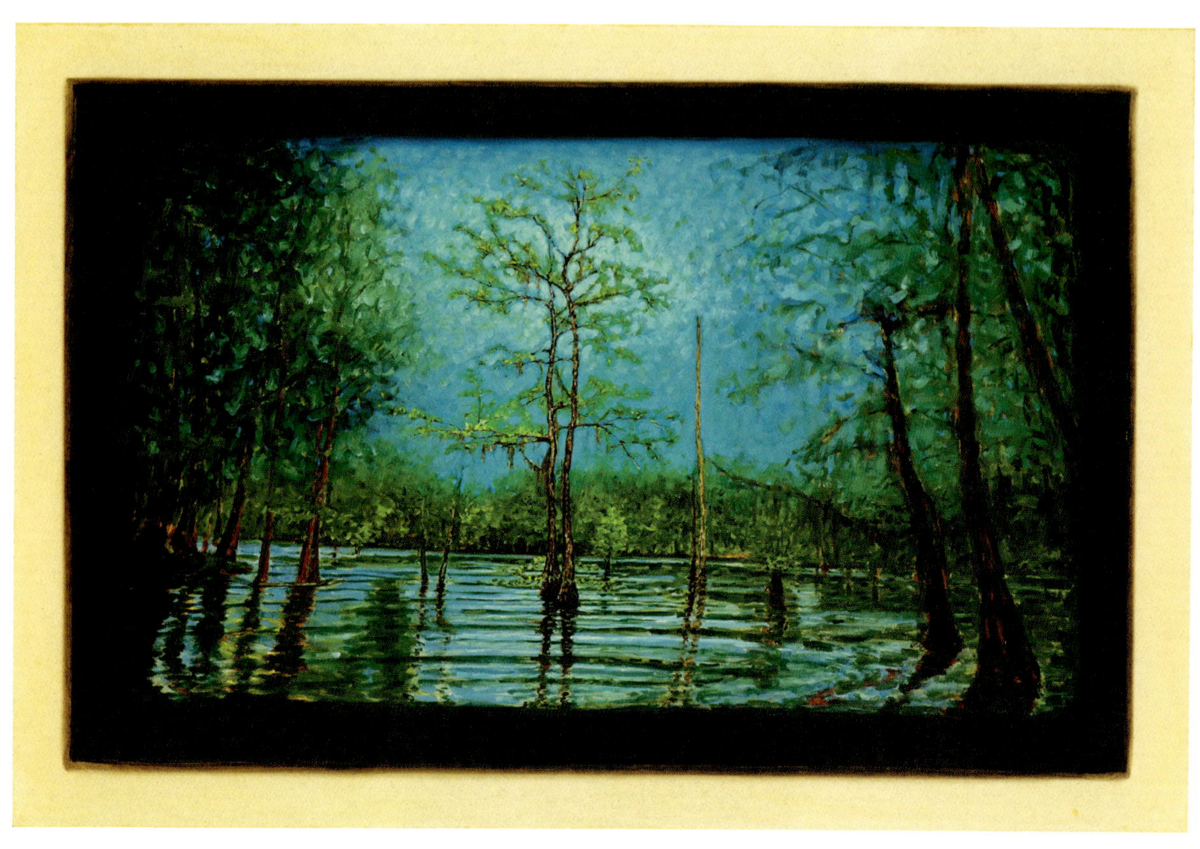

Fig. 24. *Biological Regionalism: Bayou Desiard, Monroe, Louisiana, USA*, 2012. Oil on plaster, 32" × 48". Masur Art Museum, Monroe, LA.

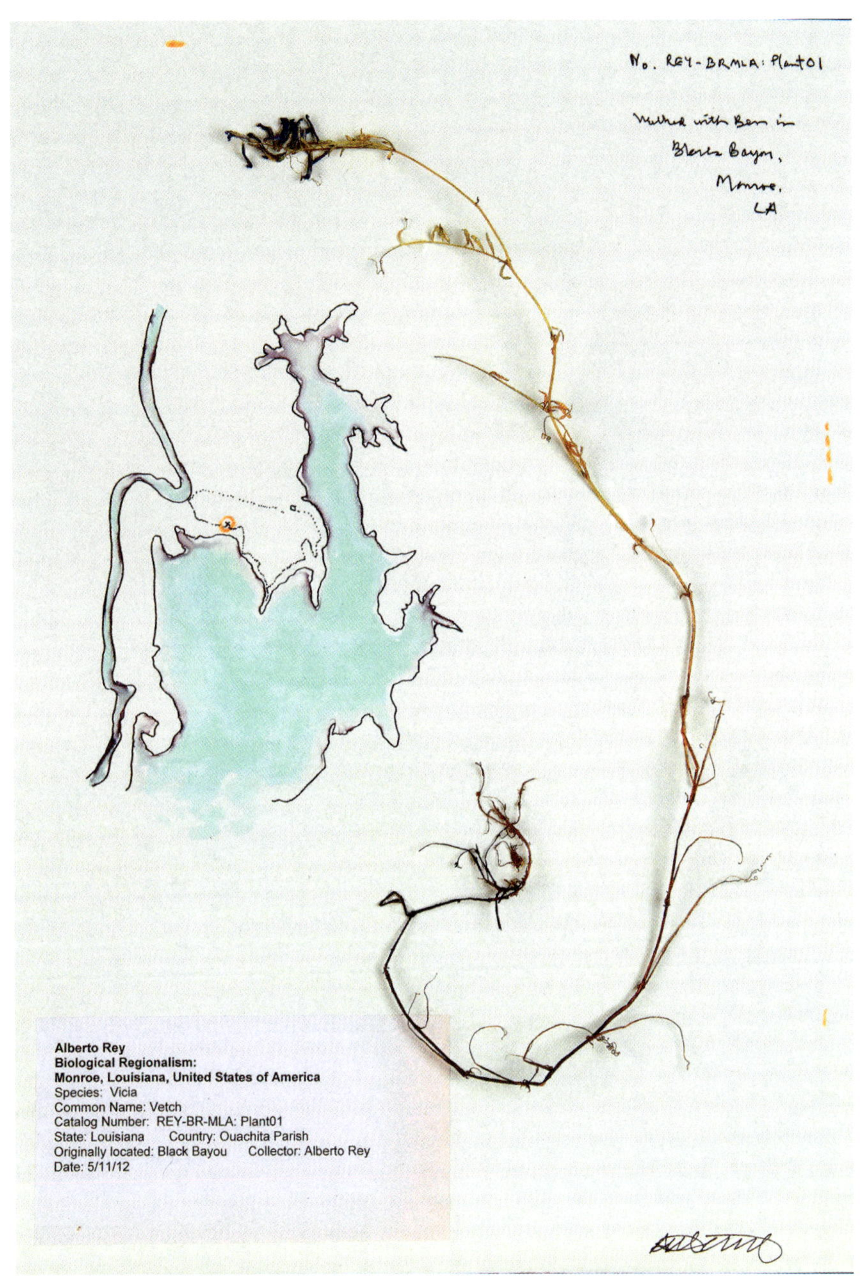

Fig. 25. *Biological Regionalism: Vetch, Monroe, Louisiana, USA*, 2012. Mixed media, 11.5″ × 16″. Masur Art Museum, Monroe, LA.

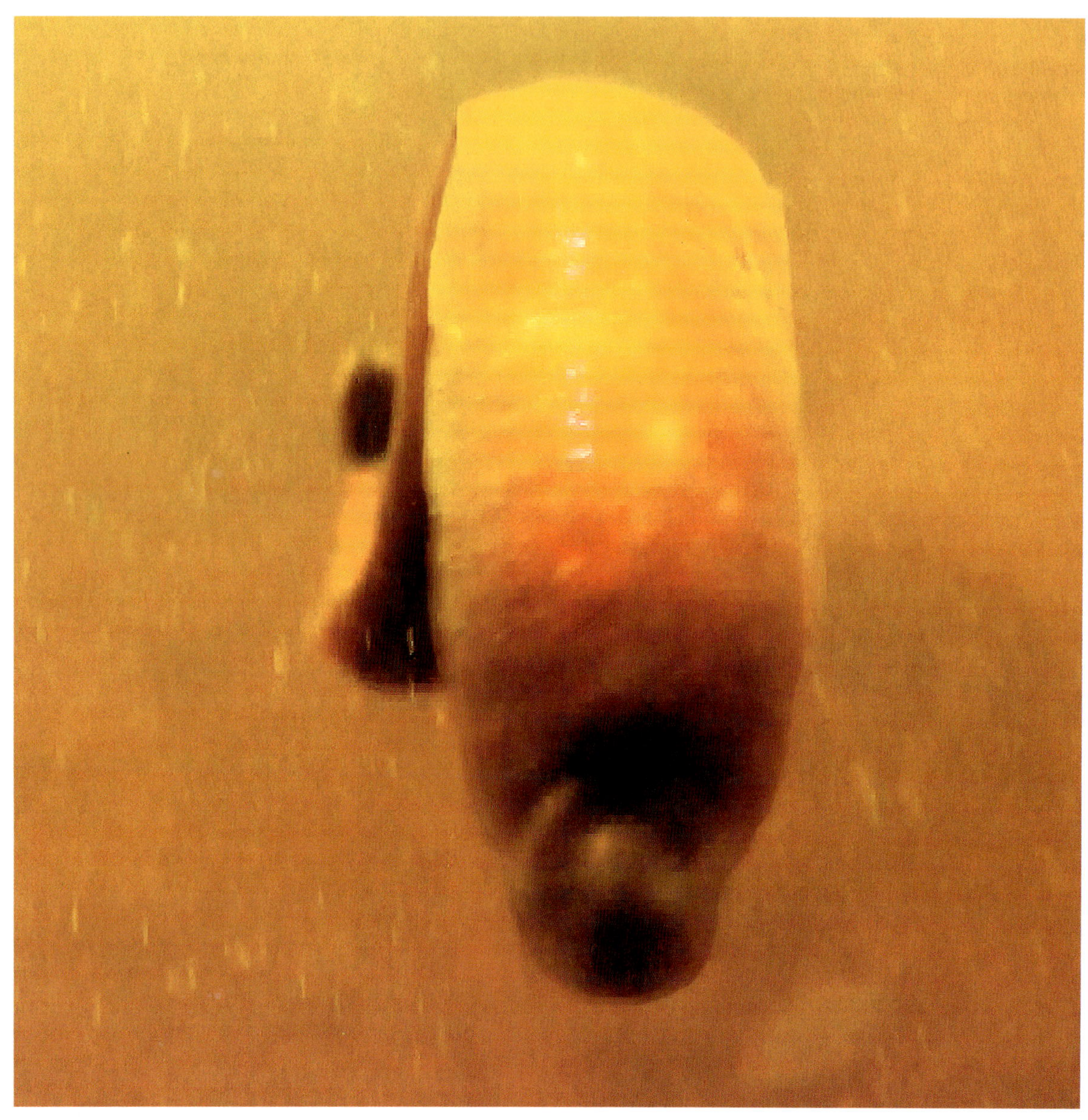

Fig. 26. *Biological Regionalism: Leech, Scajaquada Creek, Erie County, New York, USA*, 2012. Color video, 3:10. Artist's collection.

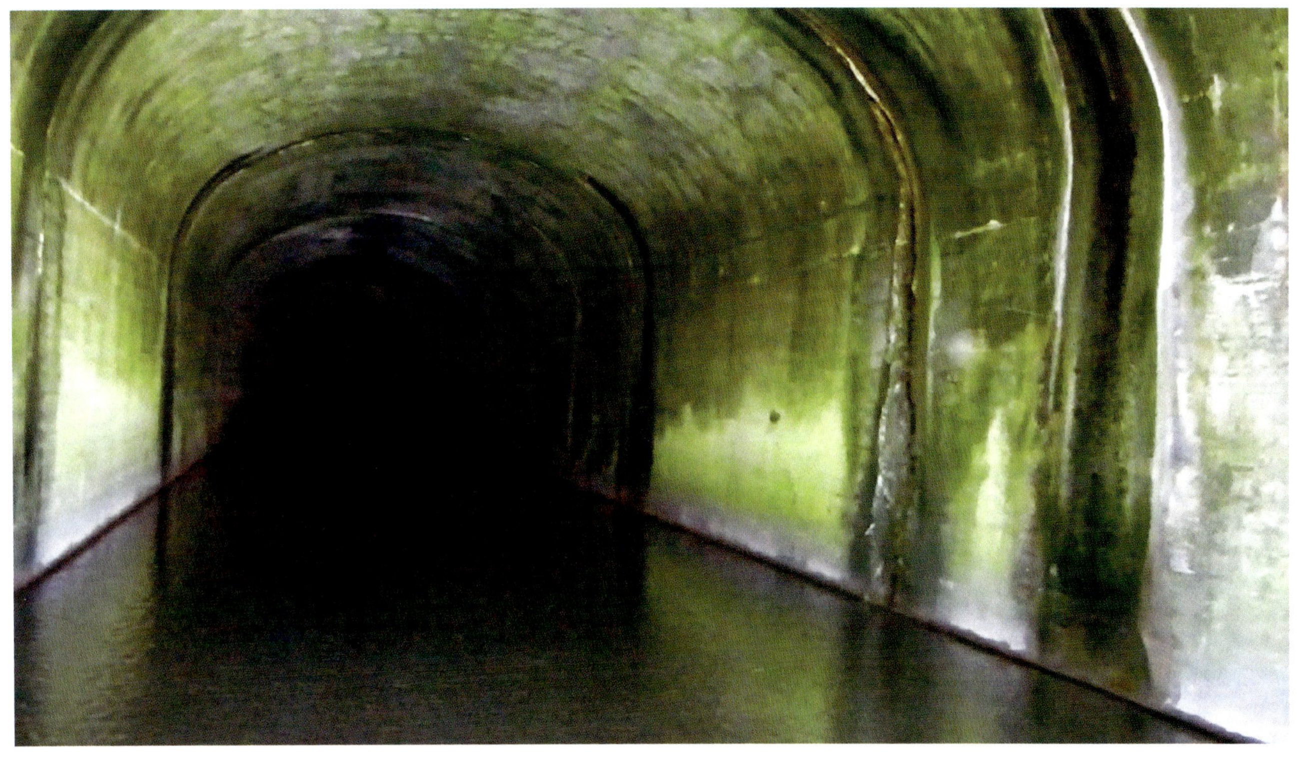

Fig. 27. *Biological Regionalism: Tunnel, Scajaquada Creek, Erie County, New York, USA*, 2012. Color video, 4:25. Artist's collection.

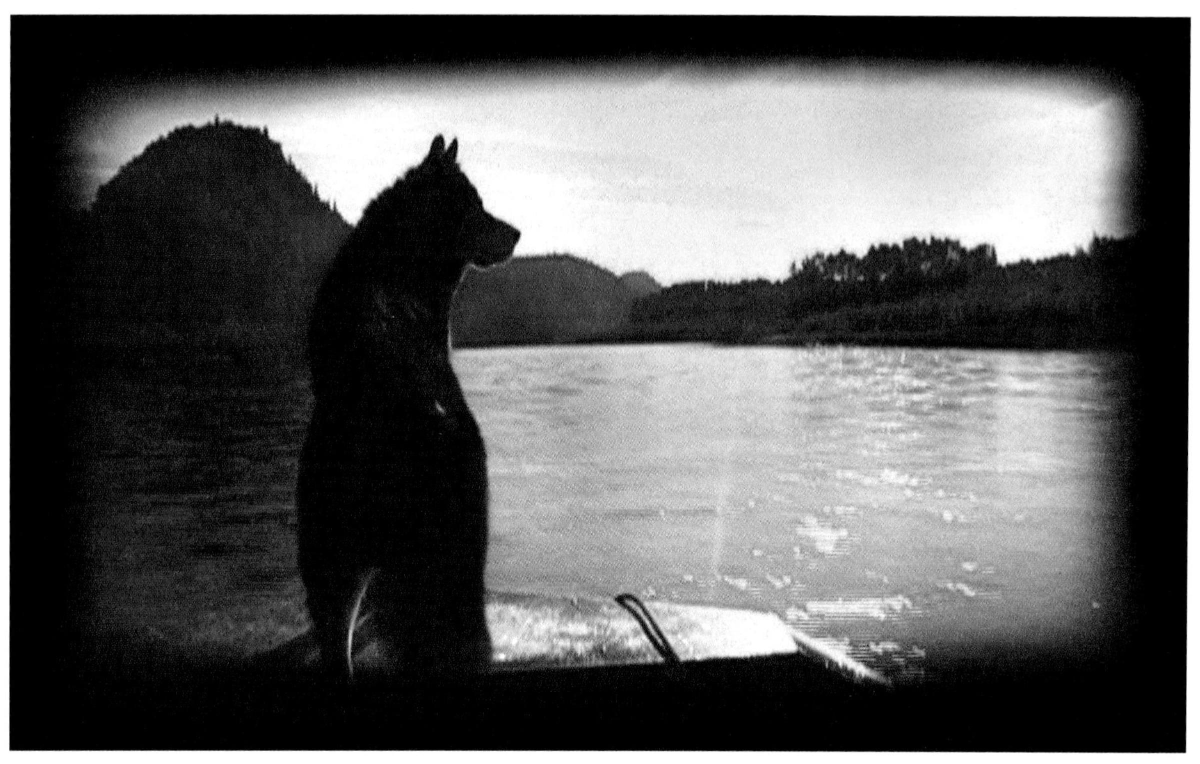

Fig. 28. *Primal Connections* (*Biological Regionalism Series*), 2006. Black-and-white video, 18:40. Artist collection.

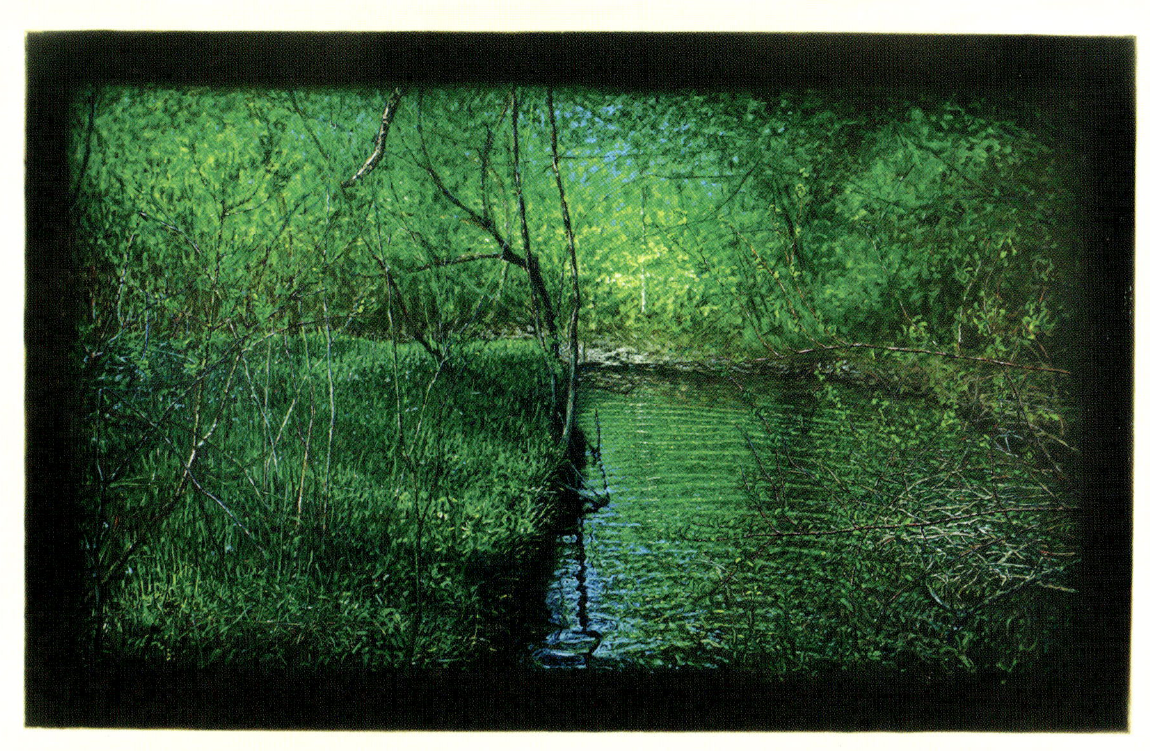

Fig. 29. *Biological Regionalism: Headwaters, Scajaquada Creek, Erie County, New York, USA,* 2012–13. Oil on plaster, 60" × 96". Artist's collection.

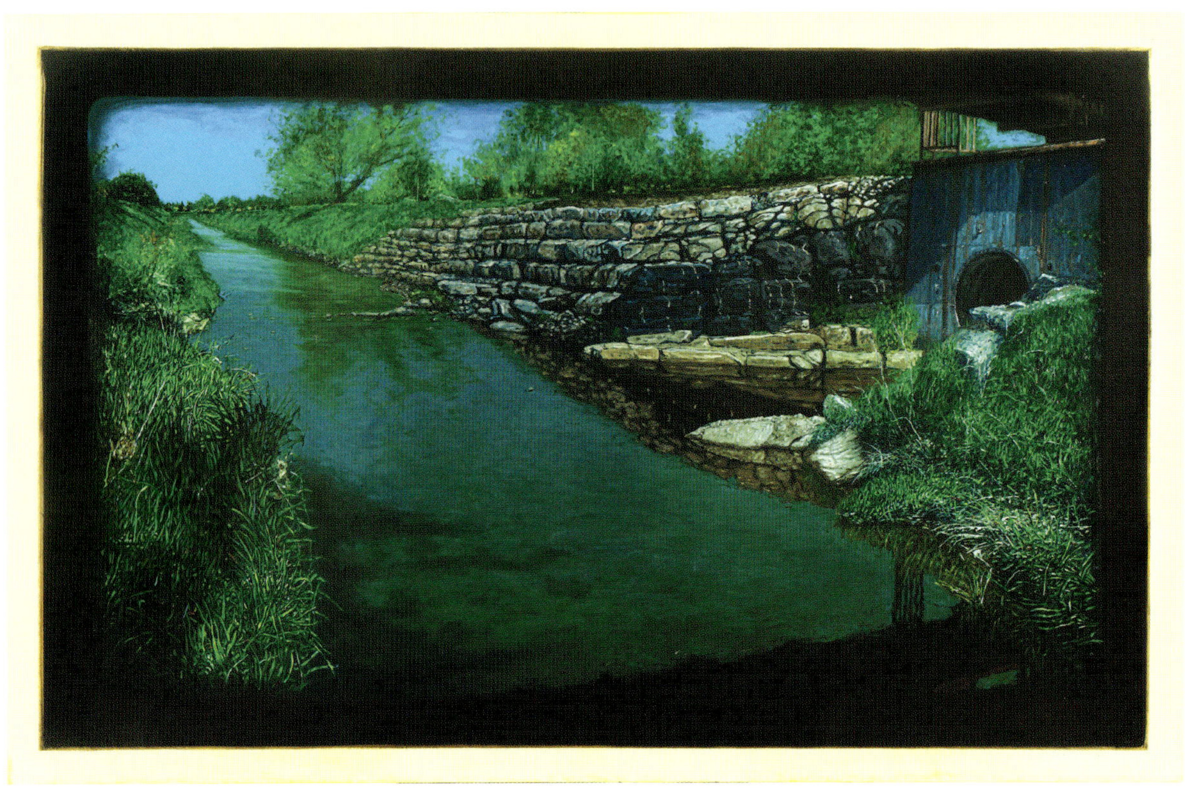

Fig. 30. *Biological Regionalism: North Creek/South Creek, Scajaquada Creek, Erie County, New York, USA,* 2012–13. Oil on plaster, 60" × 96". Artist's collection.

6

Reading the Waters
Early Works of Influence on the Literature of Fly-Fishing

JOHN ORLOCK

> In writing it I have made myself a recreation of a recreation.
>
> —Izaak Walton, *The Compleat Angler*, 1653

Back in 1957, as Harry Phillips, editor of *Sports Illustrated Magazine*, introduced a series of essays he was about to publish dedicated to the literature of fly-fishing, he wrote: "The diversion of outwitting fish with rod, line, and hook inspires devotion, meditation, and premeditation in great quantities and, in consequence, perhaps more books than any other sport."[1] In fact, an August 2012 search of the World Catalog (WorldCat)—the world's largest network of library content—reveals that there are 32,518 individual books on fishing, not counting periodicals, or various cyber-genres such as blogs. Next in line in terms of sports-related books, we find hunting (27,098), trailed distantly by football (18,102), baseball (17,108), and golf (16,304). The purposes of this essay are to serve as a brief introduction to the literature of fly-fishing, to explain when and where the literature first developed, to present certain overarching elements of style and content inherent to the genre, and finally to offer a starting-point reading list for exploring the field. In addition, I will argue that the best of the literature can be thoroughly engaging, even if one has little or no inclination to physically pursue the sport in person. At the end of this essay there is a postscript, written by Alberto Rey, that addresses how the literary culture of fishing discussed in this essay inspired and instructed him as he turned his attention to developing *Trout Encounters, Biological Regionalism*, and *The Aesthetics of Death*.

Author and angler Holly Morris, in addressing the historical breadth and popularity of fly-fishing literature, believes

there is a reason. While baseball is among the sports (some might include golf here) that inspire a certain devotion, even fanaticism, fly-fishing leads its lovers into fundamental connections, inviting a slow dance with the whimsy of the natural world, a love affair with line and rhythm and simplicity. Angling delivers the wily spiritual satisfactions that come with giving yourself to some-

thing that offers only intangible payback. . . . The angling canon displays a metaphorical range and depth unmatched by any other sport.[2]

Before proceeding further, let us define a few terms. By *fishing*, we will be referring to the sport and not the sustenance livelihood, *sport* being thought of as that activity one pursues for leisure recreation and challenge within a certain set of rules. *Fishing*, in terms of our discussion, is not providing food for the table, although this occasionally is one of the side benefits of the sport. And we will be referring mostly to fly-fishing: the sport of fishing using a rod and an artificial fly as bait.

We find the earliest references to fly-fishing in the literature of Classical Greece and Rome. There are scattered references in Oppian's *Halieutica* (169 CE) to men using clusters of feathers to attract and summarily, if of sufficient skill, catch freshwater fish. Martial also mentions Macedonians using bits of fur and cloth fastened to hooks as an artificial lure for fish.[3] In each of these sources, the rudiments of the sport are therein laid out, and remain as true today as they were in antiquity: luck and skill—fundamentals for success in any endeavor. But the references to fly-fishing in Antiquity are mentioned merely in passing, are vague, and must be viewed with much scholarly conjecture as to specifics and detail.

Almost twelve hundred years will pass before we encounter any further mention of fly-fishing: a dark age of the subject, a period for which we have no written evidence of the sport. Since a treatise on angling does arise, however, in the mid-fifteenth century, a reasonable scholarly assumption can be made that through the intervening centuries there was some sort of fishing for sport activity on an ongoing basis. The next mention of fly-fishing as a sport surfaces in 1450: *A Treatise of Fishing with an Angle*, under the authorship of Dame Juliana Berners, a woman whom tradition holds to be a nun, or perhaps even an abbess.[5] An "angle" in this case refers to a hook as the means of a fish's capture, as opposed to a net, spear, trident, or some other water hunting device.

The identity—or even existence—of Juliana Berners remains cloaked in a modicum of uncertainty. John Bale (1495–1563) in his *Lives of the Most Eminent Writers of Great Britain* rhapsodizes on the virtues of Dame Juliana:

She was an illustrious female, eminently endowed with superior qualities both mental and personal. Amongst the many solaces of human life she held the sports of the field in the highest estimation. This heroic woman saw that they were the exercise of noble men after wars, after the administration of Justice, or the concerns of state. . . . These arts therefore the ingenious woman was desirous to convey in her writings as the first elements of nobility; with the persuasion, that those youths in whose hearts resided either virtue or honour, would cultivate them to guard against vain sloth. She flourished in the year of our Lord 1460, in the reign of Henry the IVth.[5]

Raphael Holinshed (d. 1580), from whose chronicles Shakespeare drew many of his plots, writes: "Juliana Bernes, a gentlewoman endued with excellent giftes bothe of body and minde, wrote of certaine treatieses of hawking and hunting, delights greatly hirself in those exercises and pastimes."[6] These and other contemporary sources attribute to Dame Juliana attractive physical qualities and a superior intellect, as well as an ardor for sports of the field. As one reads her treatise text, a certain gentle extroverted personality—along with what appears to be a firsthand familiarity of essential angling details and skills—bubbles to the surface. Across the centuries, although much about this woman remains shrouded in legend, and other aspects of her character have crystalized into tradition, the work itself is clear and simply presented.

Whatever her origins might have been, the *Treatise* itself is a delight in respect to tone, style, and information conveyed. It begins:

> Solomon in his Proverbs says that a glad spirit makes a flowering age, that is to say, a fair age and a long one. And since it is so, I ask this question, "What are the means and cause to bring a man into a merry spirit?" Truly, in my best judgment, it seems to me, there are good sports and honest games in which a man's heart takes pleasure without any repentance afterward. Thence it follows—that good and honorable recreations are the cause of a man's fair old age and long life. Therefore, I will now choose among four good sports and noble pastimes, this is to say, among hunting, hawking, fishing, and fowling. The best, in my simple opinion, is fishing, called angling, with a rod or a pole, a line, and a hook.[9]

And she does just that, after first enumerating the reasons why each of the other three sports, while "good," nevertheless falls short of angling in the way that it brings the "good life" to the individual. For, she says of angling, even though one may lose a hook or a fish, there is always another to be had shortly thereafter. And in spite of these minor misfortunes that will always be part of the sport,

> at the very least, [the angler] will have his wholesome and merry walk at his own ease, and also many a set breath of various plants and flowers that will make him right hungry and put his body in good condition. He will hear the

melodies of the harmony of birds. He will also see the young swans herons, ducks, coots, and many other birds with their broods, which seems to me better than all the noise of hounds and blasts of horns and other amusements that falconers and hunters can provide, or the sport that fowlers can make. And if the angler catches fish with difficulty, then there is no man merrier than he is in his spirits. Also, whoever wishes to practice the game or sport of angling . . . must rise early, which thing is right profitable to a man . . . for the health of the soul, for it shall cause a man to be holy . . . it will produce bodily heath and will cause him to live long . . . it will cause him to be rich, temporarily and, you must know, and spiritually, in goods and in goodness.

Thus have I proved according to my purpose, that the sport and game of angling brings a man into a merry spirit, which (according to . . . the said teaching of medicine) makes a flowering age and a long one. . . . And therefore, I write and make this simple treatise which follows, by which you can have the whole art of angling to amuse you as you please, in order that your age may flourish the more and last longer.[9]

(As an aside to this passage, variations of Berners's thoughts on the medical benefits of a "merry spirit" are echoed today throughout the media.)

Berners then moves on to instruct on how best to construct one's tackle:

That is to say, your rod, your lines of different colors, and your hooks . . . After that, how you should angle, and in what places of the water; how deep and what time of the day for what manner of fish in what weather; how many impediments there are to angling; and especially with what baits for each different fish in every month of the year. And how you must make your braided baits, and where you'll find the material to make them. How to make your hooks of steel, and of iron, some for you to dub (dress) and some for the float . . . All these things you will find openly depicted to your eye.[10]

The narrator then proceeds in specific detail to instruct on how to do all of the above. With the rod, for instance:

You must cut, between Michaelmas and Candlemas (between September 29th and February 2nd) a fair, smooth staff six feet long, or longer if you will, of hazel, willow, or aspen; and heat it in an oven when you bake, and set it as exactly straight as you can make it; then let it cool and dry for four weeks or more. Then take and bind it tight with food cord to a bench . . . Then take a plumber's wire that is straight and strong and sharp at one end. Heat the sharp end in charcoal fire until it is hot, and pierce the staff with it through the pith of the staff—first at the one end and afterward at the other until it is all the way through. Then take a bird spit—and burn the hold as you think fit until it is big enough for you purpose and like a taper of wax, and then wax it. Then let it lie still for two days afterward, until it is thoroughly cold; then unbind it and dry it in a smokehouse or under the house roof till it is through dry. In the same season, take a rod of white hazel and (soak it in water) and let it dry. (Then) make the rod fit the hold in said staff, so that it will go half way into the staff in a continuous line.[11]

And so she lays out the rod constructing process, careful step by careful step, with a keenness of purpose and technological craft that would be eminently familiar to twenty-first-century rod builders, even though they would be working with graphite techno-fibers instead of willow.

Finally, . . . "And thus you will make yourself a rod so perfect and suitable that you can walk with it, and no one will know what you are going to do; and it will be light and nimble to fish with as you pleasure and desire."[12] Yes, she seems to say, with a twinkle in her eye, you have now built a perfect rod to give the appearance that you are merely out for a stroll in the woods with your walking staff: a benign deception of the viewer, who, due to the craft of the Dame's instruction, might never suspect that the walker is actually an angler about to indulge in one of his or her favorite pastimes.

And after laying out guidelines that cover such things as where to fish, what flies work in which months of the calendar, the kinds of fish (trout, grayling, salmon, and so forth), Dame Juliana concludes her treatise with a list of admonitions—an angler's sporting code, if you will, a set of precepts that is as much at the core of today's fishing etiquette and ethics as it was in 1450:

I charge and require you . . . that you never fish in the private water of a poor man . . . without his permission and good will; and that—you never break any man's traps, nor take away any fish caught in them. If you do as this Treatise shows you, you shall never have need to take the fish of other men; for you will have sufficient of your own catching if you are willing to work for them. It will be a very great pleasure to you to see the fair bright shining-scaled fishes deceived by your crafty means and drawn to land.

[In] going about your sport you break no man's hedge, and open no man's gate without shutting it again.

[Use this sport] principally for your solace, and to bring health to your body, and especially health to your soul. For when you go fishing you will not greatly desire many persons with you, which might set you off your game. And then you may serve God devoutly in saying well your customary prayers . . . Thus you will eschew and avoid many vices, especially idleness, well known to be the principal inducement in man of other vices.

Also, never be so greedy as to take too much game at one time [. . .], which may easily destroy your own sport, and the sport of others also. When you have sufficient game you should covet no more at that time.

Also take trouble to preserve the game in every way you can . . .

All those who keep these rules shall have the blessing of God and of St. Peter.[14]

The printer of the St. Albans book, Wynkyn de Worde, as he prepares to add Berners's work to a compilation of writings on other sports of the field, supplies the following epilogue to the treatise:

And in order that this present treatise should not come into the hands of every idle person who would desire it if it were printed alone by itself and put in a little pamphlet, I have therefore compiled it in a larger volume of various books pertaining to gentle and noble men, to the end that the aforesaid idle person, who would have but little moderation in the sport of fishing, should not by this means utterly destroy it.[14]

A further point regarding the intended readership of Berners's work is that while the early fifteenth-century treatises on hunting in England employed a hunting term that was largely Norman French, the language of the court,

the English of the Treatise on Fishing is the language of ordinary people. It is simple native prose with few long words: most are of one syllable, and most of the remainder of two syllables . . . The *Treatise of Fishing* is one of the best and most durable pieces of prose writing of its time. It is a rare thing to be able to go that far back in sport and find words so fresh and up to date (only a few words are archaic; only some of its "technology" is obsolete).[15]

And from a sociological view, there is an implication here that at the end of the fifteenth century, hunting and fishing were an acceptable combination within the same covers (of a field sports compilation), needing only a minor apology for their connection.[16] The printer's designation of his intended audience as being "gentle and noble men" did not refer to individuals of political nobility. On the contrary, the reader of the *Treatise of Fishing* in those days was likely to have been not a noble and not a landowner, since fishing had none of the dignity, ceremony, and hierarchal associations of medieval hunting. If the intended reader were to engage himself with the *Treatise of Fishing*, it would have been for practical instruction, and not to learn the manners of an aristocrat. Fishing was an inexpensive sport. As we have seen, a significant percentage of the text is devoted to the specifics of making one's own tackle. The information in the treatise is directed at the rising middle class of sixteenth-century England: merchants, craftsmen, and tradesmen whose means of livelihood might allow both time and energy enough for pursuit of recreational angling.

After 157 years from the first printing of the *Treatise of Fishing* to the first edition of Izaak Walton's *The Compleat Angler* (1653), *or, The Contemplative Man's Recreation: Being a Discourse of Fish and Fishing, Not Unworthy the Perusal of Most Anglers*. Walton (1593–1683) is one of a small cluster of authors whose titles are familiar to a multitude of people who have never read them, and in Walton's case, who have never even fished. Produced in 5 editions in Walton's life, it went through more than 300 separate

editions and reprintings in the following 300 years. Next to the Bible, *The Compleat Angler* is the most often reprinted work in English.[17] As *New York Times* op-ed columnist Verlyn Klinkenborg observes in his commentary on Walton,

Only a handful of the books first published in London in the sober year of 1653 are still read today, even by scholars [. . .]. [To us] 1653 looks like a vastly simpler time, if only because "there were fewer lawyers," as Walton puts it. But simplicity is always deceiving. "The Compleat Angler" was published just five years after England had hung its king [*sic*] and brought civil war to an end under the Puritan rule of Oliver Cromwell.[18]

In addition to the surrounding political turmoil, the course of Walton's life included the death of two wives and eight young children. He was a member of the Anglican Church and was living in London when the Anglican Archbishop Laud was executed by Cromwell's Puritan regime. Although Walton was in his early sixties when *The Compleat Angler* was first published, he was still in the early stages of his career as an author. Among his other written works were four biographies, including one of his friend John Donne. In fact, Samuel Johnson, writing in the mid-eighteenth century, regarded Walton as one of the finest biographers of his age.[19]

Yet, against the background of personal loss and grief, accompanied by over a decade of being on the fringes of religious persecution and political turmoil, Walton writes *The Compleat Angler or The Contemplative Man's Recreation: Being a Discourse of Fish and Fishing, Not Unworthy the Perusal of Most Anglers*, a reflective pastoral work of considerable charm and whimsy. The text is in the form of a dialogue between three friends, as they wander a five-day journey through the English countryside in the month of May. In the course of their peripatetic conversations, Piscator (a fisher) extols the virtues of his pastime to two jovial companions: Venator (a hunter) and Auceps (a fowler). The friends move along from stream to stream, their dialogue sprinkled with quotations and references to Classical writers, St. Augustine, and the Bible. The three occasionally encounter milkmaids, whom they regale with songs, jokes, and poetry. And then as the day wags on, the anglers retire to an inn for

pints of ale accompanied by hearty provisions at the table. After a night's rest, they continue on into further delights of walking, fishing, and lively, bantered conversation. Heading into a new day, Piscator lays out their schedule:

> It is now past five of the clock, we will fish till nine, and then go to breakfast. Go you to yon sycamore tree and hide your bottle of drink under the hollow root of it; for about that time, and in that place, we will take a brave breakfast of powdered beef, and a radish or two that I have in my fish bag.[20]

And thus as the days pass by, his two sporting companions become understandably ardent converts to angling and its pastoral social surround.

Walton follows the spirit and content of Berner's treatise in that, through the experiences and conversation of his characters in the countryside, he sets out to provide not only a guide to the angler's required skill but also a gentle instruction in the sort of meditation that should accompany the skills:

> No life, my honest Scholar, no life so happy and so pleasant, as the

life of a well governed Angler; for when the Lawyer is swallowed up with business, and the Statesman is preventing or contriving plots, then we sit on Cowslip-banks, hear the birds sing, and possess ourselves in as much quietness as these silent silver streams, which we now see glide so quietly by us. Indeed my good Scholar, we may say of Angling, as Dr. Boteler said of Strawberries; Doubtless God could have made a better berry, but doubtless God never did: And so (if I might be Judge) God never did make a more calm, quiet, innocent recreation than Angling.[21]

Here we have, laid out for the reader, a model for a pursuit of pleasure and satisfying life on both earthly and spiritual planes. And this aspect—a way of life shaped by the practice of a gentle sport, nature, God, and cordial companionship—accounts for the fact that *The Compleat Angler* stands as one of the most reprinted books in the history of British letters, with nearly four hundred editions since 1653.

But *The Compleat Angler* is a serious book, written in a serious time. By the mid-1640s in Britain, the Presbyteri-ans were in ascendance and many of the Anglican clergy (including a number of Walton's friends) were ejected from their livings, and some were imprisoned.[22] *Angler* was published less than a month after Cromwell and his soldiers entered the House of Commons and dismissed the remains of the Rump Parliament.[23] In fact, in the view of a number of scholars, *The Compleat Angler* can be read, in the context of the religious and political conflicts of Walton's time, as "The Complete Anglican." This view is strengthened by the fact that angling was one of the few recreations deemed "proper and fitting" for Anglican clergy. Furthermore,

[the] Pastoral is a rich and various mode in the English Renaissance, and yet *The Complete Angler* is a singular work in that tradition: no English pastoral has taken anything like its hold on the literate imagination. The expression the work gave [. . .] to the vision of a society coherent, communal, recreative, and nostalgic [made it] a forceful, an articulate, and, in 1653, a timely symbol.[24]

And as Canon Judith Malty of Winchester Cathedral writes:

Under the guise of a book on fishing (though an extremely detailed fishing book it must be admitted—it is a very good disguise), Walton reconstructed a society marked by community and neighbourliness—a community and a church he felt had been destroyed by religious extremism. For Walton, English Christians in the 1650s were in the grip of a false Lent imposed by religious zealots. The world of the *Compleat Angler* is one of sociability, not only of the Church but of the alehouse—of songs and shared meals. Walton's language "conveys a notion of how men should take pleasure in one another's company and of the sanctity and ceremoniousness of such pleasure."[25]

And given its context, it is a highly charged political *and* theological argument. Anglers, like Jesus' disciples, he claimed, were simple men . . . with a simplicity that was usually found in the Primitive Christians, who were (as most Anglers are) quiet men, and followed peace; men that were too wise to sell their consciences to buy riches for vexation . . . men that lived in those time when there were fewer Lawyers.[26]

Berners's A *Treatise of Fishing with an Angle* and Walton's *The Compleat Angler* each presents its advocacy of angling as a means for an individual (1) to experience the efficacy of nature to calm the mind and restore the spirit; (2) to indulge in reflection of one's life and conscience; and (3) to extend oneself to enjoy the society of fellow anglers, while at the same time they supply the skill-based information to allow the would-be angler a satisfying participation in the sport. Both texts also stand as the preeminent influential models for the predominant percentage of all fly-fishing literature that follows. Most works of fly fishing literature that come after these two will be marked to some degree, either explicitly or implicitly, with a combination of moral, spiritual, self-reflective, and skill/technique–based aspects.

Numerous variations on Walton's model appear in the eighteenth and especially nineteenth century, when the Romantic movement plunged literary sensibilities into the lushness of nature and the natural world. As we move into the twentieth century, however, the idea of angling being a catalyst for self-reflection takes on a darker tone. In Ernest Hemingway's story "Big Two-Hearted River" (1924), one of a series of stories centered on his character Nick Adams, Nick is a returning World War I veteran, suffering from what we today might diagnose as posttraumatic stress disorder. In the course of a solitary fishing and camping trip to Michigan's Upper Peninsula, Hemingway shows us how Nick begins to reconnect the pieces of a war-shattered life and psyche through the simple actions of setting up camp and going fishing in the river. In the following two excerpts from the story, we see Hemingway incorporate the kind of nature details we might read in Walton's descriptions, but in each of Hemingway's excerpts we also find a vague, yet palpable underlying tension to the narrative, an edge we never experience in Walton's prose:

> Nick looked down into the pool from the bridge. It was a hot day . . . A big trout shot upstream in a long angle, only his shadow marking the angle, then lost his shadow as he came through the surface of the water, caught the sun, and then, as he went back into the stream under the surface, his shadow seemed to float down the steam with the current, unresisting, to his post under the bridge where he tightened facing up into the current.
>
> Nick's heart tightened as the trout moved. He felt the old feeling.[27]
>
> He had wet his hand before he touched the trout, so he would not disturb the delicate mucus that covered him. If a trout was touched with a dry hand, a white fungus attacked the unprotected spot. Years before when he had fished crowded streams, with fly fisherman ahead of him and behind him, Nick had again and again come on dead trout, furry with white fungus, drifted against a rock, or floating belly up in some pool. Nick did not like to fish with other men on the river. Unless they were of your party they spoiled it.[28]

Throughout the fishing-related Nick Adams stories ("Big Two-Hearted River," "Now I Lay Me" [1924], and "The End of Something" [1927]), a solitary spirit, darkness, loss, and death move across the narrative landscape in a way that Walton never would allow to intrude on the world of Piscator and his companions. Nonetheless, the heritage of personal reflection, nature, and re-creation of the spirit are clearly evident. Within the actions of their characters, whether overtly or in metaphor or subtext, both Walton and Hemingway seek refuge from the debilitating stresses and fears of recent war and its scarring violence.

Moving much further into the twentieth century, we come to what many consider to be the quintessential work of fly-fishing literature, Norman Maclean's *A River Runs Through It* (1976). The semi-autobiographical novella tells of the loves and struggles among members of a Montana family in the 1920s who are bound together by a Presbyterian faith that is inextricably linked to fly-fishing: "In our family, there was no clear line between religion and fly fishing."[29] In her foreword to the twenty-fifth-anniversary edition of the novel, Pulitzer Prize–winning author Annie Proulx writes, "It is one of the rare truly great stories in American literature—allegory, requiem, memoir—and so powerful and enormous in symbol and regret for a lost time and a lost brother, for human mortality and the consciousness

of beauty, that it becomes part of the life experience of the reader, unforgettable."[30]

A close reading of *A River Runs Through It* reveals Maclean's masterful direct juxtaposition of two scenes starkly contrasting in respect to their setting and tone. In the first, we find his narrator in the middle of a fly-fishing sequence on a roiling river, the prose capturing all the beauty, power, and wonder of casting to trout in cascading waters. And then, several paragraphs later, the scene has shifted to the narrator claiming his brother Paul and Paul's girlfriend from the dark, puke-stenched holding cell at the county jail.[31] Throughout the novella Maclean sets up an often unexpected narrative rhythm of natural beauty, family spirituality, fly-fishing technique, love, philosophical musing, and despairing violence. With these points in mind, I would suggest that Maclean's novella could be considered a thematic and imagaic synthesis of the work of Walton and Hemingway.

In one last example of contemporary fly-fishing literature, I will mention two wide-ranging anthologies compiled by Holly Morris: *A Different Angle: Fly Fishing Stories by Women* and *Uncommon Waters: Women Write about Fishing*.[32] Contributors include such writers as Joan Salvato Wulff, Margaret Atwood, Tess Gallagher, Betsy Brown, and Annie Proulx. While an in-depth consideration of these works lies far beyond the scope of this essay, I will note that the writers included in these two collections of fly-fishing–themed prose—in addition to eliciting the resonance of Berners's and Walton's blend of the spiritual, moral, and practical aspects of the sport—also communicate a distinct sense that this sport/pastime/outdoors experience provides a level of personal satisfaction that transcends the perception that fly-fishing in its multiple dimensions is essentially a masculine form of recreation. The voices of these writers present a broad and varied range of fly-fishing explorations: stories abounding in humor, excitement, pathos, fun, reverence, and buoyant spirit.

With over thirty-two thousand books related to fly-fishing, this essay can provide only an introductory overview of an extensive catalog of the subject. And a daunting number of texts remain to be considered, a number that invites readers, whether or not they are anglers, to venture and discover passages that offer both pleasures of the highest literary merit and useful practical instruction. These books are guides. Fishing guides. Guides to where you may look. That's what a fishing guide does: it shows you where to look, how to approach, where to cast. But the experience, the adventure, is yours alone, yours to bring into reality. That is what literature of any sort does. It is an introduction to an individual's experience. It is a story that, as you move through the narration, becomes a window into your life, touching emotions, introducing new techniques through which to catch a day-to-day existence more rich in possibilities than the one in which you're currently wading, paradoxically alone, but also connected to the narrator's tale.

And so, having begun this essay with an account of a woman's voice, and come round to a collection of women's voices, I'll draw to a close with two final quotations from Holly Morris, each of which, in my view, cuts through the often nostalgic sentimentally that hovers about much of the fly-fishing literature canon, reveals that soul of the work at its mystic and humanistic best, and takes us to the depth where art and craft merge into insight and wonder:

When you fish and when you write, you enter into a staring contest with potential, a challenge devoid of guarantees. As you stand at the water's edge gazing at a glassy pool or a river proceeding with the freedom and discipline only the natural world can finesse, you are scrubbed clean of life's trivia. Watching the water, you are confronted with the unconscious as surely as you are when you stare into the humming blank screen each morning, praying that from the fathomless gray, prose will rise. Both fishing and writing are largely acts of faith: you believe that there is indeed a rich run of ideas lurking below. The convoluted first drafts, the false casts and hooked branches are all a part of some cosmic ritual designed to seduce a shiny gem to the surface. You get a nibble and your mind sings as you play the idea and reel it in. Only sometimes is it a keeper.[33]

Now nearly all those I loved and did not understand when I was young are dead, but I still reach out to them.

Of course, I now am too old to be much of a fisherman, and now of course I usually fish the big waters alone, although some friends think I shouldn't. Like many fly fishermen in western Montana where the summer days are almost Arctic in length I often do not start fishing until the cool of the evening. There in the Artic [sic] half-light of the canyon, all existence fades to a being with my soul and memories and sounds of the Big Blackfoot River and a four-count rhythm and the hope that a fish will rise . . .

I am haunted by waters.[34]

POSTSCRIPT TO JOHN ORLOCK

Alberto Rey

John Orlock's essay on the literature of fishing and angling reminded me of how I have thought about the process of fishing in connection with the trajectory of life and of my life in particular. It also made me think about how differently someone who is a angler thinks about fishing in contrast to someone who does not fish. When someone who does not fish considers the topics of "fly-fishing," "writing," and "art," they generally think of the final product, whether it is the fish at the end of a melodic cast, a finished work of art, or an example of published literature. There is a cause-and-effect relationship that is expected.

Yet, Orlock's essay has reminded me that the appreciation and understanding of art is not a simple quid pro quo, but is a complex exchange that is also a process of learning, understanding, and developing linked to how we live and perceive our lives as a source of knowledge and experience that can be shared with others. Having knowledge of fishing is not a requirement for appreciating fishing or its literary and aesthetic traditions. In the same way, it is not necessary to be an artist to appreciate art. Yet, the existence of these activities and their cultural history and influence is important for those whose lives are touched by the prevalence of these activities in our world.

It is often the results of fishing (the fish), making art (the object), or writing about fishing or making art that initially draws individuals to the activity. In reality, however, the final result can become a very small part of the entire experience for the participant or creator, once those drawn into learning about fishing

or art become aware of the process that precedes the finished product. It is rare, in fact, when a final product can transcend all the experiences that came before it or the intellectual and aesthetic investigations considered during its creation, because the processes themselves are, at least, as interesting as the end result. When these works do happen, they are moments of enlightenment that provide partial incentive to continue the activity.

Most of the time, however, the other moments of enlightenment occur during the process, when the research is compiled, the information and experiences are absorbed, the endless possibilities are contemplated, and the endless decisions are made during the execution of a work or activity. In time, the final work is a compilation of past information and experiences, skills obtained, and the intuitive technique. This process, which is the foundation for the finished work, is what is responsible for the expansion of one's knowledge, and allows for the possibility to connect with a wider range of experiences, thoughts, and feelings. These diverse experiences can be very enriching and gratifying, and when combined with the final work are usually the driving force that encourages the creator or participant to look for more complex relationships between themselves and their environments.

The examples that John Orlock has selected in his essay are wonderful examples of how these complex relationships have occurred in fly-fishing literature over the past 2,000 years. These writings reflect complexities of the process and experiences that support the activity of fly-fishing. These experiences are usually more important than the act of landing fish, and reflect the connections between society and nature. The specific interaction between the two become metaphors for the struggles and needs of the characters in the novels. Both are fragile yet steadfast forces capable of providing tremendous goodwill. Nature represents humankind's potential at its purest and most positive. Fly-fishing provides a link between the two in what Morris calls the "slow dance."

This interaction has always been important to me. The rich history of this interaction reflected in fly-fishing, art, and literature has allowed me to connect to the activities, thoughts, and feelings of those who participated in, painted about, or wrote about their society's interaction with their environment.

Fly-fishing today provides a nostalgic link to the outdoors, and an escape from the everyday. While this nostalgic vision is continually reflected in the media for commercial gain, our need for spiritual renewal remains constant. I find it refreshing that the importance of the link between society, fly-fishing, and nature is documented in Juliana Berners's writing, but it is, on the other hand, disturbing that the promotion of conservation and ethics over the past 500 years have done too little to change our society's perception on these ideals.

Although very different in approach, the restorative possibilities of fly-fishing and nature are also seen much later in the works of Isaac Walton and Ernest Hemingway, whose characters' interactions with nature are metaphors for how they dealt with their own tragedies. For Walton restoration is also found in his interaction with the community and in the social interaction of those who share similar interests and concerns. Hemingway's character, on the other hand, found solace in the solitude of one person's interaction with his environment. The more recent writings of Maclean, Joan Salvato Wulff, Margaret Atwood,

Tess Gallagher, Betsy Brown, and Annie Proulx attest to the complexities of contemporary life where the everyday is carefully woven into nature and fly-fishing, and where light and dark experiences are intrinsic to a fulfilled life. The specifics might be different in our contemporary society, but the complexities of life and society are timeless. The need to interact with nature seems to be the only constant.

It is this complexity of experiences of beauty, regret, family, community, and spiritual importance of nature that enriches my life and my work and connects me to those past writers, artists, and anglers. And it is this process in its literary and cultural history that is detailed in John Orlock's essay, which outlines the literary culture that accompanied my developing understanding that fishing has a culture and that the exploration of that culture was meaningful to my life and to my work as an artist. Yet, it isn't necessary to fish to understand that this cultural history, linked to fishing, has something to contribute to anyone who wants to explore the literary history that is the foundation for much of the representational tradition of fishing and of its visual culture.

NOTES

1. Harry Phillips, "A Special Memo from the Publisher," *Sports Illustrated Magazine* 6, no. 18 (May 6, 1957): 7.
2. Holly Morris, "Fumbling After Grace: Fishing and Writing," *New York Times on the Web*, June 8, 1997: http://www.nytimes.com/books/97/06/08/bookend/bookend.html. Accessed August 22, 2012.
3. John McDonald, ed., *The Origins of Angling* (New York: Lyons and Buford, 1963), 8.
4. William Radcliffe, *Fishing from the Earliest Times* (London: J. Murray, 1921), 152–158.
5. Dame Juliana Berners (attributed), *A Treatise of Fishing with an Angle* (West Valley City, Utah: Walking Lion Press, [1450]2006).
6. Macdonald, *The Origins of Angling*, 73–74.
7. Ibid., 77.
8. Berners, *A Treatise of Fishing with an Angle*, 37.
9. McDonald, *The Origins of Angling*, 46–47.
10. Ibid., 32.
11. Ibid., 32–33.

12. Ibid., 33.

13. Ibid., 65–66.

14. Ibid., 66.

15. Ibid., 19.

16. Ibid., 21.

17. Steven N. Zwicker, *Lines of Authority: Politics and English Literary Culture 1649–1689* (Ithaca, NY: Cornell University Press, 1993), 64.

18. Verlyn Klinkenborg, "Editorial Observer; The Wisdom of 'The Compleat Angler,'" *New York Times on the Web*, May 24, 2003: http://www.nytimes.com/2003/05/24/opinion/editorial-observer-the-wisdom-of-the-compleat-angler-at-350.html. Accessed August 22, 2012.

19. James Boswell, *The Life of Samuel Johnson* (London: Oxford University Press, 1965), 627.

20. Izaak Walton, *The Compleat Angler* (New York: Oxford University Press, [1676]2008), 66.

21. Ibid., 74.

22. Jonquil Bevan, *Izaak Walton's* The Compleat Angler—*The Art of Recreation* (New York: St. Martin's Press, 1988), 3.

23. Ibid., 2.

24. Zwicker, *Lines of Authority: Politics and English Literary Culture 1649–1689*, 61.

25. Ibid., 69.

26. Judith Maltby, "Lent Sermon Series 2012—Izaak Walton 1593–1683," *Winchester Cathedral News and Sermons*, February 27, 2012: http://winchester-cathedral.org.uk/2012/02/27/lent-sermon-series-2012-izaak-walton-1593-1683/. Accessed August 22, 2012.

27. Ernest Hemingway, "Big Two-Hearted River," in *Hemingway on Fishing*, ed. Nick Lyons (New York: Scribner, 2000), 5.

28. Ibid., 17.

29. Norman Maclean, *A River Runs Through It and Other Stories* (Chicago: University of Chicago Press, [1976]2001), 1.

30. Annie Proulx, foreword to Maclean, *A River Runs Through It*, xi.

31. Maclean, *A River Runs Through It and Other Stories*, 23–26.

32. Holly Morris, ed., *Uncommon Waters: Women Write About Fishing* (Seattle, Wash.: Seal Press, 1998) and *A Different Angle: Fly Fishing Stories by Women* (Seattle, Wash.: Seal Press, 1995).

33. Morris, "Fumbling After Grace."

34. Maclean, *A River Runs Through It and Other Stories*, 104.

7

Biological Regionalism: Scajaquada Creek, Erie County, New York, USA

ALBERTO REY

As was explained in the Introduction to this book, the catalyst for this volume was the projected exhibition at the Burchfield Penney Center for the Arts in Buffalo, New York, of Alberto Rey's *Biological Regionalism: Scajaquada Creek, Erie County, New York, USA*, planned for March 14 through June 22, 2014. While the initial chapters in this book address Rey's life and career and contextualize his work within contemporary art and the artistic traditions on which contemporary art draws, the last two chapters focus on Rey's *Biological Regionalism* series, discussed from the perspective of Rey's intentions and goals for the individual exhibitions and projects that compose this developing body of work. Rey's artist's statement about this ongoing series sets out his purpose, and Sandra Firmin's and Benjamin M. Hickey's essays analyze the significance and implications of specific installations that are part of *Biological Regionalism*.

ARTIST'S STATEMENT: SCAJAQUADA CREEK, ERIE COUNTY, NEW YORK, USA

Alberto Rey

BACKGROUND

I have been interested in streams since I was a young man growing up in the hills of western Pennsylvania. It was rare that, while exploring the streams nearby, my boyhood friend and I would catch fish, as fishing was not the goal of the explorations. We were more interested in hiking and exploring the areas around the streams. As we did so, we made continual discoveries that would affect the rest of our lives. My fascination with streams was suppressed for years, as I grew older, by my adult life and the need to earn a living, as well as by the development of my career as an artist. With time and age, and with my settling into my present position as a professor of drawing and painting at SUNY Fredonia, the layers of responsibilities and duties that kept me from continuing my early interests seemed slowly to dissolve. I began to look at streams anew as I drove over bridges, and subsequently I started to seek out naturalists and sportsmen/women who shared my interests. In so doing, I researched the history of the local streams near my home and began to learn about other comparable streams in other states. I was looking for similarities and differences between these other streams and my home waters that would help me to better understand the topography and specific character of my region.

As with many mid-to-late-career artists, change in artistic direction often occurs slowly, as ideas are fleshed out and allowed to mature and develop. My work for the past thirty years has been about my role in contemporary society, much of it focused on exploring the Cuban and Cuban American side of my identity. But around the year 2000, my early interest in science and in biology became more pronounced, and I began to understand that I was seeking to become more rooted in the region in which I lived as an American and as someone who had a family within a local community. Looking at streams, whether large or small, has become a window leading me into the life of different communities that live along the banks of streams. These communities reflect the society fostered by the existence of neighboring streams and human interaction with them. I am interested in the contemporary relationships that form between streams and communities, and in the history of the developments that led to the current coexistence of streams, wildlife, and people. I am also interested in the cultures of such communities and what these communities mean for our contemporary lives. In our own national history, the connection between our everyday lives and nature has been deteriorating, as most of what we depend on for our social and economic needs has moved to an urban setting. I am interested in how art can reconnect a community to its natural environment when such a connection has been diluted or even severed. Thus, when I paint fish, their environments, and the topography of the landscapes of streams, I seek to bring my experience of these places to the spectators who come to see the exhibitions that present my work. It is my hope that I can, in a way, take the spectators to the places I have seen so that they too can become immersed in these natural environments and feel, once more, that they are part of the communities created by these natural settings.

ART AS AESTHETIC NATURAL DOCUMENTATION

When I started the *Biological Regionalism* series, I was intrigued and excited about how the artists of the Hudson River School of the nineteenth century had connected communities with what was then the mostly inaccessible wilderness. These artists documented the expanding American landscape for a general public that had little exposure to this new environment, because its population was mainly concentrated in urban areas.

As the Hudson River School artists documented the flora, fauna, and landscapes of the United States, their work assisted scientific studies of biology, botany, and geology. The people acquiring these paintings were new or relatively recent arrivals to the United States who were interested in seeing the areas being explored, and who wanted to know more about the plants and animals scientists were studying. The association between the sciences and art was very close, as many artists accompanied geological survey expeditions and visually documented, in drawings, watercolors, and oil and mixed-media paintings, the aspects of nature that were of interest to scientists and surveyors.

As the urban centers grew and scientific inquiry became more specialized, the accompanying shift in populations created more distance between urban dwellers and nature. New modes of transportation, such as the expansion of railroads, meant that the wilderness was no longer inaccessible. Yet, as more areas were domesticated, the primal connection to nature became more tenuous, and urban life increased the alienation from nature that began with large-scale industrialization.

Biological Regionalism, in its ongoing development, is a body of work in which I attempt to reestablish a subtle connection to nature and the bodies of water that are in close proximity to the exhibition venues. The connection is attempted by bringing paintings, videos and specimens from these rivers, streams, and creeks into the exhibition spaces. By visually reintroducing the spectators in a community to their local fish and landscapes, in paintings and/or videos as well as other media, I also hope to create an opportunity for the audience to reconnect with its local natural environment. Once a local natural link is made, other connections can begin to develop that can reach to other waterways across the country and the world. The incorporation of paintings, drawings, videos, and wall plaques with historical and biological information into my exhibitions also creates a complex network of associations that can function as a foundation for additional dialogues between historical and contemporary theories of aesthetics, social development, and environmentalism.

SCENARIO SHARED BY THE SCAJAQUADA AND OTHER STREAMS ALONG DEVELOPED COMMUNITIES

The Scajaquada Creek is reflective of many other bodies of water that run through developed communities. Ever since the glaciers receded from Western New York, indigenous groups were drawn to streams to address their basic needs for water and food. The groups moved every five to ten years, as their environments became stressed from hunting and human waste. The tribes would move up and down the stream in search of new resources and could return every twenty years to older sites that had been naturally renewed. As the communities became more stationary and began to grow and develop, the streams became a natural resource for energy and transportation, while creating a cleansing vehicle for human and industrial waste. The stream that had sustained early communities eventually became polluted when the population increase interfered with the renewal of water quality. At that point, the Scajaquada's water was no longer suitable for drinking, farming, or sustaining wildlife populations. The stream was no longer the vibrant resource of a community. It had become a nuisance and a potential hazard to the community and to wildlife, as it hosted a multitude of diseases, flooded regularly, and negatively affected the communities near its banks.

The efforts to transform and restore previously ruined bodies of water have been part of ecological concerns for the past thirty years, and one complex success story is that of the Hudson River in New York City, which has undergone a remarkable transformation from a sterile and polluted river to one where marine life has returned. Yet, such efforts are recent compared to the lengthy history of geological formations, and are slowed down by the ongoing rate of development and the economic benefit of that growth, which comes at the cost of nature. The financial cost of stopping pollution can be overwhelming to an urban area, and efforts to renew natural areas can be complicated by a diverse range of opinions about how to best proceed while causing the least amount of change to the communities and businesses. At times, even a body of water's original structure and flow, as well as the environment along its banks, have been changed and diverted to best suit the needs of the local popula-tion. What remains is an artificial construct that displaces the natural resource that attracted the original community. Streams ruined by misuse lose their original character and life, and, in extreme cases, what is left is a dead channel.

While this exhibition focuses on the Scajaquada Creek and its history, I hope that the issues and concerns raised here can be useful to other communities, because they are of universal significance. Ultimately, I hope that this exhibition will enable a new connection to the Creek for those who live in the region through which the Scajaquada flows.

IN CONCLUSION

I am drawn to streams for many reasons, but mostly because of their potential to transform those who embrace their life. What the Scajaquada once was and what it once again could be exists in other bodies of water that have not been disturbed. These models can inspire the restoration of the Scajaquada: many community, conservation, and government groups are interested in the waterway's restoration, because it continues to affect the community, whether in a positive or negative manner. Because of this community and local government interest, there is potential for improvement and for positive change. This change might happen slowly, and it might not be all-encompassing, but it will nurture future restoration efforts.

A HISTORICAL OVERVIEW BY LYNETTE M. F. BOSCH

For the Buffalo area, the Scajaquada Creek is an historical body of water. The Scajaquada Creek itself is a tributary of the Niagara River and part of the watershed of the Lake Ontario basin. The Scajaquada's watershed includes Delaware Park, designed by Frederick Law Olmsted, who was part of the design team responsible for New York City's Central Park. In 1960, Olmsted's design was severely altered by the expressway that divided the park and changed the topography. As the Olmsted design was altered, the surrounding natural elements of the Watershed area were also subjected to changes that did not improve the environmental quality of what was once a pristine body of water. Different species of fish, such as herring, trout, carp, and shiners, along with snapping turtles and such birds as blue- and black-crowned night heron, which were once plentiful, have dwindled in number and quality and have disappeared from some parts of the creek.[1]

Margaret Wooster's book on the Creek, *Living Waters: Reading the Rivers of the Lower Great Lakes*, traces and documents the Creek's decline, even the ongoing hostility toward it on the part of Buffalo-area residents, and the recent attempts that have been made to save the Creek, despite the incursions of developers, who have been steadily destroying the Creek, its surroundings, and the wildlife that once thrived along its banks.[2] Wooster has also chronicled the pollutants that were dumped into the river, including: acetylene gas, acid, ammonia, bleaching powder, chlorine, dextrin, disinfectant, enamel, fungicide, glucose, insecticide, lacquer, linoleum, paint, paper, pulp, perfume, potash, printing ink, shellac, starch, turpentine or varnish, or grinding colors by machine; manufacture, refining, or distillation of asphalt, carbon, coal, coke, creosote, gas, and tar. These chemicals continue to appear in the bodies of local wildlife and are, of course, being absorbed by Buffalo's inhabitants as well. Yet, development along the Creek that adds more toxic substances continues largely unhampered by regulations that are supposed to be in place to prevent the loss of more natural habitat and to control pollution.

According to Wooster, the Creek's turnaround began when Jessie Kregal, who was a timpanist with the Buffalo Philharmonic Orchestra, began to campaign for a turnaround for the Creek.[3] Although slowly and intermittently, the local government and community have begun to take action to reverse the Creek's decay. The Scajaquada Creek's decline is now in turnaround, as the local government and community have begun to take action to reverse the Creek's decay and once again to make it into a living body of water. Since the year 2000, the oversight of this project is under the management of The Scajaquada Creek Watershed Advisory Council, which has several initiatives underway to bring the community into the project and to share in environmental concerns.[4] Rey's goal in studying such waterways is to bring attention to what has happened and what can be done to reverse damage and to allow a space in which spectators can come to their own conclusions about diverse situations and events.

Close to 94,000 people live within the Scajaquada Creek Watershed, which runs through the City of Buffalo, the Town of Cheektowaga, the Village of Depew, the Town of Lancaster, and part of the Village of Lancaster. The Creek Watershed is connected to urban residential areas, parks, hospitals, industrial sites, cemeteries, and vacant land, and so affects the territory of Buffalo State College, Canisius College, and Buffalo-Niagara International Airport. In Buffalo, the Scajaquada runs through Forest Lawn Cemetery and Delaware Park, the largest park designed by Frederick Law Olmsted (1822–1903). Next to the creek are Cheektowaga Union High School, McKinley High School in Buffalo, and the Walden Galleria Mall. The project to clean up the Scajaquada was spearheaded by Legislator Judith P. Fisher (District 4) and is funded by a grant from the legislature. The Council's mission is simply stated: "to develop and implement a community-based Watershed Management Plan to protect, restore and revitalize the Scajaquada Creek watershed, to encourage and support environmental stewardship efforts, and to provide for improved opportunities for public enjoyment of the watershed." If the Council is successful, the next generation may see the Scajaquada Creek restored closer to its natural state.

NOTES

1. In an e-mail to Alberto Rey, dated July 17, 2013, Margaret Wooster gave a list of some of the fish and birds that once populated the Scajaquada Creek.

2. Margaret Wooster, *Living Waters: Reading the Rivers of the Lower Great Lakes* (Albany, N.Y.: State University of New York, 2009).

3. Margaret Wooster, Albany, State University of New York Press, 2009, 43–50, where she describes the area around the source of the Creek, which is continuing to be polluted by development.

4. http://scajcreek.net/. Accessed August 22, 2012.

8

Time Submersion

A Portrait of Two Creeks

SANDRA FIRMIN

Just prior to the turn of the Common Era, Cicero coined the term *second nature* to expound on how humanity has sculpted the raw material of the natural world to serve its needs and cultural aspirations through the creation of agriculture, transportation networks, the development of cities, and, not to forget, art—as pigments, plaster, and marble were turned into frescoes, friezes, and temples. This philosophical belief distanced Roman society from nature by situating land and waterscapes as something to be manipulated for economic, political, or religious purposes while, at the same time, transforming it in the dramatic, literary, and visual arts. Although no division between nature and culture can exist—because we are always in and of nature—as cognitive animals we are constantly repositioning ourselves vis-à-vis the natural world.

While human modifications to ecosystems have been ongoing since the dawn of civilization, with the rise of the industrial revolution, the acceleration and magnitude of our incursions have taken on Frankensteinian proportions. We have blown off mountaintops for mining, straightened and buried rivers underground, and drained wetlands to build cities below sea level. "The closer we look at the land," as the environmental writer Ginger Strand succinctly describes it, "the more it appears to be a human sandbox, cluttered with our construction toys and sculpted by our ongoing efforts."[1]

If the vast majority of scientists, environmentalists, and news media outlets are to be believed, there is no one else but ourselves to blame for an all too conceivable extinction. And as humans are wont to do, we will not go down quietly, but in our polluting wake greatly diminish biodiversity by producing ideal conditions for the proliferation of a few species at the expense of untold others. With their science fiction designation, so-called invasive species feed into our apocalyptic vision of an environment in peril. We are confronted daily with images of kudzu engulfing trees and houses, beetles decimating pine forests, algae blooms removing oxygen from rivers and oceans, and zebra mussels clogging the machinery of nuclear power plants. Further feeding our cultural anxieties are shifting weather patterns due to global warming, which are causing drought in the United States, flooding in Pakistan, more powerful and plentiful hurricanes, and melting glaciers. Polar bears stranded on detached icebergs haunt the imagination. And if these events were not enough, to this deeply disturbing vision of the future could be added human vulnerability to superbugs, wide-spread exposure to industrial and pharmacological toxins, and lack of access to safe drinking water.

Alberto Rey wades into these murky waters of present-day geopolitical and environmental realities armed with a paintbrush and video camera. His stated agenda in his *Biological Regionalism* series is to establish a connection between viewers and local landscapes by introducing fish found in bodies near the exhibition venue into the gallery space through video and piscatorial painting. Rey, however, unsettles the conventionally romantic representations of the American landscape tradition. The most well known of these are by the nineteenth-century Hudson River School and Luminist painters, who habitually depicted the Atlantic Ocean and the rivers of the northeast United States bathed in the pink hues of daybreak or the golden light of dusk. Human presences are rare.

Recent theories in cognitive science and evolutionary biology explain the continuing popularity of these spectacular vistas on an evolutionary level, as they simultaneously provide pleasing views and safe lookouts to scan the terrain for signs of danger.[2] When ships, wagons, or trains with their ominous plumes of smoke appear, their presence is kept to the far background so as not upset the tranquillity of the compositions. A leading authority of nineteenth-century landscape paintings, Barbara Novak, notes, "That happiness was implicit in the nature paintings of the nineteenth century, recording a vulnerable present, offering images of a past we presently regret, as axe, train, and man only hint at the future to come. . . . The outlines of that future were blurred by optimism and submerged in the unconscious assumptions of a chosen people."[3] One needed to turn to novelists like Herman Melville and Edgar Allan Poe, Novak claims, for a darker appreciation of the role nature played in the human psyche.

On the cusp of the Industrial Revolution, Manifest Destiny justified exploration and settlement of already occupied land, an agenda that the Hudson River School, unwittingly or not, furthered by presenting nature as landscape to be contemplated and consumed. As scientist-explorers, nineteenth-century landscape painters and photographers joined military expeditions, or struck out on their own, to explore the far reaches of the Americas, pursuing knowledge of the frontier and recording its flora, fauna, and geological terrain. As entertainers, Hudson River School painters, in particular, offered popular entertainment for a nascent middle-class who would pay modest entry fees to be wowed by baroque spectacles of a wilderness waiting to be tamed.

In the years following the Civil War, increased mobility spurred the creation of destination tourism and leisure economies. Sporting art, and especially angling painting, became a popular subject matter for nineteenth-century painters like Winslow Homer, who reproduced his scientifically precise illustrations of fishes in motion and fly-fishing scenes in recently minted sporting magazines. During this time, fly-fishing evolved from an activity rooted in local traditions to a national pastime for an elite who could afford expensive equipment, travel to far-flung places, and enjoy private sporting club memberships.[4]

In his *Biological Regionalism* series, Rey depicts the same rivers, brooks, and streams that inspired nineteenth-century landscape and angling painters. Some of his paintings are stocked with brightly colored fish energetically swimming and feature ice-cold streams into which viewers could imaginatively dip their toes, or secluded locations where fishers could wait for hours in quiet contemplation. Others, in contrast, depict tributaries that have been repeatedly polluted by industry and commercial development, and neglected by a public oftentimes oblivious to their very existence. He accomplishes this by introducing waterways located in the vicinity of the museum where his work is to be exhibited through a combination of large-scale video projections, riparian landscape and angling painting, and notes and samples from his field and historical research. Altogether, he presents to visitors a vision of nature that is variously peaceful, beautiful, terrifying, dangerous, inscrutable, or knowable through scientific empiricism. These representations of the local ecology underscore how images and language convey deep-rooted ideological beliefs.

Biological Regionalism: Ellicott Creek, Amherst, New York, USA, 2010, which was shown at the University at Buffalo Art Gallery, is a case in point (fig. 22). Like many places in the United States named after people long-forgotten, the name of Joseph Ellicott, surveyor and land agent for the Holland Land Company, has faded from memory, but he had an enduring impact on the topography and, by extension, the economies of Western New York. He laid out the villages of Buffalo and Batavia, strongly advocated for the construction of the Erie Canal, and supervised the sales of tract, mostly to small farmers, mill operators, and innkeepers. Villages, buildings, and roads throughout the region are named after him, including Ellicott Creek, a forty-five-mile stream that begins in the Town of Darien, New York, and flows through much of the land he surveyed in the late 1700s, before releasing into Tonawanda Creek.

In *Biological Regionalism: Ellicott Creek*, visitors entered a tightly enclosed light-well with walls soaring upward two stories and painted a deep charcoal gray. In this square, silo-like space, they immediately confronted a floor-to-ceiling three-screen vertical projection of underwater footage of Ellicott Creek. The dark-greenish cast of the video makes it difficult to distinguish it from the architecture. As one's eyes adjust to the dimness, vague shapes, and movement emerge that correspond to three viewpoints of a river typically unavailable to human perception. Rey trained the camera's eye first on a sandy bed, which is surmounted totem-like by a straight-on view piercing the water and topped by a skyward gaze directed at the glassy surface where glints of sun rhythmically fluctuate with shadows.

Rey created this aquatic phantasmagoria by blurring the boundaries between the screen and the gallery walls with a diffused black edge and suffusing the space with the hypnotic sound of lapping water. It was as if the visitor had actually been submerged and was now experiencing the muddled sounds of life aboveground. The slow deliberateness of Rey's videos disorients one's sense of space and time. He transfixes viewers with long, static shots, which also serve as antidotes to the chase scenes, explosions, or juggling of complicated narratives that fill our fast moving media-scape. Writing on artists who employ video to explore the social construction of time, curator Jessica Morgan evokes Gilles Deleuze's suggestion that, "rather than thinking of ourselves or our actions as 'in time,' we should think of time as being 'in us' or 'in them' in a way that may divide us from our given selves (private and public). This awareness, then, exposes us to other worlds, other possibilities, other paths and trajectories."[5]

By employing this flexible—and empathetic—time consciousness, time ceases to be an absolute that exists separate from humans, but forms a constellation of intersecting temporalities of human, animal, and plant time, as well as cosmological, planetary, and meteorological time. The experience of time changes throughout the day, the year, one's life, and the generations. It splinters into multiples. It can be cyclical, like annual migrations, or repetitive, like Ground Hog's Day. Teleological time in the nineteenth century drove the faith in technological innovation to propel the onward march of civilization. Then the West believed that invention and control over natural processes could alleviate social ills. But now the endlessly repeating forty-hour-plus workweek, structured around international markets, labor, and the promise of leisure, holds us captive. Progress has lost its potency in the face of market forces, the vast chasm between rich and poor, pollution and ecological destruction, and the loss of local traditions due to the homogenizing force of global capitalism.

Before entering the gallery to view *Biological Regionalism: Ellicott Creek*, visitors were first presented with a map showing the river's proximity to the Buffalo Niagara Airport and the University at

Buffalo's North Campus, and its eventual dispersal into Lake Erie. It also pinpointed the site represented in the installation. At this point, visitors might have experienced the pleasure of being able to orient themselves geographically in the "you are here" sort of way. But it wasn't much help in identifying how to access the river, which bypasses public and private lands, including golf courses, suburban homes, and a landfill. Even those who interact with the creek on a daily basis are likely see it as pleasing backdrop to their walks, canoe trips, or backswings rather than a living ecosystem suffering the corrosive forces of urban development.

Yet, Rey does not seem to advocate an actual adventure into the physical landscape to commune with the creek. Rather, by presenting hauntingly beautiful images of a river and its inhabitants, Rey encourages an introspective state of mind in which we can contemplate how we coexist with other organisms in interlocking cycles of birth, illness, and death. He wants us to think about what this connection would look like and toward what goal it might be directed. Does our endurance as a species require that we find equilibrium with nature through conservation? And who decides how nature is

to be managed and to what end? The animal activists want the Town of Amherst to stop trapping beaver at Ellicott Creek. But what about those concerned about the trees the beaver are gnawing down? Does nature care what we do? And why should we care?

People make and appreciate art, attend their respective places of worship, care about ideas and ethics. But we also value jobs and economic gain. We are constantly measuring the immediate cost versus rewards that a fundamental realignment—from one of dominion to one of mutual dependence—would have on our livelihoods and the oil-driven lifestyles to which we have grown accustomed. We would need to radically increase our awareness of the ripple effects our behavior has on vast and complex systems of species and their environment. While we can begin to do this through the acquisition of knowledge and activism, Rey's work proposes that it is equally necessary to acquire an intuitive understanding of how nature lives inside us. Fast-paced modern existence is not solely responsible for humanity's alienation from nature. The rift is rooted in the beginning of Western civilization. Recognizing the power of landscape art to offer pretty pictures of nature to assuage our fears, Rey strategically uses characteristics of the sublime, like darkness, obscurity, and slowness, to channel this original trauma and induce feelings of dread and longing in the viewer.

To step into the cathedral-like space at the University at Buffalo was akin to crossing a threshold into a dream or a kind of netherworld. Often there was not much activity in the three mammoth projections, and visitors would naturally gravitate to the two oil paintings on plaster installed on either side of left- and right-hand gallery walls. One painting featured a riparian landscape, and the other presented a profile of a largemouth bass depicted several times its actual size. Ambient noise from the video provided a hypnotic soundtrack for picture viewing and seemed to animate the paintings. This uncanny sense of motion through sound was enhanced by the large size of each painting in which the central images fade into a mirage-like blackness.

In the psychologically charged landscape painting on the left-hand side of the gallery, it is as if we were looking into the inky depths of a portal to see ripples emanating from the bottom edge of the painting. The current would ratio-nally come from the audience's viewing position, thereby connecting pictorial and literal space. Are we standing in the water? Fisherfolk are always on the look-out for the slightest movement of water suggesting the presence of fish. Is there something in the water we do not see? An unearthly light penetrates the tight-ly enclosed scene in which there is no reassuring view downriver. Rather, the tree-lined bank forms a boundary at the fore and middle ground, forcing a bend in the river as it veers imperceptibly out of the frame. Rey's deft, impressionistic strokes and bold colors convey a dazzling light that skims the glassy water and flits about in the trees. These paintings are also infused with an interior luminos-ity, technically achieved by a basecoat of white plaster and a final layer of glazing, which removes any traces of brushwork. By reducing the evidence of the paint-erly process, like the Luminists before him, Rey minimizes his presence, and by extension his ego, and shifts the viewer's focus from appreciating specific passages of painterly bravura to becoming com-pletely absorbed in the entire vignette.

Out of the corner of one eye, a viewer might catch a glimpse of a largemouth bass swimming into the central projection.

Painting and video in the gallery demand our attention in different ways, and by situating them together in the same space, Rey pits our ability to control how long we look at painting against the unpredictability of video as a disruptive force. Painting's fixed presence is always theoretically available for us to contemplate, even if our mood or the knowledge we bring to the work varies. Video, on the other hand, constantly changes, producing a suspicion in the viewer that he or she might miss some crucial bit of information, a condition exacerbated by the fact we are in a constant state of distraction, moving from artwork to artwork, overhearing conversations, reading wall labels, taking pictures. Video art tends to eschew the traditional narrative structure of beginning, middle, and end in favor of the loop, which presents time as cyclical. Like photography, video cannot escape its connection to reality and truth, and is often read as a form of reportage. The media theorist Boris Groys connects video in the museum to our real-time existence: "In life, we are always only accidental witnesses of certain events and images, whose duration we cannot control."[6] Did the gargantuan fish on screen cause the modest ripple effect in the painting? Is the fish in the painting on the right-hand wall the same one as in the video? Is the fish going to do something other than kick up sand? Jump out of the water? Spawn? Undergo a metamorphosis? Are we willing to wait and see?

In the painting of the largemouth bass, we look through crystal-clear water at morphological details to which we would not have access to in nature. Rose-tinted cheek and gills give way to sun-dappled scales of light and dark greens, while fins surrounding the body on all sides offer a fascinating study of propulsion. Frozen in calm repose, the painting of the fish is a memento mori, a reminder of our own fragile existence, whereas the bass in the video is inscrutable. The image is slowed down by 30 percent to give the impression of the bass languorously swimming in and out of the frame, instead of darting to and fro as is its natural inclination. Rey recorded the bass on its annual migration to shallows and shoreline areas to spawn. While the video seduces us into experiencing part of its life cycle through balletic movement, an undercurrent of Lilliputian dread remains when our thoughts turn to the fact that we are dwarfed by a six-foot-high by eight-foot-long fish.

Since their inception, recording devices were thought to possess the ability to connect people to the spirit world. The vast watery void in the video conjures Gothic visions of a voyage on the River Styx, which separates the world of the living and that of the dead. Are we seeing an apparition, or a new being of our own making? Fish, after all, can be telltale signs of polluted waters, and science has hypothesized that increased estrogen in our waterways can cause male fish to develop ovaries.[7] In his *Biological Regionalism: Scajaquada Creek, Erie County, New York, USA*, 2013, the sense of dread expressed in nature grows more pronounced. Rey maintains that he does not seek out polluted waterways, but just responds to the parameters of the project. In the case of Scajaquada Creek, near Buffalo State College in New York, Rey confronts the Creek's long history of pollution and the manmade alterations imposed on it by industry and urbanization, as well as recent attempts by grassroots organizers at renewal. Rey's concentrated focus on specific rivers aligns his project with political movements that advocate for biodiversity, native species, and small-scale farming in the face of unconstrained globalization. Waterways, in particular, are vulnerable to the free movement of goods evidenced by the reckless introduction of the Asian Carp to the United States, which is currently making its way up the Mississippi and threatening the Great Lakes system.

Margaret Wooster, an expert on the history and current status of Scajaquada Creek, bluntly describes it a "veritable Frankenstein" that has been engineered into a sewer. The Creek begins with a spring in Lancaster, New York, ten inches deep and a foot wide, magically bubbling up to form a river that empties thirteen miles later into the Niagara River. What we know about streams aboveground is only a small part of the story. Everyone lives in a watershed, defined by the Environmental Protection Agency as an "area of land, a bounded hydrologic system, within which all living things are inextricably linked by their common water course and where, as humans settled, simple logic demanded that they become part of a community."[8] This hydrologic system not only includes the visible river, which during the summer months and times of drought often dries up, but underground flows that are responsible for naturally filtering water and have been measured to a depth of thirty feet and for miles laterally.[9]

Given water's tendency to disregard county, state, and national borders, it is a potent symbol for society's inability to contain the disastrous effects of pollutants on a finite resource necessary for our survival. The Scajaquada Creek watershed runs through five municipalities, including the City of Buffalo. Although an influential Seneca Chief is the river's namesake, the Seneca referred to the creek historically as Ga-noh'-gwaht-geh, "after a peculiar kind of wild grass, that grew near its border."[10] Knowledge of what this native grass might have been has long since disappeared with the introduction of rampant nonnative plant species. Like most urban waterways, it has been variously manipulated to suit the immediate needs of an expanding population: it has been channelized, or straightened, and buried underground in two locations, once for close to four miles in a tunnel fifteen feet or more below the surface and thirty-three feet wide. This marvel of engineering was built "between 1922 [and] 1928, after locals could no longer stand the smell of dead animals, garbage, and sewage that had been continuously dumped in the creek."[11] In the early 1970s, it was first tied into and then disconnected from the Buffalo sewer system right before it enters Forest Lawn Cemetery, where it is reportedly replenished by over thirty springs. Frederick Law Olmsted dammed it in advance to form "Gala Lake" (now Hoyt Lake) in the 1880s, but due to sanitation concerns, it was detached from the lake and forced underground again only to emerge into an industrial district where it meets the Niagara River, which, in turn, empties into Lake Ontario.

Prior to the late 1960s and 1970s, when concern for the environment was not widespread, smokestacks and water tinted green with chemicals signaled economic prosperity, not health hazards. But in 1969, when the Cuyahoga River in Cleveland, Ohio caught fire, followed by one spectacular environmental catastrophe after another, the United States and Canadian governments took note and started to listen to the outcry of activists and those impacted most by the lack of government oversight: poor and working-class families. A flurry of environmental regulations were passed, including the Great Lakes Water Quality Agreement of 1978, followed by the Great Lakes Strategy 2002, which seeks to provide a healthy habitat for humans and wildlife, clean drinking water, beaches for swimming, and fish safe to eat. Whatever its good intentions, this treaty is more about leisure and human habitation than a philosophical and ethical insistence that we have a moral responsibility to find a balance with nature. It assumes that if people realize that their actions have a detrimental impact on their enjoyment, behaviors will change. Once again it begs the question of what kind of connection to nature we should strive for.

Because Scajaquada Creek is a tributary of the Niagara River, the history of its contamination from industrial, municipal, and residential development is integral to the success of the binational agreement. Rey worked with the Buffalo Niagara Riverkeepers, one of the principal nonprofit watchdog agencies involved in monitoring and cleaning up the Creek, as he was developing *Biological Regionalism: Scajaquada Creek*. Buffalo Niagara Riverkeeper Riverwatch captains regularly take samples of the water and sediment at predetermined sites, five of which provide the source imagery for the paintings in *Biological Regionalism: Scajaquada Creek*. Gallery-goers begin at the woodsy headwaters and follow it through successive scenes depicting remnants of urbanization. Overgrown culverts, floodwalls, channels, debris collection grates, and

concrete pathways are eerily devoid of people. In their shallow depths and large-scale sequential procession, the paintings call to mind natural history dioramas and the nineteenth-century panoramas of the Mississippi that traveled around the country entertaining and educating audiences about the river's history and characteristics. Likewise, Rey's paintings are accompanied by informational material such as maps of the Scajaquada and bottled sediment samples, which, while seemingly innocuous, elicit a sense of dread once the content is considered.

The unassuming tone of Rey's paintings, videos, and didactic material are quietly suggestive, not prescriptive. He reminds visitors that the spectacles of environmental disasters that we see in the media, such as rivers grotesquely catching fire and birds slathered with oil—images that readily point to an industrial culprit—are now a small part of a much larger and mostly invisible problem. Far more insidious and harmful are the pharmaceuticals we flush down toilets, the soaps we use to rinse our hands, and fertilizers that run off our lawns when it rains and wind up in nearby rivers. Journalist Alex Prud'homme states it this way: "The effect of long-term multifaceted pollution on the ecosystem is not well understood. What, for instance, is the cumulative effect of a 'cocktail' of old and new contaminants—sewage, plastics, ibuprofen, Chanel No. 5, estrogen, cocaine, and Viagra, say—on aquatic grasses, water bugs, bass, ducks, beavers, and on us?"[12]

Accompanying Rey's paintings are two video projections. One shows a small, serpentine form undulating in golden water that is reminiscent of Andre Serrano's notorious *Piss Christ* (1987). Here we witness the hypnotizing body of a leech, the only living creature Rey found during his documentary expeditions, in which, it should be noted, he was careful to wear rubberized waders. In a self-reflective moment, this being can almost be seen as a Christ-like character sacrificed for our spiritual attainment. The theme of human redemption continues in the next video, in which Rey walks toward a tunnel. The jerky camerawork and sound of sloshing water delivers creepy *Blair Witch* moments, which, through its amateurism, connects us more directly to the action and the images of trash and sludge-stained walls. Sun glare causes a blinding light that brackets the experience of entering and, shortly thereafter, exiting the darkness of the tunnel. Scajaquada Creek, with its cemetery pass-through

and manmade alterations, provokes poignant meditations on the current state of human existence by presenting a textbook study on how societies attempt to manage natural processes for their own gain, resulting in forlorn landscapes.

One of Rey's first videos, *Primal Connections* (2006), is uncharacteristically narrative, but strangely arresting. It opens with the viewer in the subject position on a propeller plane staring over the shoulder of a young girl transporting a fish in a bag. The first-person perspective of the camera sets us adrift in a black-and-white, symbol-laden dream experienced in high definition. Soon we are on a motorized boat, with a dog on the prow, swiftly heading toward fishing grounds. Although it was filmed in the far reaches of Alaska, we do not encounter native peoples or the high-keyed bird's-eye view of glaciers and mountaintops characteristic of the high production value of sporting channels. Rey has stated that "our culture has developed outdoor recreational activities, zoos, and pets as ways to reconnect with our innate need to be close to nature." Close to nature, "this film investigates one way to reconnect. It also documents how far we have to go and what efforts we have to take to find wilderness in our contemporary society."[13]

The bond between use and nature, however, is not established through embodied travel, since we inevitably encounter goods and services imported from faraway and detect signs of encroaching global warming. Rather, Rey's makes this connection through the disembodied medium of video, which possesses an uncanny power to transport us into achingly strange images of transience. In the end, though, we do not remain in this defamiliarized landscape, but are brought back to reality with Charon at the helm. Where we go from here is one of the great, unsolved mysteries of the twenty-first century.

NOTES

1. Ginger Strand, "At the Limits: *Landschaft*, Landscape and the Land," in *Badlands: New Horizons in Landscape*, ed. Denise Markonish (North Adams, Mass.: Mass MOCA, 2008), 82.

2. Ibid., 85.

3. Barbara Novak, *Nature and Culture: American Landscape and Painting, 1828–1875*, 3rd ed., with new preface (New York: Oxford University Press, 2007), 169.

4. See Patricia Junker, "Pictures for Anglers," in *Winslow Homer: Artist and Angler*, Patricia A. Junker, Winslow Homer, Sarah Burns, and William H. Gerdts (New York: Thames & Hudson, 2003), 47.

5. Jessica Morgan, "Time After Time," in *Time Zones: Recent Film and Video*, ed. Jessica Morgan and Gregory Muir (London: New York: Tate, 2004), 16.

6. Boris Groys, *Art Power* (Cambridge, Mass.: MIT Press, 2008), 88.

7. Prud'homme, *The Ripple Effect: The Fate of Freshwater in the Twenty-First Century* (New York: Scribner, 2011), 75.

8. United States Environmental Protection Agency, available at: http://water.epa.gov/type/watersheds/whatis.cfm (March 6, 2012). Accessed August 23, 2012.

9. Margaret Wooster, *Living Waters: Reading the Rivers of the Lower Great Lakes* (Albany, N.Y.: State University of New York Press, 2009), 3.

10. Ibid., 49.

11. Scajaquada Creek: Info Central About the Creek, available at: http://scajcreek.net/?page_id=18 (December 15, 2009). Accessed August 24, 2012.

12. Prud'homme, *The Ripple Effect*, 11.

13. Alberto Rey, available at: http://www.albertorey.com/video-ar/primal-connections/ (2013). Accessed August 22, 2012.

9

Alberto Rey

Beneath the Surface

BENJAMIN M. HICKEY

Alberto Rey was recently Artist-in-Residence at the Masur Museum of Art in Monroe, Louisiana. My experiences working with him on his research regarding the waterways of Northeast Louisiana as well as his forthcoming exhibition at the Masur will inform my interpretation of art from his series *Biological Regionalism*. As I see it, *Biological Regionalism* contains four deeply interconnected conceptual layers or themes: they are the idea of high and low art; regionalism as it relates to supposed "avant-garde" culture in a globalized world; the specific histories of the area in which he works; and environmentalism. These themes consistently overlap, like ripples on water colliding and melding as they flow into one another. In order to embrace this phenomenon while still presenting Rey's work in a straightforward fashion, I will separate the aforementioned themes into four focused sections. Each section will eventually merge into the thematic whole, carrying readers through the chapter as they engage with the varied eddies of meaning that give Rey's work its complex and sometimes surprising cohesion.

HIGH AND LOW ART

Alberto Rey's series *Biological Regionalism* uses research conducted in aquatic ecosystems to re-create a localized narrative history. His histories often speak to the interconnected nature of our species and our environment by exploring the impact on our environment of factors such as pollution, overfishing, invasive species, human encroachment, and, sometimes, recovery. This series conveys a sense of urgency because it utilizes the formal components and systems of meaning from diverse art historical antecedents—not often associated with contemporary art—while still addressing today's most pressing environmental issues. *Biological Regionalism* operates on several conceptual levels, combining the empiricism of John James Audubon with the sensitivity to ecological issues possessed by artists such as Thomas Cole and the Hudson River School. Additionally, Rey often juxtaposes the sense of scale in his work with seemingly mundane or antiheroic imagery, a strategy not unlike that of Courbet. Specifically, he works in a monumental scale, using ostensibly unfashionable "low art" imagery featuring fish to create fine art with a cerebral Pop sensibility similar to that pioneered by Andy Warhol.[1]

The *Biological Regionalism* series is projected to include the current work-in-progress focusing on the region of Northeast Louisiana and its waterways. As part of this series, the Northeast Louisiana project will be related to previous projects, such as *Biological Regionalism, Ellicott Creek, Amherst, New York, USA* (fig. 22) and *Biological Regionalism: Brown Trout, Hosmer Creek, Sardinia, New York, USA*. Photographs of those projects give an idea of the forthcoming addition to this series and represent how Rey's work incorporates aspects of high and low art into a conceptual whole. Rey's exhibitions are composed of paintings, videos, and explanatory text and they are dominated by large-scale, closely cropped paintings of fish; in these two exhibitions, the central works depict a largemouth bass and a brown trout, respectively. While each exhibition's featured species displays a different artistic sensibility, they both rely on extreme contrasts in tone and hue to produce a vibrancy that hints that they are more than sentimental images documenting the fruits of leisure activities. These works imply, but do not make explicit, a narrative that will be discussed below.

BIOLOGICAL REGIONALISM: LARGEMOUTH BASS, ELLICOTT CREEK, AMHERST, NEW YORK, USA ·

The installation photographs from the University at Buffalo feature a largemouth bass highlighted by a shaft of light in the murky waters of Ellicott Creek. Its powerful tail is frozen in midstroke, implying that the fish will soon leave the image's foreground. The much larger than life depiction of such a fleeting moment fixed in place gives *Biological Regionalism: Largemouth Bass, Ellicott Creek, Amherst, New York, USA* a mythical quality that overlays and supersedes its minimalist title. The physical details visible in the video recording the bass and its environment unavoidably elicit contemplation. Why does this fish hold such an important place in Rey's life? The specific answer will come later, when I situate Rey within the context of environmentalism, but succinctly the answer is because it is symbolic of transience and power within an ecosystem.

BIOLOGICAL REGIONALISM: BROWN TROUT, HOSMER CREEK, SARDINIA, NEW YORK, USA

Biological Regionalism: Brown Trout, Hosmer Creek, Sardinia, New York, USA employs the same visual strategies as *Largemouth Bass, Ellicott Creek*, but features an increased use of brightly shimmering light throughout. The brown trout, a European sport fish introduced to North America, dominates the fore-ground. The image in Rey's work represents the moment after the fish was successfully caught from Sardinia Creek. Rey's depiction of water glistening off the trout's skin is detailed and graphic. It is easy to imagine the fish jumping and flopping on the ground as it tries to find the sanctuary of nearby water. The harvested fish firmly establishes the trout's position within the food chain in Sardinia Creek as a consumer of flies. Incidentally, Rey used a fly, modeled after a lowly mayfly, to capture the trout. Rey was able to take advantage of Sardinia Creek's biological bounty, for sport and possible sustenance, by mimicking the cycle of life in Sardinia Creek, and in so doing connected the angler to the fish, to the fly, and to the environment in which all live.

Rey's realistic depiction of fish and ecosystems gives visual form to his interests in conservation and in the restoration of our environment, an increasingly pressing issue. In addition, he juxtaposes and reinforces this concept with an antiempirical visual device, wherein he encloses each fish—*Largemouth Bass* and *Brown Trout*—with an irregular black halo, thereby forming a vignette composed of fish and halo. It is a pictorial device that gives a viewer's eye a place to rest and is endowed with other implications. Like the halos found on Christian icons, Rey's pictorial device connects the fish to the pictorial and iconographic history of otherwise invisible spirituality or religiosity. Rey started using this compositional element in the early 1990s in his *Madonnas of Western New York*, in the *Madonnas in Time*, and in the *Icons* series (figs. 5–7, respectively). Since then he has frequently used such halos to indicate an unseen bond between an object or location and an idea. In the context of *Biological Regionalism*, it is a multivalent symbol for the inexplicable urge for all life to persist, the idea of ecological interconnectedness, and especially the importance of human stewardship. Rey's images reaffirm the human idea of the sublime—the dual sense of exaltation and terror in the face of the nature in its purest forms—and the metaphysical connection we feel to our environment. Rey's very subtle incorporation of pictorial devices evoking spirituality in many of his compositions connects the works to potential spiritual experiences of nature on the part of spectators. While Rey does not overtly equate his vignettes of fish to direct religiosity, he is not opposed to the idea that the spectator can make such connections.

These intimations of spirituality represent only one aspect of Rey's engagement with the relationship between low and high art: his titles represent an additional aspect of this dialectic in that they are overtly scientific, often undercutting the otherwise romantic sensibility one may detect in his work. They are reminiscent of Audubon's austere titles like *Swallow Tailed Hawk, 1821, Drawn from Nature, Oakley Plantation, Louisiana*. Titles of this nature allow Rey to use Audubon to justify some of his choices as accepted aesthetic conventions, while simultaneously pointing to the traditionalism of the format in relation to currently accepted avant-garde practices. Ironically, this embrace of the traditional in a contemporary art context gives his work an unexpected edgy quality. In addition, his engagement with spiritual themes, depending on one's perspective, could be characterized as either skirting camp and a commentary on the sort of postmodernist art criticism often stereotyped as antireligious or atheist. Rey accepts this relationship between high and low art as a part of life and gives form to it in art by exploring the interaction between the different ways in which nature has been used, studied, and exploited; thus, he indicates how different ecosystems (including those of academia and the art world) can be bound together for better or worse. In so doing, Rey plays on the complexity of aesthetic traditions to argue for the validity of *Biological Regionalism*'s diverse references to high and popular culture. The dialogue or conflict itself affirms Rey's project and serves to being together a variety of audiences and voices from the world of nature and the world of artifice.[2]

REGIONALISM—*BIOLOGICAL REGIONALISM: BAYOU DESIARD, MONROE, LOUISIANA, USA*

My goal in this section is to provide commentary related to Rey's artistic practice in order to pinpoint his status within specific art historical and environmental discourses. *Biological Regionalism: Bayou Desiard, Monroe, Louisiana, USA* does this in several unexpected ways (fig. 24). Bayou Desiard is the lifeblood of Monroe, Louisiana. It represents the biological diversity and health of the area, and provides the City of Monroe with its water. It is fitting that Rey chose Bayou Desiard as the subject of a major painting to reflect the history and artistic traditions of Northeast Louisiana. One of the bayou's topographical features is a pair of

bald cypress trees, slowly growing into one another, which stands in the bayou like two great blue herons. Around them, the only discernible evidence of human presence is the slowly spreading wake from the Louisiana State Department of Wildlife and Fisheries boat on which Rey and I traveled, while we were looking for source material for his work. The finished work, which employs the horizon line Rey observed while in the boat, is a faithful recreation of his experience in the Bayou. Rey's rendition of the landscape is important because it is a straightforward assessment of the existing topography with its fixed horizon line. Bayou Desiard can be interpreted either as a static, mythical land, impervious to mankind's encroachment, or as a resource destined to be dominated and used without regard for the consequences. The fixed horizon provides an entry into Rey's landscapes from which his work can be interpreted, much as a map guides a traveler through unknown territory. The correspondence is made clear in Rey's frequent use of cartographical imagery as documentation of an area.

Rey's realistic depiction of Bayou Desiard includes a fish vignette, the metaphysical implications of which were addressed above. While this undermines my analysis of *Biological Regionalism: Bayou Desiard, Monroe, Louisiana, USA* to a point, it does support my broader agenda of discussing Rey's parallel understanding of complexity of various ecosystems, be they social, cultural, or natural. This facet of his work is best seen in the artist's handling of light. *Bayou Desiard* is bathed in a warm luminosity and easily conveys a sense of movement as light refracts off the Bayou's gently but constantly moving water. Rey's gestural treatment of tree limbs and foliage also implies movement in the form of a humid, sun-soaked breeze, which illustrates the actual moving parts in the real world observed in *Bayou Desiard*'s vegetation. The use of this motif additionally emphasizes the sense of flux and uncertainty about the Bayou's future that is part of its present.

To most people who read this essay, Bayou Desiard is not a familiar place, but it is recognized that its fauna includes alligators and its flora Spanish moss. These elements embody aspects of America's frontier past and to those who live in Desiard, these elements are part of their identity. Monroe, Louisiana is on the westernmost edge of the Mississippi Delta, and its sloughs, bayous, and creeks are

iconic pillars of the ecosystem. They serve as filters for the largest river system in North America, supporting a huge diversity of plants and wildlife as well as cleaning the Mississippi's vast watershed (with mixed results in recent years) before its water is ejected into the Gulf of Mexico. The Bayou is important for the specific history of Northeast Louisiana, and it is an element that represents the region and the identity of the people who live in this area.

The idea of regionalism in contemporary cultural studies is an area of inquiry that seeks to define the identifying markers for the shared culture of an area for groups that are inherently bound to geographical specificity and the cultural traditions associated with an area. Regionalist art often has less cultural capital associated with it than art from metropolitan centers simply because it originates in areas with less political, economic, and human capital. An example would be a comparison between art being made and sold in Crested Butte, Colorado, and art being made and sold in New York City. Because the prices are lower, and the content and subject may be more local than universal and speak to a smaller audience, the differences between such art centers can create the perception that regional art is a lesser form of art. However localized, such art does not restrict the quality of the statement or its presentation, yet regional artistic production can have difficulty competing with art produced in major centers that is free of localized specificity. Such art is additionally perceptually hampered by the term *regional*, which, in many aesthetic circles, can be used in a pejorative manner to marginalize dialogue related to cultural identity in areas that exist on the periphery of the dominant culture. Nevertheless, many regional art historical movements benefit from their proximity to a powerful political, economic, and or cultural center with enough critical mass to validate them within a broader context. Hence, the interaction between center and periphery is not simple or straightforward.

A good example of this is the Hudson River Valley School and Thomas Cole. Cole became a forefather of the American cultural establishment because his art was used to justify New York City's ascension as a major urban center of culture and economic power, which was already evident in Cole's time. Cole's legacy is important because it operates in two separate ways. It conveyed the idea of Eden by empha-

sizing the purity and bounty of the New World. Yet, Eden was slated for destruction in the wake of human advancement, ironically to create a new, ideal world.[3] The duality of Cole's message was evident to him, but later critical appraisal presented a simplified view of his work as representing the idea of Manifest Destiny, even before the term existed.[4] This meant that Cole's work came to symbolize the providential nature of the United States of America's expansion across the continent, as the fledgling country became a world power. The cultural misappropriation of Cole's art is representative of what can happen when works of art are interpreted through different cultural filters.

Other examples of this phenomenon is the reception of Grant Wood's work. Wood's work is often held up as portraying a manly, rough-and-tumble ideal to which Midwestern America aspires or is rejected as a mocking caricature of his home state of Iowa and other states that share common traits. His work has also been seen as an alternative to the cultural and aesthetic hegemony of the contemporary, New York–based, seemingly more cosmopolitan movement of Abstract Expressionism.[5] Wood's outsider status as a citizen of the American hinterland nonetheless gave his work enough validation to enable it to maintain its continued relevance. Thus, both center and periphery can be comparably validated, even if they can be differently regarded by the critical establishment.

Rey's conception of regionalism creates an important dialogue that simultaneously questions and responds to the traditions and history of an area. Each aspect of Rey's approach is intrinsically important to his project. Rey's thought process situates him as being both a regional and a global artist. While his artistic center is found within the mainstream, he has created his place at the center by focusing on studying the regional and the local, as he functions in the role of itinerant postmodern arbiter of aesthetic taste—even as he injects himself into cultural milieus with which he had little previous involvement. One could justifiably ask why he thinks he is uniquely qualified to further cultural traditions from areas to which he is not directly tied. Is he just a cultural tourist?

The considered answer is no. While acknowledging his limitations as an outsider to many of the regions he represents as well as his responsibility to research his topics thoroughly, Rey is nevertheless skeptical of the notion of an "authentic" regional perspective: "There is no perfect vantage point from which to reflect on a region. Even residents have limited perspective created by past experiences, by the repetitive nature of their everyday lives, and by the group of the folks they regularly correspond with. I do the best I can to bring my skills and past experiences into each unique situation."[6] Rey is invested in documenting a variety of ecosystems or geographical locales because he is concerned with environmentalism, with the practice of fishing, and with merging his personal activity with much larger traditions. Thus, he engages in site-specific dialogues that bring the local, the regional, the national, and the global in touch with one another. *Biological Regionalism* fills a need to document the resources we possess while also leveling and questioning the aesthetic playing field with unique combinations of painting, installation, video, text, and sculpture. Rey's conceptual base is intrinsically bound to complex ideas of high and low art and the applicable qualitative indicators, while he retains an earnest and well-executed artistic practice. By participating in regional culture and by transcribing this culture and its natural environment into works of art, Rey seeks to combine the diverse aspects of American culture into his work. While Rey is not seeking to revolutionize aesthetic and ideological practices in contemporary art, he does seek to engage a diverse population in the dialogues he creates in his individual projects.

NORTHEAST LOUISIANA

Biological Regionalism: Fish Shadows, Black Bayou Lake National Wildlife Refuge, Monroe, Louisiana, USA is a video Rey created for his forthcoming exhibition at the Masur Museum of Art. The picture frame shows the forest floor while Black Bayou Lake is at flood stage in the spring. Rey's forays into new media always involve the incorporation of slow-motion imagery. As a result, many of his new media works closely resemble his paintings when initially viewed. Perceptive observers who slow their viewing process to match the pace of Rey's videos literally see the moving microcosm of life he that is implicit in his paintings. *Fish Shadows*, for example, features lazy air bubbles drifting to the surface, implying oxygen, gases, rot, and nature's ability to create life from death. The air bubbles slowly draw viewers into the small section of forest floor until they are capable of seeing thousands of tiny creatures swimming in all directions. These creatures' identities remain anonymous, but they illustrate the sheer wealth and complexity of life even in such a tiny part of a larger ecosystem. In this case, moreover, the underwater camera captures the very life forms that normally emerge only when humans leave, thereby reflecting, according to Rey, "the unseen environment of the Bayou."[7] Unlike the subjects of most of Rey's works, the namesakes of *Fish Shadows* are more implicit than explicit: perhaps the last part of this work most people are likely to see are the shadows of several small fish feeding at the surface of the water. The ability of *Fish Shadows* to slow down the viewing process illustrates the contemplative nature of Rey's work. The video is unusual in that a monumental image of a fish is not the primary emphasis, but for the purposes of Rey's project in Monroe, it is perfect.

In advance of Rey's arrival in Monroe, he asked Masur staff to find several types of research materials for him. He was most interested in seeing historical examples of landscape paintings and other examples of fine art from Monroe's more distant past. Such artifacts do not appear to exist within Monroe's cultural milieu. There are many historical examples of art documenting the landscape and culture of Southern Louisiana, but similar equivalents do not exist in Monroe. The lack of local artistic documentation of Monroe's environment means that Rey's project is powerful, because it is almost unique in documenting and continuing the history of art in this part of Northeast Louisiana. Rey is currently beginning this process of creating regional art using documentary photographs, lithographs, and etchings culled from newspaper archives. He is also becoming familiar with ancient Native American artifacts that are part of local collections. Rey's investigation of these resources brings attention to the importance of his project for the cultural life of Monroe, and it has the potential for creating long-term and lasting changes at the Masur Museum of Art.

In a strange and unexpected way, Rey's trip to Monroe closely resembles the journeys of exploration undertaken by two historic figures that inform his work, Frederic Edwin Church and Alexander von Humboldt. Humboldt, a German naturalist who influenced the American artist, and Church were contemporaries from different generations during the nineteenth century. Humboldt is known for his travels throughout Latin America, primarily documenting flora and fauna. His empirical approach expanded scientific knowledge of the new world and furthered an enlightenment viewpoint informed by his belief that nature transcended reason.[8] Church's artistic enterprise had similar goals. He regularly mounted research expeditions to isolated or exotic locations, later creating spectacular large-scale images. His depictions of landscapes are sometimes fictional composites, but they are rendered with an extreme sense of realism that parallels Enlightenment thought. However, he consciously incorporated aspects of technique that rendered his landscapes with an undeniable sense of the sublime and the breathtaking. He attained these effects through the use of expansive use of scale and depictions of natural phenomena such as rainbows that indicate his theistic or romantic aims.[9]

While he does not directly advocate a specific spiritual or religious viewpoint within his current artistic practice, Rey acknowledges this element within his work.[10] This is supported by my previous discussion of his use of light, halos, and the slow and contemplative pace of his videos, all of which are resonant and evocative of Humboldt and Church. Rey's holistic appreciation of a landscape or ecosystem in the form of environmental documentation is understated in comparison to Church's spectacular landscapes or Humboldt's unrelenting scientific detail, but Rey's work is as clearly articulated in its intention. Rey's engagement with a locale presents it simultaneously and paradoxically as exotic and authentic, fragile and durable, romantic and empirical. His self-conscious creation of this complex system of meaning that accepts diverse interpretive possibilities is meant to create dialogue between contrasting positions and perspectives, as Rey does not dogmatically dictate a specific perspective for his work or its content. He feels that enriching environmental debates and making them complex is the only way to ensure progress and prevent one-sided, adversarial dialogue.

Rey's approach is particularly well suited to the region he has chosen for this project. Monroe's current population is less than fifty thousand people, and its poverty rate is 34 percent.[11] Both statistics are typical of the region. Although investment in infrastructure is impressive when these facts are taken into account, it is not surprising that a strong historical narrative of visual arts never took root. Rey's project will serve as the impetus for the creation, potential rediscovery, and close continued maintenance of a canon of Northeast Louisianan art history at the Masur. Rey's participation at the Masur Museum will assist in making different aspects of Northeast Louisianan culture more accessible within and outside the area. It will also improve the region's ability to successfully capitalize on its frontier identity and the resources it has retained. Among those resources, the most important cultural, economic, or political development specific to Northeast Louisiana after World War II is arguably the founding in 1997 of Black Bayou Lake National Wildlife Refuge. The refuge represents an interesting response to the history of the area: instead of viewing the environment solely as a means of recreation, subsistence, or profitability, it has pushed an agenda of educational outreach and holistic thinking in regard to resources management. Along with its highly involved community auxiliary group, the Black Bayou Lake National Wildlife Refuge represents an unexpected confluence of constituencies, who understand that their quality of life depends on the natural environment. Significantly, their agenda of inclusion mirrors Rey's approach to his art and environmental advocacy.

While in Monroe, Rey visited Black Bayou Lake several times and held a sketchbook workshop there as well. He further injected himself into Northeast Louisiana's environmental and artistic discourse by hosting a fly-tying workshop at the Masur and a joint lecture with Kelby Ouchley, former Manager at Black Bayou Lake. This second event focused on the local ecosystem and Rey's career as an artist. Rey also partnered with local citizens and other institutions, drawing on many resources within the community to make his project at the Masur as rich as possible. Fishing with the community auxiliary group Friends of the Masur and breaking bread with Northeastern Louisianans will hopefully expand the reach of Rey's message by creating strong bonds within the community.

More important to Rey's artistic practice, he worked with staff members at Louisiana State Department of Wildlife and Fisheries as well as University of Louisiana at Monroe's Museum of Natural History. As previously mentioned, the Department of Wildlife and Fisher-

ies took Rey to Bayou Desiard to gather specimens of indigenous fish and plant species to serve as source material for his project. Gathering flora and fauna, then preserving them in the manner of scientific specimens, is something new to Rey's practice, but it would seem to be a natural progression for his investigations and research. This new practice was assisted by the University of Louisiana at Monroe's Museum of Natural History, which boasts the third-largest university collection of fish specimens in the world. Their staff members' willingness to assist Rey with the task and the art of preserving and documenting specimens in an appropriately scientific manner made this addition to his practice seamless.

ENVIRONMENTALISM BY WAY OF A CONCLUSION

Biological Regionalism: Vetch, Monroe, Louisiana, USA and *Biological Regionalism: Largemouth Bass, Sunfish, Spanish Moss and Sawgrass, Bayou Desiard, Monroe, Louisiana, USA* are examples of Rey's incorporation of biological specimens into his installations and artistic projects (figs. 25 and 23).[12] *Vetch* and *Largemouth Bass and Sunfish* represent Rey's dedication to an interdisciplinary approach and his desire to strike a balance between the empiricism of science and the aesthetics of fine art. *Vetch* uses a dried member of the bean family collected near the park to communicate this thematic interplay while maintaining a sense of refined simplicity. The work presents Black Bayou Lake in the style of frontier or expeditionary cartography, with a bird's-eye viewpoint often associated with omnipotence or omniscience. The gentle balance between these two elements of *Vetch* is driven home by the very fragility of the specimen itself and the play of line within the composition that represents the area on a proportionately larger scale than it has on proportional maps, which is seen in the manner in which the vetch mirrors the contour of the east side of Black Bayou Lake as well as the course of Bayou Desiard off to the west. This layering of looping lines in *Vetch* is underscored by the contouring of the text of its scientific plate and label information.

Largemouth Bass and Sunfish accomplish the same thematic ends in a manner more in keeping with Rey's large-scale fish imagery from *Biological Regionalism.* The two fish are preserved in formalin and sealed inside their jar with paraffin wax. The impasto application of paraffin is imperfect and painterly, drawing attention to the implied ruthlessness of sacrificing fish in the name of science and stewardship of the species. The wax also gives *Largemouth Bass and Sunfish* a sense of importance by emphasizing that through art, the fish is fulfilling a higher cultural purpose and becoming a type of reliquary. It is important to recognize Rey's continued use of scale to convey his message. The bass is so large that it blocks the sunfish from view and completely fills its container. It appears uncomfortable, and its tail was indeed doubled back on itself before Rey placed the dead fish in the jar. Replete with Spanish moss and saw grass, two plants pulled directly from the fish's former home, *Largemouth Bass and Sunfish* functions as a reminder of origins and indicates how, through human agency, the fish has been removed from its ecological place. This juxtaposition raises serious and potentially unsettling questions about the struggle for life within an ecosystem, and what Rey identifies as "the nostalgic quest for information through science," ultimately inviting its viewers to reflect on their own quests for knowledge and their experiences with the species and its environment.[13]

A further examination of Alberto Rey's recent personal history will clarify how he came to engage with the Masur Museum of Art, as this chapter concludes. Angling has long been an important part of Rey's life. His engagement with it as a segment of his identity gives *Biological Regionalism* a sense of purposeful unity with his past series and his life long journey to reconcile his conception of self with his place in the world. The most significant difference between Rey's current and previous work, aside from the inclusion of angling imagery, is his determination to use his artistic practice as a means of making a direct impact on issues in which he believes strongly. In 1999, for example, Rey enrolled in Sportfishing and Aquatic Resource Educational Programming (SAREP) workshops hosted by Cornell Cooperative Extension. This training prompted him to help found the SAREP Youth Fly Fishing Program with funding from the Chautauqua County Industrial Development Agency. The program places equal emphases on inclusion, environmental consciousness, ethics, scientific training, and sport fishing. The Canadaway Creek Conservation Project, in which Rey is involved, is equally emblematic of the Youth Fly Fishing Program's mission and is comparable to the SAREP program. It features an annual event focused on garbage collection, the management of creek sediment, and the reestablishment of both the native brook trout population and native plant species to further stabilize the creek's health. During the rest of the year the Youth Fly Fishing Program uses Canadaway Creek as a site for many of its other activities and outreach.[14]

In his trajectory as a fisher, an environmentalist, and an artist, Rey follows a pattern established by Winslow Homer, perhaps the best-known American painter of landscapes and wildlife. Rey has been aware of this facet of Homer's career for some time, and his influence on Rey is undeniable. To Homer, an angler was a member of a fraternity who was in touch with his bonds to other men and their smallness within nature.[15] According to Homer, anglers understand the balance between humanity's right to exploit natural resources for their benefit and the responsibility to show respect for the environment to ensure its continued productivity. Finding a balance between these concerns has been at the forefront of the environmental movement from its origins with Rachel Carson's book *Silent*

Spring in 1962. This desire for balance seems to inform Rey's practice on nearly every level, including his pragmatism, educational outreach, interdisciplinary collaboration, and advocacy for the finer things in life by creating the finer things in life. In my estimation, the work offers us a provocative challenge as well as a course of action worthy of emulation.

NOTES

1. Alberto Rey, "Biological Regionalism, Ellicott Creek, Amherst, New York," lecture presented at State University of New York at Buffalo: UB Art Galleries, April 4, 2010.

2. Alberto Rey, interview with author during field research at Black Bayou Lake National Wildlife Refuge, April 11, 2012.

3. David Bjelajac, "Thomas Cole's Obow and the American Zion Divided," *American Art* 20, no. 1 (2006): 60–83.

4. Robert Hughes, *American Visions: The Epic History of Art in America* (New York and Toronto: Alfred A. Knopf, Incorporated, 2009), 211; Allen Wallach, "Thomas Cole's 'River in the Catskills' as Antipastoral," *Art Bulletin* 84, no. 2 (2002): 334–350.

5. R. Tripp Evans, *Grant Wood* (New York and Toronto: Alfred A. Knopf, 2010).

6. Alberto Rey, personal correspondence with author, August 19, 2012.

7. Ibid.

8. Michael Dettelbach, "Alexander von Humboldt Between Enlightenment and Romanticism," *Northeastern Naturalist* 8 (2001), 9–20.

9. David Huntington, *The Landscapes of Frederic Edwin Church: Vision of an American Era* (New York: George Braziller, 1966); Timothy Mitchell, "Frederic Church's 'The Icebergs': Erratic Boulders and Time's Slow Changes," *Smithsonian Studies in American Art* 3, no. 4 (1989): 2–23.

10. Alberto Rey, interview with author during field research at Black Bayou Lake National Wildlife Refuge, April 11, 2012.

11. United States Department of Commerce, 2010 Census, City of Monroe, http://quickfacts.census.gov/cgi-bin/qfd/location, July 20, 2012.

12. The specimen in *Biological Regionalism: Vetch, Monroe, Louisiana* was first seen inside Black Bayou Lake National Wildlife Refuge. A different

example of vetch was gathered from another site.

13. Alberto Rey, personal correspondence with author, August 19, 2012.

14. Alberto Rey "Biological Regionalism, Northeast Louisiana," lecture presented at Masur Museum of Art: Alberto Rey Artist-In-Residence, 12 April 2012.

15. Patricia Junker et al., *Winslow Homer: Artist and Angler* (Fort Worth and San Francisco: Amon Carter Museum and Fine Arts Museum of San Francisco, 2002).

10

Conclusion

Bioregionalism and Animal Studies

LYNETTE M. F. BOSCH AND MARK DENACI

In writing and editing this study, it became clear to us that there is much future scholarly work that can be done about Alberto Rey and his work. The manner in which Rey's work addresses a cross-section of life, art, social issues, nature conservancy, trout and fish populations, identity, and place means that it is naturally interdisciplinary and open for study by specialists in the humanities, the sciences, as well as the behavioral sciences. Contemporary regionalism studies is another perspective from which Rey's work can be explored, as his life, art, and philosophical considerations are rooted in places and in identifying that which is local and belongs to specific places, and which defines the environmental and social culture of individual regions.[1] Art, literature, music, and other aspects of culture are to a degree determined by the natural environment that shapes the social groups who settled in different places in our world.

Bioregionalism as a field of study encompasses study of natural environments and their flora and fauna, and the identification of geographic and environmentally linked areas, independent of political boundary designations. Such studies classify and differentiate between native and invasive species, and in conservation projects, attempts are made to restore natural diversity and to remove invasive species that threaten areas with the destruction of diversity of wildlife and plant life, as invasive organisms displace the original ecological balance. The aesthetics of natural landscapes vary and preserving and restoring that which is untouched is valuable in and of itself because biodiversity ensures survival, even as it encourages evolution in a gradual manner that enables a natural selection of species diversity. Part of Rey's project to preserve regional species and to study the local culture that recognizes these species as markers of their identity, enables the creation of a valuable record that can be used by scientists to determine the health of specific areas.

For the groups that inhabit these varied regions, their sense of self is linked to the animals and plants that share their part of the world. Regional biodiversity affects the formation of identity in profound ways and the displacement of these natural forces, as they give way to pollution or to the rapid advance of what does not assimilate but destroys and causes disorientation and alienation among the groups that lose such an important part of their identity. As Rey studies that which is diverse and that which defines identity, he also records the interaction between humans and their environment as he preserves the knowledge of a balance that exists between land and survival of all of the species that need a healthy environment to thrive. With the destruction of nature comes the destruction of those who destroyed it, because human beings are not independent from nature. Thus, much of Rey's work is about giving back regionalist roots to the people who live in different places by making them remember the essence of what defines them. Rey is not an artist who takes in and renders aesthetic diversity as a tourist of lovely environments; he is a keen observer of what is necessary to nourish the soul and the body. Having spent his life living on the hyphen, what Rey seeks is to remind those who can still rebuild and save their regions that these regions define who they are and who they can become.

In turning from the earlier, more-or-less overt themes of human identity and culture to representations of living and dead fish and their natural environments, Rey's recent work cannot help but to engage with many of the concerns of the currently small but growing academic field of animal studies, also known as human-animal studies. This interdisciplinary body of scholarship, mainly centered in the humanities, has evolved out of (and within) the continental philosophical tradition, drawing on a combination of poststructuralist thinkers, most notably Giorgio Agamben and especially Jacques Derrida, whose late writings such as "The Animal That Therefore I Am (More to Follow)" (2002) and "Violence Against Animals" (2004) seem to have provided the field with a kind of nodal point around which to coalesce.[2] Recent work by such scholars as Kari Weil, Cary Wolfe, and Matthew Calarco explore the fundamental questions raised by the aforementioned philosophers (in conjunction with other lines of thought, such as the "post-humanism" of Donna Haraway) about the lines drawn between the human and the animal, and the way we define each category in relation to the other, as well as the relationship of these definitions to concepts of consciousness, sentience, language, and even ethics in general, applying insights derived from these explorations to virtually all aspects of cultural production, including art.[3]

Many scholars within this field seek to differentiate themselves from the more long-standing animal rights movement, suggesting that most concepts of "rights" depend too securely on anthropocentric foundations, particularly to the extent that animals are claimed to deserve rights mainly because (and therefore only to the extent that) they resemble humans.[4] This antihumanist perspective, therefore, goes beyond animal advocacy to involve a broad critique of contemporary thought; according to Matthew Calarco, "to allow . . . anthropocentrism to go unchallenged renders thoroughly unradical and conservative much of what today goes by the name of radical politics and theory."[5] While some scholars, such as Calarco, explicitly or implicitly position animal studies in strict opposition to anthropocentrism, others, such as Weil and Wolfe, seem more interested in deconstructing that very opposition. Wolfe, for example, claims that "the other-than-human resides at the very core of the human itself, not as the untouched, ethical antidote to reason, but as a part of reason itself—the 'trace' that inhabits it, to use Derrida's term."[6] Weil, for her part, while acknowledging the necessity of understanding animality as a form of radical alterity, nonetheless argues for a "critical anthropomorphism," in which "we open ourselves to touch and to be touched by others as fellow subjects and may imagine their pain, pleasure, and need in anthropomorphic terms, but stop short of believing that we can know their experience."[7] As examples of artwork occupying the opposing ends of the spectrum between radical alterity and anthropomorphic empathy, Weil offers up Bill Viola's 1986 video *I Do Not Know What It Is I Am Like*, with its disorienting account of a nonhuman vision, to account for the former pole, and Frank Noelker's 2002–2006 series of disarmingly dignified portraits of formerly abused chimpanzees, to represent the latter.[8]

Where, then, do Rey's relatively (but never absolutely) naturalistic "portraits" of living and dead fish fit into this discourse? While none of this volume's contributors approaches Rey's work from an explicit animal studies perspective, several of them raise these issues implicitly, alternately exploring both the artist's "anthropomorphic" identification with the fish, on the one hand, and his attempt to reach outside himself (and an earlier desire to connect with cultural "origins") to an exploration of the nonhuman world, on the other. Arguably, part of what makes Rey's fish paintings so compelling is their refusal to occupy either pole of Weil's spectrum, putting viewers in a kind of

ambivalent position between empathetic identification and confrontation with radical otherness. The fact that Rey's interest in representing fish began around the same time as the emergence of this particular strain of animal studies is fascinating; both his work and this nascent body of scholarship seem to be responding to a related set of cultural and philosophical questions, and examinations of his work grounded more thoroughly in this body of inquiry may well yield fruitful results.

NOTES

1. See Mike Carr, *Bioregionalism and Civil Society: Democratic Challenges to Corporate Globalism* (Vancouver, BC: University of British Columbia Press, 2004); Michael McGinnis, editor, *Bioregionalism* (New York: Routledge: 1998); Gary Snyder, *A Place in Space: Ethics, Aesthetics and Watersheds* (Berkeley, Calif.: Counterpoint: 1995); Robert Thayer, *LifePlace: Bioregional Thought and Practice* (Los Angeles: University of California Press, 2003).

2. Though necessarily partial, any list of the field's foundational texts would have to include the following:

Giorgio Agamben, *The Open: Man and the Animal*, trans. Kevin Attell (Palo Alto, Calif.: Stanford University Press, 2004); Jacques Derrida, *The Animal that Therefore I Am*, trans. David Wills, ed. Marie-Louise Mallet (New York: Fordham University Press, 2008); Jacques Derrida, *The Beast and the Sovereign,* vol. 1, trans. Geoffrey Bennington (Chicago, Ill. University of Chicago Press, 2009); Donna Haraway, "A Manifesto for Cyborgs: Science, Technology, and Socialist Feminism in the 1980s," in Elizabeth Weed, ed., *Coming to Terms: Feminism, Theory, Politics* (New York: Routledge, 1989); Donna Haraway, *When Species Meet* (Minneapolis, Minn.: University of Minnesota Press, 2008); Vicki Hearne, *Adam's Task: Calling Animals by Name* (Pleasantville, N.Y.: Common Reader Editions, 2000); Thomas Nagel, "What Is It Like to Be a Bat?" *Philosophical Review* 83, no. 4 (October 1974).

3. Matthew Calarco, *Zoographies: The Question of the Animal from Heidegger to Derrida* (New York: Columbia University Press, 2008); Marianne DeKoven and Michael Lundblad, eds., *Species Matters: Humane Advocacy and Cultural Theory* (New York: Columbia University Press, 2012); Kari Weil, *Thinking Animals: Why Animal Studies Now?* (New York: Columbia University Press, 2012); Cary Wolfe, *Animal Rites: American Culture, the Discourse of Species, and Posthumanist Theory* (Chicago, Ill.: The University of Chicago Press, 2003); Cary Wolfe, ed., *Zoontologies: The Question of the Animal* (Minneapolis: University of Minnesota Press, 2003).

4. See, for example, Wolfe, *Animal Rites,* 190–193. For the most frequently cited "foundational texts" on the animal rights movement, see Tom Regan, *The Case for Animal Rights* (Berkeley: University of California Press, 1983) and Peter Singer, *Animal Liberation* (New York: Avon, 1975).

5. Calarco, *Zoographies*, 13.

6. Wolfe, *Animal Rites*, 17.

7. Weil, *Thinking Animals*, 20.

8. See the chapter "Seeing Animals" in Weil, 25–50.

Biographical Timeline

August 7, 1960—Born in Havana, Cuba. Family lived in Agramonte, a small farming community (three hours by car from Havana). The family was composed of farmers, small business owners, and teachers and lived modestly in a small rural, agricultural town.

Father: Enrique Rey, family from Canary Islands (mother's side) and from Escalante, Spain (father's side).

Mother: Olga Guerra Rey, family from Santander, Spain (mother's side).

Both parents were born in Agramonte, as were his father's parents.

April 18, 1961—The day after the Batalla de la Playa de Girón (Bay of Pigs) invasion, Alberto's father, Enrique, was jailed in a chicken farm for ten days because he was a known dissenter of Fidel Castro's plans and policies.

Rey Comments: "All the locals knew that my father was against Fidel. The day after the Bay of Pigs, everyone who was against Fidel was imprisoned in separate locations across Cuba. My mother's two brothers, her father, and my father were held at Palmar del Jonco Stadium in Matanzas, for three days, and then moved and were imprisoned in a large, commercial chicken farm for another week."

1963—Enrique Rey, Alberto's father, was granted political asylum in Mexico and moved to Tlalnepantla, a suburb of Mexico City. He worked for Monsanto, using his expertise as a math teacher, with a PhD in education from the University of Havana. By August, Enrique borrowed and saved enough money to bring Alberto and the rest of the family over from Cuba.

Rey Comments: "My family collected money from friends and family with which they paid $8,000 to the Mexican Embassy and he was picked up by car on a predetermined corner of a street. He had met a Mexican engineer, in Cuba, who arranged for the job in Mexico. My dad worked a year and then borrowed more money from his boss to pay for the visa and airfare to bring my mother, my sister Mayda, and me to Mexico. We were the first in our family to leave Cuba. We were allowed to take three changes of clothes, but were not allowed to take any money or anything else."

Family Remaining in Cuba

Mother's Side: Fredy Guerra and Pepito Guerra (mother's brothers), remained to continue farming the family farm and to take care of their parents, Victoria Pascual Guerra and Jose (Pepe) Guerra, and their Aunt Celina. They died in Cuba. Amparo, Fredy's wife, remains in Cuba, farming the same family farm.

Father's Side: Father's brothers (Manolo, Fernando and Juan) and his sister, Luisa, stayed with their parents, Enrique and Mercedes Rey. Paola Liberata Prieto Baéz also remained in Cuba. She was originally from Bolondrón in the Province of Matanzas, where her parents, José María Prieto and Dominga Baéz, had settled.

Rey Comments: "The folks, who stayed in Cuba—my mother's side of the family—were my uncles, Fredy Guerra and Pepito Guerra (my mother's brothers). They stayed to work the farm and take care of their mother and father, Victoria Pascual Guerra and José "Pepe" Guerra and Aunt Celina. They all remained in Cuba until they died. From that group, only Amparo remains in Cuba. She is still there working on the farm. On my father's side, his brothers, Manolo, Fernando, and Juan and their sister, Luisa, stayed with their parents—Enrique and Mercedes Rey. Manolo followed us to Mexico four months later, with his wife, and they flew to Miami a year later. A year later, Fernando also passed through Mexico, then flew to Miami. Juan stayed in Cuba with his father, Enrique, because he was not allowed to leave during the Mariel boatlift. He had to remain in Cuba because he was a dentist, but his wife, Elsa, and his mother, Mercedes left through Mariel, in 1980. The boat was overloaded and capsized. Ten passengers died, including Mercedes. Enrique received permission to leave Cuba, in 1982 and Juan got permission to leave through Spain, then Mexico and finally to Miami, where he joined his wife. They now live in Spain, near Madrid, where he is still a dentist. Pepe died in 1978, in Cuba."

1964—The Rey family moved to Miami and settled in a small house on NW Third Street, which was located a few blocks from the old Orange Bowl.

Rey Comments: "We left by bus through Brownsville, Texas, to Miami. My parents wanted to live in the United States and we had an aunt in Miami, Lucía Prieto; she and her husband, La Grana, lived in Miami, so we went there."

1965—Rey family moved to a second-floor apartment on Twenty-first Street and Seventeenth Avenue, next door to where the Orange Bowl parade floats were made.

Rey Comments: "My father worked in the sugar refinery, then as an airplane mechanic, fiberglass boat manufacturer,

cutting aluminum sheets for windows. He had skills that you get when you grow up in a small, rural, farming town. My mother worked at home. She built fishing rods and as a seamstress, doing piece-pockets for shirts. She was also an Avon salesperson and worked at the Ancel packing plant in packaging. As with my father, she had work skills from growing up in a rural community, where people did their own sewing and repairs."

1966—Rey family moved to a small house near the apartment on NW Seventeenth and Twenty-First Streets to live with Rey's uncle, Fernando Rey. His father and uncle worked for the Ancel guava factory a few blocks away. Rey's father worked in packaging and as a representative at food fairs. His uncle worked cooking the guava for the guava paste. This is the house about which Rey retains the most memories. His Aunt Mirta, Uncle Pepe, and cousins—Mirta, Omar, and Joel Álvarez—moved next door soon after. Currently, the Álvarez family lives near Rey's parents in Perrine, South Miami.

1967—Pepito, Alberto's uncle, died, in Cuba, in the fields of Isla de Pinos prison, where he was detained as a political prisoner and forced to do agricultural work. Reportedly, he was hit by lightning while working.

Rey Comments: "My mother's cousin was working in the fields with him. During a lighting storm, four workers took shelter under a truck and the truck was hit and they all died."

1967—Rey family moved to Steele Avenue in the outskirts of a small coal-mining town, Barnesboro, Pennsylvania (population, 2,500). Rey's father had achieved his recertification to teach and found a job teaching Spanish at Northern Cambria High School. No one in the Rey family spoke English very well at this point, and as they looked very ethnically Cuban, they stood out in the small, rural community, composed of mainstream Americans. There wasn't a Latino community in Barnesboro. The Reys were the only Cubans in the region, and while the family did not experience discrimination, it took a long time for them to feel comfortable in the United States.

Rey Comments: "My father had participated in an educational program in Rutherford, New Jersey, that had been set up for Cubans who were teachers, to get recertified to teach in the United States. He had been a teacher and school director of a high school in Cuba, with a PhD, in math education. The program guaranteed that they would find jobs for the graduates, and my father decided to take the job in Barnesboro, because there weren't many jobs in Miami, which was then a much smaller city."

1968—The Rey family moved to a second-floor apartment over a women's clothing store on Philadelphia Avenue in downtown Barnesboro. This was the same year that Alberto's mother's sister and her family moved to Miami from Cuba. The Rey family spent every summer in Miami from this date on to 1978. While the Rey family didn't have a Cuban or Latino community in Barnesboro, these annual trips provided Rey with an idea of what Cuban culture had been and still was, transported to Miami. He learned about Cuban customs and family history from stories, ate "Cuban" food and observed his Cuban relatives continuing to be Cuban among Cubans. Then the family returned to Barnesboro, and to the solid American world into which he assimilated every day, as much as was possible for a member of an ethnically Cuban family, who spoke English with accents.

Rey Comments: "My parents, my sister and I were the only Cubans around, and other Cubans were about an hour away. They were professors at Indiana University of Pennsylvania and they helped us move to Barnesboro. We became good friends. My father taught Spanish at Northern Cambria High School, and my mother worked in a clothing factory in Hastings, Pennsylvania."

1972—The Rey family bought a house (610 Seventeenth Street—now called Jupiter Street) in North Barnesboro (now called Northern Cambria).

Rey Comments: "We lived in a small, rurual coal-mining town of about 2,500 residents and two traffic lights. In front of the house was a large bony pile (a mound made of coal waste and slag) that was left from an old coal mine, and behind the house was a forested hill, where we hunted, slept out, and ran up and over on the way to the town swimming pool. A scene right out of the Michael Cimino movie, *The Deer Hunter*, which was filmed, in 1978."

1978—Pepe Liberata, Rey's grandfather on his mother's side, died of pancreatic cancer, in Cuba. Rey has no memory of his grandfather.

Rey Comments: "I remember the scene vividly. We had been sitting and waiting in our living room in Barnesboro. We knew Pepe was not doing well and my mother had been praying all day. We could not watch TV or listen to music. Evening crept up on us, and the entire house grew dark, except for the one candle that my mother had been praying in front of. I remember watching that candle and thinking about how this was all very foreign to me. I had no memory of my grandfather, but respected what was happening. A few minutes later, the candle went out for no reason. My mother started to cry and a few seconds later, we got a call from Cuba that he had passed. No one seemed surprised by what had happened and it was never discussed."

1978—Rey received an appointment to West Point Military Academy. Later, he left with an honorable discharge to start his studies in biology at Indiana University of Pennsylvania (IUP).

Rey Comments: "I had several letters of interest from several schools due to my track record of football achievements. I was then thinking of attending a few schools with degrees in oceanography. At the time, I was not part of a culture that did a lot of research into colleges and universities. I looked at a few catalogs and was ready to make my decision.

"I remember getting a call from our congressman's representative, asking me if I was interested in attending West Point. I was a bit surprised to get the call, since I had not applied to the academy, but it was due to my past athletic experience and favorable grades. I would not even have known about West Point if it had not been for a recent high school graduate, who had gone there a year before. I had no plans for the summer, so I decided to attend. A couple of months later, I grew to respect the Academy, their education, their philosophy, and career options, but it became clear that this was not what I had planned for my life.

"I had not envisioned myself as an artist at this point. War and killing is unfortunately a reality of life and of global societies, but if I had the option, I did not want to make it a career option. I grew up a lot in those few months. My father was not pleased about my decision, and it created a lot of dissension in the family over the next four to six years.

"I had been interested in art and biology since I was around ten, but being an artist had never been a realistic career choice. In high school, I copied drawings from *Mad* magazine and portraits from photographs, while also copying paintings from the Hudson River School and Frazetta. I knew nothing about art history. After leaving West Point, I attended Indiana University of Pennsylvania. I enrolled in several biology and chemistry classes my first semester and decided to try drawing class my second semester, along with my other science classes. I was encouraged to pursue drawing, by Professor Paul Ben-Zvi, and to continue my studies in art."

1979—Rey changed his major to art and moved to Toms River, New Jersey in the summer to work as a cook at Sodl's on the boardwalk.

1980—Rey moved to Cape May, New Jersey during the summer to work as a bellhop at the Colonial Hotel.

Rey Comments: "I enjoyed working in the summers on the Jersey shore. New adventures, new challenges, new experiences—very little employment was available in Barnesboro."

1980—Paula (Mercedes) Liberata died in an overcrowded boat in an attempt to reach the United States. Manolo Rey, Rey's uncle, identified his mother after her body was recovered, in the waters off Key West. Rey has no memory of his grandmother.

Rey Comments: "My grandmother's death was rarely discussed. It was difficult for my father and his brothers. The motor on the boat exploded in the middle of the boat, *Olo Yumi*. All of the fifty-two passengers, who were crammed into the boat, moved to the back when the explosion happened and it capsized—ten died (including my grandmother), thirty-eight survived, and four were not found. Elsa, my aunt, was found but there were not enough life jackets. Many died from burns from the gasoline."

1980–1981—Rey moved to an apartment with his friends, Joe di Febo and Brian Shuliger, on Chesterfield Street in West Oakland, near Carnegie Museum of Art and Natural History in Pittsburgh and enrolled for a year in Visual Communication at the Art Institute of Pittsburgh, in affiliation with IUP. Rey worked as a darkroom technician and messenger for Focal Point Photography and made weekly pilgrimages to the Carnegie museums.

Rey Comments: "The Art Institute had established a relationship/affiliation with IUP, where you could get your concentration in Illustration. I went for a year and discovered after finishing the curricular requirements, within the first few weeks of each semester and receiving an "A," that no one cared about my education more than me. A friend, from IUP, Don Diehl and I spent every morning at the library, doing research on the history of illustration, formalism, and aesthetics. Those mornings were filled with investigating art and taking control of our education and our lives; it was one of the most fulfilling experiences I had had up to that point. The only highlight of being at the Art Institute was taking life classes with Henry Koerner. He was a true master, a committed artist and a real character. Working for Focal Point Photography was also very important in my artistic life. I learned the business of being a professional and fine-tuning a print to that finite point, where it would come to life."

1981—Rey returned to IUP to receive his BFA in drawing and painting and to finish his BA.

1982—After graduation, Rey saved money stocking shelves at the A&P grocery store in Barnesboro, and moved to Boston, MA. He worked part-time doing cut-and-paste work at a design firm and doing illustrations for the *Christian Science Monitor.*

Rey Comments: "I had always wanted to go to Boston, and I had met a friend, a fellow resident hall counselor, at IUP, who had moved there. I stayed with her while I was showing my illustration portfolio around town and tried to make enough money to settle down there, but I was not able to make enough money. I returned to Barnesboro to regroup and save up some more money to try again somewhere else. All of these experiences gave me more confidence and more knowledge about the realities of making a living."

1983—Not able to make a living in Boston, Rey moved to Miami to begin interviews with galleries and design firms. He was hired as a worker on Christo's *Surrounded Island* project.

Rey Comments: "My aunt and uncle, who I had been visiting in the summers since I was a child, offered to let me stay with them, while I tried to get my career started. I had been interviewing with galleries since I was in Pittsburgh, and now I also had an illustration portfolio that I was showing to secure a job. While on one of my interviews, I saw some things going on in Biscayne Bay, and started to do some drawings from hotel rooftops, since it was one of the few places you could get a perspective on the project. I was young and it seemed exciting to do this. After doing a little more research, I found out that the headquarters was on Pelican Island. I walked in, asked about the job and gave a brief overview of my past experiences. I started the next day and worked around sixty hours a week for the next few weeks. Christo and Jeanne-Claude were very accessible, and working within a community of international artists and nonartists made me appreciate the scale of possibilities in contemporary art."

1984—Rey moved to Davie, Florida, and worked on designing and etching large panels of fine art glass at Joan of Art Studio, Fort Lauderdale, Florida.

Rey Comments: "While in Miami, I met a friend, Scott Witcoscki, who I had worked with on the Jersey Shore. He was able to get me a job, and we shared rent with a few other workers from the studio."

1984—Rey moved to South Goodman Street in Rochester, New York, and worked at Light Impressions archival photo supplies and did freelance work for Lichtenstein Marketing Communications.

Rey Comments: "I started thinking about graduate school, and had been dating a friend since my days back at IUP. She was living in Rochester, and it seemed like the right time to move up there, work to save money, and try to get into graduate school."

1985—Rey moved to Buffalo and began graduate studies at the University of Buffalo (UB), and started the *Father and Sons* series.

Rey Comments: "I had done some research although it is always difficult to select a graduate school for painting. I had the list down to two schools. I applied to the Art Institute of Chicago because of a recent write up and ranking in an art magazine and to UB because I had heard good things about the program. I got rejected from the Institute and got an assistantship to UB. The decision was made."

1986—Enrique Rey, Rey's grandfather, died a few years after getting permission to leave Cuba and coming to Miami. Rey was in graduate school at the University of Buffalo. This death began Rey's work investigating Cuban and American identities and culture as he started his *Auto-geographical* series.

Rey Comments: "He lived a good life during the last few years, while in Miami. He continued to smoke cigars, got married, visited families, and he had several friends. My parents were still in Barnesboro, but most of the rest of my family—aunts, uncles and cousins—continued to live and prosper in Miami. My sister and her family lived in Morgantown, West Virginia. We talked by telephone, and I took bus trips to Barnesboro to visit my folks for major holidays. I bought a used Gremlin, in 1988, and was able to visit my folks more often. Trips to Florida did not occur for a few years, while I was in graduate school."

1987—Rey received an MFA from UB in drawing and painting and traveled to Spain (Madrid, Valle de los Caídos, Santa Pola, Malaga, Marbella, and Gibraltar) and Morocco. He returned to Buffalo and moved to West Buffalo where he began to teach Spanish full time in inner-city schools. He began the *Black Lace* series.

Rey Comments: "My uncle lived outside of Madrid and had been asking me to come visit his family. I also wanted to experience Spanish culture, which had deep connections to my heritage. I asked a fellow rugby friend, Matt McCarthy (who later became Graciela's godfather) to come with me, and we drove from Madrid to Gibraltar and then took the ferry to Morocco. We stayed in hostels along the way and slept in the car one night. I worked all summer painting houses from dawn to dusk to get the money. I had just received my MFA in drawing and painting, and there I was painting windows, trim, and doors. It was very humbling, but it wasn't needed. I had been humbled my whole life by being different and by not having much money. My family was generally supportive, but they didn't understand the world I was moving into.

"In Madrid, I visited every major art and anthropological museum. I saw many of the paintings I had adored in books since I was young. I also set up interviews with galleries to show examples of my work in slides and printouts. I ended up finding a very well respected gallery, that offered me an exhibition a year later and then began to represent my work in Spain and in Miami—Galería Emilio Navarro. We also took a trek to Granada on our way south to Gibraltar. As we traveled along the coast, we had no schedule. We stopped and snorkeled along the coast at various places, as we saw interesting waters to investigate.

"There are too many ways to describe how it affected me, but let me give you an overview. All travel makes me question how each society and culture views their lives, jobs, family, environment, art, and food. It made me more aware of diversity in cultures and traditions and how these impact art. It also made me realize that there are many significant artists in the past and in contemporary art who are not well known in the United States. It was a bit of a wake-up call that very few artists ever find major, international recognition.

Art in its many diverse forms, seemed to be appreciated by a wider segment of the public in Europe, and more artists seemed to know about their culture's historically significant artists. All of these experiences and many more have provided me with a wider perspective on what creates a culture and broadened my perception of what directions my work could take. Unscheduled stays in unknown towns and cities also made me more capable of accepting and welcoming situations, as they occurred. This made me flexible, confident, and capable of dealing with diverse issues and situations."

1988—Rey moved to Boston and began teaching art full time at Lincoln Sudbury High School as a sabbatical replacement. He also did adjunct teaching at the Museum of Fine Arts, The Art Institute, in Boston, and The New England School of Art and Design. He traveled to Mexico (Isla de Mujeres, Valladolid, and Chichen Itza). Rey attended classes in contemporary art history and environmental studies at Harvard University and began the *Binary Forms* series. He had his first solo exhibition in New York City at the Museum of Contemporary Hispanic Art (MoCHA).

Rey Comments: "I really liked Boston, and wanted to live in a city that was a bit more manageable than New York City. There was a small-town feel to the city. My family came from a small town, I grew up in a small town and I was comfortable in the culture of small towns. I bought a *Boston Globe* in Buffalo and applied for an art teaching position at Lincoln Sudbury, for an instructor who was on sabbatical. When the instructor returned, they created a position to keep me on board. When I got to Boston, I went through the yellow pages and called every college to see if they needed any adjuncts. I got several calls back and submitted my résumé. I was given a studio, while at Lincoln Sudbury, and created works from the *Prenuptial Binary Forms* series and the *Black Lace* series. Marriage was on my mind.

"A year after graduate school, I was represented by Pat Stavaridis Gallery, on Newbury Street. I was exhibiting with artists I had read about and admired in art magazines while in graduate school. It was very exciting. Pat was the first major gallery that represented my work. She was a wonderful owner and supporter of my work. She was a pleasure to work with but the gallery closed in a couple of years later."

1989—Rey traveled to the Caribbean (Isla de Saintes, Guadalupe, St. Kitts, and Antigua) and moved to Dunkirk, New York, and accepted a position as an assistant professor at the State University of New York at Fredonia. He married Janeil Cam Strong from Gloucester, Massachusetts.

1990—Rey and Janeil traveled to Italy (Rome, Florence, Capri, Sorrento, Venice, and Ferrara).

Rey Comments: "I had just gotten married and was working on the *Binary Forms* series, which was about marriage, abstraction, religion, and spirituality."

1991—Rey worked as a crew captain on Christo's *Umbrellas* project in the Tejón Pass in California, and later traveled to Mexico City. He began the *Madonnas of Western New York* series.

Rey Comments: "I heard Christo was planning this project in Tejón, and so I called him and mentioned my involvement in the *Surrounded Islands* project and I was asked to be one of the crew captains, who were installing the umbrellas. For the *Madonnas of Western New York*, I wanted to document elements of American popular culture and selected to work realistically, so that I could make the work and the content more accessible to the public. I also wanted to make contemporary versions of Mexican *retablos* and *ex votos*."

1992—Rey was promoted to associate professor at State University of New York at Fredonia, and his works were accepted into the permanent collections of the Albright-Knox Museum, Brooklyn Museum of Art, and Bronx Museum of Art.

Rey Comments: "Everything was moving nicely. There seemed to be interest in the *Binary Forms* and the *Madonna Series*. I had gotten tenure and life was good, but this was around the time that I realized that my career was not going to progress as quickly as I had envisioned, because of my move from Boston to Fredonia and because teaching was going to take up a good deal of my professional time. I didn't realize at this point that a career does not need to progress in a linear manner, but that it can occur by embracing divergent directions that come from diverse intellectual interests. Everything was holding steady on all fronts."

1993—Rey traveled to Spain (Madrid, Alicante, and Santa Pola) and began *Madonnas in Time* and *Icon* series.

Rey Comments: "Inverna Lockpez was the director of the MOCHA in New York City, and she continued to support my work over the years, as we also became friends. In Boston, after Pat Stavaridis closed, the Harcus Gallery represented my work for a few years, until this gallery closed, and then I was picked up by Howard Yezerski Gallery. Howard and I continued to work together for several years, until the long distance between us made it difficult for collectors to see the work regularly. In Buffalo, I was represented by Nina Freudenheim Gallery, until she closed her gallery and then reopened in a smaller venue. Art Dialogue Gallery handled some of my work as they had done since I was in graduate school."

1994—Rey received the William T. Hagan Young Scholar/Artist Award for distin-

guished scholarly and creative activity as junior faculty and the Minority Visiting Scholar Award from Central Missouri State University.

1995—Rey traveled to Aruba.

Rey Comments: "We decided to celebrate Janeil's parent's fiftieth anniversary on an island that rarely experiences hurricanes. I remember flying over Cuba and thinking how far it seemed to be."

1995—Rey traveled to Venice, Italy, for the Venice Biennale and to Key West and Stock Island, to research Cuban Refugee center. He begins *Las Balsas* series.

Rey Comments: "I wanted to return to Italy and dedicate two weeks to experiencing Venice again (my favorite city in the world), and I wanted to have the time to experience the culture and lifestyle, while also getting to see every venue for the Venice Biennale. I enjoyed the bounty of historically significant work mixed in with some of the most important contemporary artists from around the world. Again, I saw many interesting artists that I had never heard about. It was a very stimulating experience. Upon returning to the States, I went to the University of Miami and Key West Library to investigate their collection of Cuban archives for the *Appropriated Memories* series. While I was in Key West, I stopped at the Cuban Refugee Center to do my research for the *Balsas* and *Balsas Artifacts* series.

1996—Rey was promoted to professor at State University of New York at Fredonia, and his parents retired and moved to South Miami/Perrine, a small town near Miami. From this point on, Rey made regular trips to Miami, at least once a year. He traveled to Mexico City and Teotihuacán for a solo exhibition at Galería Nina Menocal, where his traveling solo exhibition had arrived after being presented at the Meridian Gallery in San Francisco, California and Southern Oregon University in Ashland, Oregon.

Rey Comments: "A few months after finishing the *Balsas* series, the work was exhibited at the Bronx Museum by Marysol Nieves. Emilio Navarro Gallery, in Spain, opened another gallery, in Miami, and represented the work in exhibitions held at Gramercy International Contemporary Art Fair and at Art Miami."

1996—Rey began the *Las Balsas Constructions* series and the *Appropriated Memories* series.

1996—Rey accepted a temporary, part-time, position as the director/curator at the Chautauqua Center of the Visual Arts at Chautauqua Institution, while remaining at State University of New York at Fredonia. Soon afterward he was appointed to the New York State Council on the Arts and to the Artist's Advisory Panel of the New York Foundation for the Arts.

Rey Comments: "I had been asked to consider the position, and it allowed me to restructure the professional practices of how the Center promoted contemporary art. The restructuring moved the Center toward its acceptance and integration into the Chautauqua Institute's ambitious future plans. I was also invited to be on both advisory groups in New York City. These experiences provided a holistic vision of the inner workings of granting institutions and exhibition spaces. It sensitized me to the needs of each organization and its relationship to artists and supporters."

1997—Rey was selected to the New York State Council for the Arts, Visual Arts Panel, New York, New York.

1998—Rey traveled with his mother, Olga, to Cuba (Agramonte, Havana, Varadero, and Viñales) for the first time in thirty-five years. Graciela Victoria Rey, Rey's first child, was born. Rey began the *Balsas Artifacts* series and *Studio Retablos* and started the SAREP Youth Fly Fishing Program (Dunkirk, New York). He was selected to the New York Foundation for the Arts, Artist Advisory Board, New York, New York.

Rey Comments: "My mother wanted me to go with her so that she could share her memories of specific locations in Cuba, while also introducing me to family members. Back home, I thought I wanted to give something back to the inner-city community, in Dunkirk, New York. I thought fly-fishing would provide a lifelong positive outlet for the youth in the city. I hoped it would also provide something that would take them outside the city and bring solitude to them in a positive and thoughtful way. When traveling back to New York City, I learned a lot about the workings of NYFA and the grant-review process. It was very enlightening. It also provided me with regular opportunities to visit galleries and museums.

"The trip to Cuba dramatically influenced my life and work. It provided the realistic perspective on what was actually happening in Cuba. I experienced extreme highs at being back in Cuba and experiencing what I had seen in photos, heard through family stories, and listened to in songs over the past three decades. Extreme lows were also an important part of the overall experience. It was very depressing seeing the poverty and struggles that my family and other Cubans were experiencing. I collected film footage and documented images of family members and friends for the *Cuban Portrait* series, which would be the last body of work that dealt with Cuba (apart from a couple of works I did as part of the *Biological Regionalism* series that included work from the Jardines de la Reina, in Cuba).

1999—Rey is diagnosed with chronic migraine variant, which plagued him with several months long periods of light-headness and nausea. He moved to a new home and larger studio in Fredonia, New York and began working on his first documentary on sixteen millimeter film, *Seeing in the Dark*; the video incorporated footage shot during the trip to Cuba taken the previous year.

Rey Comments: "This was the most difficult period of my life, as the condition took a long time to diagnose and I continued to have bouts of it. At times, I wondered if I would regain my health. As the condition continued, I realized that I would need to reconsider my health, my work ethic, and my life, and I began to understand that this was not a temporary condition. I learned to cope with it and to plan and execute projects ahead of deadlines in case of a recurrence.

2000—Rey began the *Trout Encounters* series, which was a major change of direction in his work.

Rey Comments: "In 1998, I returned to Cuba, for the first time since I left as a child. I experienced the real difference between "nostalgia" and "reality." Apart from the *Balsas* series, my work for the last fifteen years had dealt with a romantic vision of the past and present. The work fulfilled my need to reconnect with my culture, while still trying to relate it to the present. The work had brought a great deal of fulfillment and it provided a sense of spirituality to my everyday life.

"After that trip to Cuba, I saw everything around me quite differently. I still found value in the work I had done but it was from a completely new perspective. Apart from the trip, I was also ending two major series of works, putting together a complicated installation, preparing to install three solo shows simultaneously and was moving into a new house and studio. I knew that I was at the pivotal point in my artistic career. After all the chaos subsided, I realized that this was a perfect time to carefully examine the work and the future.

"I decided it was time to move in another direction. At first, I wasn't sure what that next series would be but I knew that it could not be about Cuba any longer. I had to gather my thoughts about the past work and see if there was anything new I could bring to it. I also realized that most things in life were cyclical and that I might return to examine issues related to Cuba again but it would be from a new perspective.

"At that moment, I knew that I would have to go in a completely different direction to completely separate myself from the past work and begin to investigate a new intellectual direction. A short time later, my answer was clear and I was very excited to begin the series. The new work would combine my interest in art history, biology, contemporary society's connections to our environment, and the lost artistic notion of regionalism and angling art.

"It all seemed very clear. As most of our social and economic reliance had moved to an urban setting, the connections between nature and culture in contemporary society seemed to have been lost over the last few generations. This series would try to mend these lost connections by presenting paintings of fish and landscapes that were characteristic to a specific region and that were local to the exhibition site. While the regions are specific, the issues raised would be universal."

2001—Rey accepted the Kasling Lecturer Award for distinguished scholarly and creative activity as senior faculty member. Diego Cressy Rey, Rey's son, was born. Rey traveled to rivers in Montana, Wyoming, Idaho, and Yellowstone Park and traveled to Phoenix, Sedona, and the Grand Canyon.

Rey Comments: "Victoria Guerra, my grandmother on my mother's side, passed away, in Cuba. I returned to Montana with the youth fly-fishing program, and then went to Iceland to investigate other rivers and other fish species, while adding documentation to the *Biological Regionalism* series and took a family trip to visit some friends and to investigate the galleries and museums in Phoenix, while fishing and documenting fish and landscapes in Sedona and the Grand Canyon."

2002—Rey returned to Cuba, on assignment for *Fish and Fly Magazine*, Seattle, Washington. He visited: Havana, Agramonte, Santa Clara, Jardines de la Reina, and Jardines Del Rey/Cayo las Brujas. When he returned to the United States, he traveled to rivers in Montana, Wyoming, Idaho, and Yellowstone Park and traveled to rivers in Iceland (Minnivallalaekur and Grenlaekur). Rey became an Orvis Endorsed Guide.

Rey Comments: "I had met Tom Pero, the editor, before and he asked me to come with him to do an article about fly-fishing, in Cuba, at the Jardines de la Reina and Jardines del Rey/Cayo las Brujas. I took the opportunity to visit my aunt and uncle, in Agramonte. When I returned, I flew to Montana. I also traveled to Iceland because of its unique landscape, location, and fish culture. I made those trips to the islands over the years to document the native fish and the landscapes that exist in Iceland. I had made previous trips to Montana, when I was a mentor for a youth fly-fishing program.

"It is always difficult to return to Cuba because of the extreme emotional highs and lows experienced. The lack of an American Embassy always makes me a bit wary about not being able to return to my family in the States if anything goes wrong. Nonetheless, returning to Cuba is something that I always think about. I was going to return this summer but family illness, in Miami, made me change my plans. Every trip to Cuba adds a bit more to my soul and to who I am but it was not appropriate for me to continue to do work on Cuba, when there were other things going on around me. I do not exclude the possibility of doing more on Cuba—especially if I return again. My work is a reflection of my life, of what I experience and my thoughts about my role in contemporary society."

2003—Rey accepted the Chancellor's Award for Excellence in Scholarship and Creative Activity. He traveled to England (London, Bath, Castle Combe, and Cotswells); Wales (Breton Beacons, Swansea, Cardiff, The Mumbles, Carmarthen, Llandello, and Usk); rivers in Montana, Wyoming, Idaho and Yellowstone Park; as well as in Iceland (Hrutafjardara, Laxa in Nesjum, and Breiddalsa).

Rey Comments: "Janeil took a group of students on a study abroad trip to Wales. I took advantage of the trip to document many of the rivers and its fish for the *Biological Regionalism* series. I returned to Montana with the youth fly-fishing program and to Iceland to investigate other rivers and other fish species, while adding documentation to the series.

2004—Mayda, Rey's sister, died at the age of forty-seven from pancreatic cancer. The death deeply affects his work and life. Neil Strong, his father-in-law, also passed away a few months later with lung cancer.

Rey Comments: "This was a tough year, one of several that came in a row. We shed a lot of tears and we just tried to survive that year. After it was over, I realized that I had been changed forever and could be brought to tears at the slightest discussion about family, my sister, or anything sentimental. It made me much more sensitive to everyone's struggles. I started collecting a lot of images of dead or dying fish and other animals, although I wasn't sure what I would do with them. It took me a couple of years to organize my thoughts about the *Aesthetics of Death* series, which created large paintings of dead or dying steelhead. The work was an unflinching look at death and at the fragility of life. By making the paintings very painterly and colorful, they represented the vitality of life and the decay represented the reality of its temporality. The series is another example of using large-scale format in order to investigate a metaphor for investigating contemporary social issues through traditional media. The scale of the work also links my series—*Binary Forms, Icon Series, Appropriated Memories,* and *Biological Regionalism*—to that used by the Hudson River School and who, to me, represented an American culture of representations of fish and fishing."

2005—Rey accepted the Chancellor's Research Recognition Award and began Biological Regionalism series and traveled to Anchorage and Aniak River in Alaska.

Rey Comments: "I was invited to come out to Alaska and I was excited to document more fish species and rivers in the true wilderness. The video I created documented how difficult it is to find wilderness in contemporary society and what it is that you will find when you are there. During this period, I started to use my past research to create international/global extensions to the *Trout Encounters,* as that series transformed into the *Biological Regionalism.*

2006—Rey's wife, Janeil, was diagnosed with breast cancer. Rey began the *Aesthetics of Death series* and traveled to Portland, Oregon (Deschutes and Metolius Rivers).

Rey Comments: "I was invited by an advocacy group, Cascade Resources Advocacy Group, in Portland, to work with other guides to find and document the threatened bull trout.

"Since 1998, I have been the founder and director of the SAREP Youth Fly Fishing Program. We meet weekly to tie flies and discuss various biological topics and then go on bimonthly field trips. For the past eight years, we have organized the Canadaway Creek Conservation Project, where we have a community picnic, provide educational programming, plant 200 trees, remove trash from the stream, and remove invasive species.

"Apart from Canadaway Creek project, we have been raising funds to finance the reintroduction of trout into the Canadaway Creek. That fish species was eradicated from the stream about 100 years ago due to pollution, development, and the consequential changes to its environment.

"The Children in the Stream Conference is our newest venue, which started in 2012. The conference brings educators and community leaders from around the country together as a way to discuss issues related to fly-fishing, with the ultimate goal of having the students incorporate outdoor activities with a discussion of related issues based on literature, science, social studies, and art."

2007—Rey was promoted to State University of New York Distinguished Professor and traveled to Iceland (Reykjavik, Vik, Gullfoss, Jokarlson, Geysir, Stykkshólmur, Hellnar, Budhir, Skogar, and Blue Lagoon) and Spain (Madrid, Bilbao, Argonos, Santona, Alicante, Santa Pola, Escalante [his grandfather Enrique's birthplace].

Rey Comments: "In Iceland, I returned with my family and documented non-fishing landscapes that I had not documented before and also set up meetings with museum curators and visited several art and historical museums around the island. I also wrote and illustrated a travel article that was published in *Buffalo Spree* magazine. The idea of combining my writing with my artwork and elements of my family together into a published work was very fulfilling. I returned to Spain for the first time with my children to visit my uncle, in Madrid, while also developing a taste for local foods, such as black-hoof Iberian ham, as I revisited the major art museums in Madrid and Bilbao. During this trip, I continued investigating the places from which my family emigrated to Cuba from Spain."

2009—Rey traveled to Nassau, Bahamas, and to rivers in Montana and Yellowstone Park.

2010—Janeil Rey was diagnosed with breast cancer for the second time. Rey began installing large video projections with his large paintings as part of his *Biological Regionalism* series (Lightwell Gallery, University of Buffalo, New York).

Rey Comments: "This was another personally difficult year for Janeil and me, and we tried to keep everything stable for our children. Professionally, the exhibition at the University of Buffalo provided an opportunity to create an ambitious site-specific installation that combined a series of large video projections with a couple of eight-foot paintings of an indigenous fish species, largemouth bass, and the landscape where it was documented. The exhibition opened up into the possibility of creating more of these types of work in the future. This approach will be used at the solo exhibition at the Masur Museum, Monroe, Louisiana in November 2013 and at the Burchfield Penney in 2014. At this point in my career, I am more interested in doing large-scale ambitious projects with publications. I realize that I am at a point in my life when I might have, hopefully, around two decades to create large, ambitious bodies of work and would like to use that time on special projects."

2012—Rey travels to Rome to see his work in an exhibition at the American Embassy in the Vatican City. He travels with his family to Pompeii, Florence, Siena, Venice, and San Sano. While in San Sano, he travels to the headwaters of the Tiber River to document the native brown trout and their environments.

Rey Comments: "It was wonderful to bring the family to Italy and share all the experiences together. I have come to a point in my life where traveling alone is not as exciting as it has been in the past. There have been too many experiences that I have not been able to share with my family.

Rey begins a two-part residency at Masur Museum at Monroe, Louisiana, which concludes in 2013.

"The two-part residency provided a wonderful opportunity to work with local biologists to collect flora and fauna from local waterways and incorporate the specimens into the installation that is planned for the following year. These artifacts will be presented with site-specific paintings and videos. Installation approaches used for this exhibition will be incorporated into the installation at the Burchfield Penney Art Center two years from now."

2013—Rey has his first solo, European museum exhibition at the Extremaduran and Latin American Museum of Contemporary Art, Badajoz, Spain, as his solo museum exhibition opened at the Masur Museum, Monroe, Louisiana. While in Europe, Rey traveled to Portugal to document brown trout and their environments on the Ceira and Alva Rivers in Portugal.

Rey Comments: "The exhibition at Badajoz was wonderful. Since the museum is round, I was able to see several large video projections at one time. I have never been able to see the work in this manner, and I was very proud of it. The five site-specific videos that I had created for the space worked well together, and when you stood in the middle of the five projections, you felt as though you were in the environment that I had documented. The videos were synchronized so that each video went underwater at the same time and you could see the migrating steelheads around you. The videos, maps, and text documented in a small stream a few miles from my house. It was nice to see what I had envisioned on the floor plan come together so well."

2014—Rey's forthcoming exhibition at the Burchfield Penney, Buffalo, New York—the occasion for which this book was written—is set to open on March 14, 2014 and will close on June 22, 2014.

"I have been working on this exhibition for about three years. This is the most ambitious site-specific installation, publication, and programming to date. While I have had other projects also going on at the same time, it has been a luxury to have had this time to fully formulate all aspects of the exhibitions and related activities. At the date of this final manuscript editing in July, most of the work is finished, with only a couple of optional paintings yet to be created and a couple of videos still to get their final revisions. The installation of the work is tentatively planned, with only the programming to be realized."

Rey Comments: "This exhibition is an opportunity to share information about a stream that runs underneath the city of Buffalo and around the Burchfield Penney Center. Very few folks know about the stream and its history. This ambitious exhibition will combine aesthetics with issues related to conservation and commercial and social progress."

Locations Investigated by Alberto Rey

PENNSYLVANIA (1972–1978) AND (1997–2013)

Spring Creek
First Fork Creek
Fishing Creek
Fisherman's Paradise
Twenty Mile Creek
Sixteen Creek
Walnut Run
Elk Creek
Neshannock Creek
Black Run
Beaver Run
North Branch of Blacklick Creek
Prince Galitzen State Park
Duman Lake
Kettle Creek

CANADA (1995, 1997, 1998)

Smoke Lake (Algonguin Park)
Trout Lake (Algonguin Park)
Ragged Lake (Algonguin Park)
Gull Feather Lake

NEW YORK (1996–2013)

Cassadaga Creek
Salmon River
Cassadaga Lake
Chautauqua Lake
Findley Lake
Cayuga Creek
Cazenovia Creek
Derby Brook
Eighteen Mile Creek

Hosmer Creek
Oak Orchard Creek
Irondequoit Creek
Oatka Creek
Slater Creek
Upper Niagara River
Lower Niagara River
Red House Brook
Quaker Run
Ischua Creek
East Branch Delaware River
West Branch Delaware River
Delaware River
Johnson Creek
French Creek
Lake Erie
Pendergast Creek
Wiscoy Creek
East Koy Creek
Upper Cattaraugus Creek
Lower Cattaraugus Creek
South Branch of Cattaraugus Creek
Clear Creek (Arcade)
Clear Creek (Ellington)
Clear Creek (Seneca Reservation)
Ellicott Creek
Esopus Creek
Willowemoc River
Beaverkill River
Batavia Kill River
Keg Creek

Sandy Creek
Four Mile Creek
Allen Creek
Genessee River (Lower Falls)
Upper Genesee River (Scio)
Canadaway Creek
Little Canadaway Creek
Beaver Creek
Scott Creek
Chautauqua Creek
Upper Chautauqua Creek (Mayville)
Little Chautauqua Creek
Corell Creek
Walnut Creek
Silver Creek
New Albion Lake
Bear Lake
Bear Lake Outlet
Mill Creek
Crooked Brook
Hudson River
Boreas River
Ausable River
West Branch of Ausable River
Johns Brook

MASSACHUSETTS (1996–2013)

Fish Brook
Crane Beach
Rafe's Chasm

Halibut Point
Essex River
Rust Island
Plum Island
Half Moon Beach
Gloucester Harbor
Pebble Beach

FLORIDA (1996–2013)

Cumberland Key
Big Pine key
Matecumbe Key
Everglades
Big Pine Key
Islamorada Key
Bahia Honda Key
Matheson Hammock Park
Alligator Point
Tiger Tail Beach

NEW MEXICO (1998, 1999)

San Juan River
Cimarron River

NEW HAMPSHIRE (1999)

Powwow River

CALIFORNIA (1999)

East Fork of San Gabriel River

ARIZONA (2001)

Oak Creek
Page Spring Creek

MONTANA (2001, 2002, 2003, 2009, 2010, 2013)

Madison River
Mill Creek
Lower Madison River
Tom Miner Creek
Upper Ruby River
Ruby River
DePuy Spring Creek
East Gallatin River
Gallatin River
Yellowstone River
Hyalite River
Merrill Lake
Boulder River
Big Hole River
Big Horn River
Gallatin River
Warm Spring Creek

YELLOWSTONE PARK (2001, 2002, 2003, 2009, 2010, 2013)

Firehole River
Little Firehole River
Sheep Eater River
Pebble Creek
Gibbon River
Soda Butte River
Lamar River Slough River

CUBA (2002)

Jardines de el Rey
Jardines de la Reina

ICELAND (2002, 2003)

Grenlaekur River
Minnivallalaekur River
Hrutafjardara River
Breiddalsa River
Laxa i Nesjum River

WYOMING (2001, 2002, 2010)

Beartooth Lake
Flat Creek
Hoback River
Granite River

ENGLAND (2003)

By Brook

WALES (2003)

Teifi River
Towy River
Usk River
Taf Fechan River
Taff River

ALASKA (2005)

Aniak River
Kuskokwim River
Holitna River

OREGON (2006, 2012)

Metolius River
Deschutes River
Grand Ronde River
Wallowa River

VIRGINIA (2008)

Big Mary's Creek
North Fork of Moorman's Creek

LOUISIANA (2012)

Black Bayou
Bayou Desaird
Horseshoe lake
Ouachita River

ITALY (2012)

Tiber River

PORTUGAL (2013)

Ceira River
Alva River

Selected Curriculum Vitae

EDUCATION

1988

Harvard University, Cambridge, MA: Additional courses in Visual and
Environmental Studies

1987

State University of New York at Buffalo, Buffalo, NY: MFA, painting and drawing,
National Hispanic Scholarship

1982

Indiana University of Pennsylvania, Indiana, PA: BFA, painting and drawing;
concentration in visual communication
Distinguished Alumni Award (2007)

1981

Art Institute of Pittsburgh, Pittsburgh, PA: Affiliation with Indiana University of
Pennsylvania, concentration in visual communication

1978

West Point Military Academy, West Point, NY: Honorable discharge

EMPLOYMENT

1992–PRESENT

SUNY Distinguished Professor for Research and Creative Activity (2007), State
University of New York at Fredonia, Fredonia, NY;

1991

Christo's Umbrellas Project, Tejón Pass, CA, Captain of an Installation Crew

1988–1989

Instructor, Art Institute of Boston, MA
Instructor, New England School of Art and Design, Boston, MA

1987–1988

Instructor, Museum of Fine Arts, Boston, MA

1986–1987

Instructor, Albright-Knox Art Gallery, Buffalo, NY

1986–1987

Instructor, State University of New York, Buffalo
Director and Curator of Exhibitions, Bethune Gallery and Pfeiffer Theater Gallery,
State University of New York, Buffalo

1985–1986

Teaching Assistant, State University of New York, Buffalo

1983

Assistant in Communication and Construction, "Christo's: Surrounded Islands Project,"
    Miami, FL

AWARDS

2012

Visiting Artist, Masur Museum, Monroe, LA

2008

MARK Professional Practice Program, New York Foundation for the Arts, New York, NY

2008

Visiting Artist, Washington and Lee University, Lexington, VA
Visiting Artist, Residency, Peabody Essex Museum, Salem, MA.

2006

Visiting Artist, Residency, University of Virginia, Charlottesville, VA

2005–2007

Visiting Faculty, Chautauqua School of Art, Chautauqua Institution, Chautauqua, NY

2005

Chancellor's Research Recognition Award

2004

Artist-Teacher, Union Institute, Vermont College, Montpelier, VT

2003

Chancellor's Award for Excellence in Scholarship and Creative Activity

2001

Kasling Lecturer, for distinguished scholarly or creative activity as senior faculty
member

1996–1997

Director/Curator, Chautauqua Center for the Visual Arts, Chautauqua Institute, NY

1994

William T. Hagan Young Scholar/Artist Award, for distinguished scholarly or
creative activity as a junior faculty member

1994

Minority Visiting Scholar Award from Central Missouri State University,
Warrensburg, MO

MUSEUM COLLECTIONS

Albright-Knox Art Gallery, Buffalo, NY
Art Museum, University of Virginia, Charlottesville, VA
Frost Art Museum, Florida International University, Miami, FL
Bronx Museum of the Arts, Bronx, NY

Brooklyn Museum, Brooklyn, NY
Burchfield Art Center, Buffalo, NY
Catskill Fly Fishing Museum, Livingston, NY
Castellani Art Museum, Niagara University, NY
Centro de Arte Contemporáneo de Caja de Burgos, Burgos, Spain
El Museo del Barrio, New York, NY
Erie Art Museum, Erie, PA
IGFA Museum, Fort Lauderdale, FL
Lowe Art Museum, University of Miami, FL
Masur Museum, Monroe, LA
Extremaduran and Latin American Museum of Contemporary Art, Badajoz, Spain
Museum of Art, Fort Lauderdale, FL
Museum of Latin American Art, Long Beach, CA
National Museum of Wildlife Art, Jackson, WY
Peabody-Essex Museum, Salem, MA
Richard F. Brush Art Gallery, St. Lawrence University, Canton, NY
Roger Tory Peterson Institute of Natural History, Jamestown, NY
Tampa Museum of Art, Tampa, FL

SOLO EXHIBITIONS

2014

Burchfield Penney Art Center, Buffalo, NY

2013

Masur Museum of Art, Monroe, LA
Extremaduran and Latin American Museum of Contemporary Art, Badajoz, Spain

2012

Octagon Gallery, Westfield, NY
Northeastern Seminary at Robert Wesleyan College, Rochester, NY
Arts Council for Wyoming County, Perry, NY

2011

Chace-Randall Gallery, Andes, NY

2010

Roger Tory Peterson Institute of Natural History, Jamestown, NY
Lightwell Gallery, University of Buffalo Art Gallery, Center for the Arts,
    Buffalo, NY

2009

Chace-Randall Gallery, Andes, NY

2008

Washington and Lee University, Lexington, VA

2007

Case Western Reserve University, Cleveland, OH
Peabody Essex Museum, Salem, MA

2005

El Museo Francisco Oller y Diego Rivera, Buffalo, NY
Abud Foundation for the Arts, Lawrenceville, NJ
Erie Art Museum, Erie, PA

2004

IGFA Museum, Fort Lauderdale, FL

2002

Erpf Gallery of the Catskill Center, Arkville, NY
Roger Tory Peterson Institute of Natural History, Jamestown, NY
Buffalo Arts Studio, Buffalo, NY

2001

Adams Art Gallery, Dunkirk, NY

1999–2000

Bertha V. B. Lederer Gallery, State University of New York, Geneseo, NY
Hallwalls Contemporary Art Center, Buffalo, NY
Big Orbit Gallery, Buffalo, NY
Weeks Gallery, Jamestown Community College, Jamestown, NY

1997

Sharidan Art Gallery, Kutztown University, Kutztown, PA
Richard Brush Art Gallery, St. Lawrence University, Canton, NY
Miramar Gallery, San Francisco, CA

1996

Galería Nina Menocal, Mexico City, Mexico
Meridian Gallery, San Francisco, CA

1995

Schneider Museum of Art, Southern Oregon State College, Ashland, OR
Wayne County Council for the Arts, Lyons, NY
Castellani Museum, Niagara University, NY
Howard Yezerski Gallery, Boston, MA

1993

Mercer Gallery, Monroe Community College, Rochester, NY
INTAR Gallery, New York City, NY

1992

Olean Public Library, Olean, NY
Nina Freudenheim Gallery, Buffalo, NY

1990–1991

Rockefeller Art Center, State University of New York, Fredonia, NY
Harcus Gallery, Boston, MA
Art Dialogue Gallery, Buffalo, NY

1988–1989

Museum of Contemporary Hispanic Art (MOCHA), New York City, NY
Art Dialogue Gallery, Buffalo, NY
Stavaridis Gallery, Boston, MA

1986

Mercer Gallery, Monroe Community College, Rochester, NY
El Museo Francisco Oller y Diego Rivera, Buffalo, NY

INVITATIONAL EXHIBITIONS

2013

Abud Family Foundation for the Arts, Lawrenceville, NJ
American University Museum, Washington, DC
Anderson Galleries, University of Buffalo, Buffalo, NY

2012

Iris and B. Gerald Cantor Gallery, College of the Holy Cross, Worcester, MA
Latino Arts Gallery, Milwaukee, WI
Stark Galleries, Texas A&M University, College Station, TX
Davison Art Gallery, Robert Wesleyan College, Rochester, NY, *Thaw: Realms and Origins: Paintings by Jim Condron and Alberto Rey*
UB Anderson Art Gallery, Buffalo, NY, *Fifty at Fifty: Select Artists from the Gerald Mead Collection*
Buffalo Arts Studio, Buffalo, NY, *Evolution/Revolution*

2011

Centro de Arte, Caja de Burgos, Burgos, Spain, *(I+E)2*
Marion Gallery, Rockefeller Arts Center, State University of New York, Fredonia, NY, *Then and Again: Faculty/Alumni Invitational Exhibition*

2010

Memorial Art Gallery, Rochester, NY, *Fourth Rochester Biennial*
Iris and B. Gerald Cantor Gallery, College of the Holy Cross, Worcester, MA, *Jorge Luis Borges: Encuentro del Arte Visual con la Ficcion/Visual Art's Encounter with Fiction.* The exhibit traveled to the following places: Universidad Católica Argentina, Puerto Modero, El Pabellón de las Bellas Artes, Aires, Argentina.

United States Embassy, Vatican City, The Holy See, Italy, *Art in Embassies Exhibition*
Strohl Art Center, Chautauqua Institution, Chautauqua, NY, *Cuban Connections: Works by Contemporary Cuban Artists*
Erpf Gallery, Catskill Center, Arkville, NY, *Almanac Artists*

2009

Museum of Latin American Art, Long Beach, CA *Selections from the Permanent Collection*
Burchfield Penney Art Center, Buffalo, NY, *Gateways: Space, Place and the Transformative*
Center for the Arts, University of Buffalo, Buffalo, NY, *UB Art Alumni and Faculty from Gerald Mead Collection*
Chace-Randall Gallery, Andes, NY, *Curator's Choice*
Patterson Library Octagon Gallery, Westfield, NY, *North Shore Artists*

2008

Chace-Randall Gallery, Andes, NY, *Curator's Choice*
Abud Family Foundation for the Arts, Lawrenceville, NJ, *Fifth Anniversary Exhibition*
Chace-Randall Gallery, Andes, NY, *One New Work*

2007

Art Museum, University of Virginia, Charlottesville, VA, *Complicit! Contemporary American Art and Mass Culture*
Hallwalls Contemporary Arts Center, Buffalo, NY, *Exquisite Horizon*
Cantor Art Gallery, College of the Holy Cross, Worchester, MA, *Layers: Collecting Cuban-American Art*
Chace-Randall Gallery, Andes, NY, *One New Work*

2006

University of Buffalo Art Gallery, Buffalo, NY, *Layers: Collecting Cuban-American Art*

Castellani Art Museum, Niagara University, NY, *From Aguirre to Zuniga: The Figure in Latin American Art*
Rockefeller Art Center, State University of New York, Fredonia, NY, *Faculty Exhibition*
Art Museum, University of Virginia, Charlottesville, VA. *Allyson Mellberg and Alberto Rey*

2005

M & T Center, Buffalo, NY, *Concerning Heritage*
Burchfield Penney Art Center, Buffalo, NY, *Abstraction from the Collection*
Burchfield Penney Art Center, Buffalo, NY, *Concerning Heritage*

2004

Burchfield Penney Art Center, Buffalo, NY, *Art on the Hyphen: Cuban-American Artist of Western New York*

2003

Museum of Art, Fort Lauderdale, FL, *Selections from Permanent Collection*

2002

Burchfield Penney Art Center, Buffalo, NY, *A Second Look: Selections from Four Decades of Western New York Artists*
Anderson Gallery, Buffalo, NY, *Big Orbit Gallery: Ten Years of Spin on Western New York Art*
Allyn Gallup Contemporary Art, Sarasota, FL, *Boxes Boxed*
Russell Jinishian Gallery, New York, NY, *Union League Club*

2001

Chautauqua Center for the Visual Arts, Chautauqua Institution, NY, *Nature: Reflections from the Natural World*
Museum of Art, Naples, FL, *Breaking Barriers*

2000

Russell Jinishian Gallery, *Alberto Rey*, Fairfield, CT
Bronx Museum of Art, Bronx, NY, *Selections*
Atrium Gallery, Corning Community College, Corning, NY, *Transferred Sensibilities*

1999

Conlon Siegal Gallery, Santa Fe, NM, *Transferred Sensibilities*
South Shore Art Center, Cohasset, MA, *Uncommon Perspectives*

1998

Tampa Museum of Art, Tampa, FL, *Nature: Friend, Foe and the Spiritual Muse*
Tampa Museum of Art, Tampa, FL, *Breaking Barriers: Contemporary Cuban Art*
Conlon Siegal Gallery, Santa Fe, NM, *Uncommon Perspectives*
PaineWebber Art Gallery, New York, NY, *Histories (Re)membered*
Museum of Art, Fort Lauderdale, FL, *Breaking Barriers: Selections from the Permanent Collection*
Concept Art Gallery, Pittsburgh, PA, *Artists as Curators*
Bronx Museum of Art, Bronx, NY, *Talk Back! The Community Responds to the Permanent Collection, Part III*

1997

Bronx Museum of Art, Bronx, NY, *Talk Back! The Community Responses to the Permanent Collection, Part II*
Richard Brush Art Gallery, St. Lawrence University, Canton, NY, *Past Cuba: Identity and Identification in Cuban-American Art*
Thomas Walsh Art Gallery—*Past Cuba: Identity and Identification in Cuban-American Art*, Quick Center for the Arts, Fairfield University, Fairfield, CT
Gramercy International Contemporary Art Fair, Miami, FL, *Emilio Navarro Projectos Contemporaneo*
Art Miami, Miami, FL, *Emilio Navarro Projectos Contemporaneo*

1996

Burchfield Penney Art Center, Buffalo, NY, *Toys: The Artist at Play*
Forum Gallery, Jamestown, NY, *Regional Review*
Lucky Street Gallery, Key West, FL, *Gallery Artists* (group exhibition)
Bronx Museum of Art, Bronx, NY, *Amidst the Silence: Enrique Martinez Celaya and Alberto Rey* (two-person exhibition)

1995

Adams Art Gallery, Dunkirk, NY, *AIR Show*
Philharmonic Center, Naples, FL, *Engaged Cultures* (touring exhibition)

1994

Bronx Museum of Art, Bronx, NY, *Building the Collections: Recent Acquisitions and Selected Works from the Permanent Collection*
Hofstra Museum, Hempstead, NY, *Engaged Cultures*
Rockefeller Art Center, State University of New York, NY, *Engaged Cultures*
College of St. Rose, Albany, NY, *Engaged Cultures*

1993

Castelanni Art Museum, Niagara University, NY, *New Additions*
Mercer Gallery, Monroe Community College, NY, *Gods Greatest Hits*
Art Museum, University of Wisconsin–Milwaukee, WI, *Verging on Emergence*
Rockefeller Art Center, State University of New York, Fredonia, NY, *Explorations*
Harnett Gallery, University of Rochester, Rochester, NY, *Engaged Cultures*

1992

Hallwalls Contemporary Arts Center, Buffalo, NY, *The Second Skin*
Burchfield Art Center, Buffalo, NY, *The Nude Figure in Art from the Collection*
Tower Fine Arts Gallery, Brockport, NY, *Faculty Exchange Exhibition*
Art Dialogue Gallery, Buffalo, NY, *Regional Art Exhibition*
Forum Art Gallery, Jamestown, NY, *Wit and Wisdom: Humor in Art*

1990–1991

Harcus Gallery, Boston, MA, *Boston Through the Years*
Burchfield Art Center, Buffalo, NY, *Personal Territories: Artists from the Southern Tier*
Circle Gallery, Olean, NY, *Personal Territories: Artists from the Southern Tier*
Forum Gallery, Jamestown, NY, *Personal Territories: Artists from the Southern Tier*
Oxford Gallery, Rochester, NY, *Drawings and Prints*
Memorial Art Gallery, *Unique Works on Paper*, Rochester, NY
Albright-Knox Art Gallery, Buffalo, NY, *Selections from Marine Midland Collection*
Bank of Boston, Boston, MA, *South Street Collections*
Oxford Gallery, Rochester, NY, *Selections* (group exhibition)

1988–1989

Adams Memorial Art Gallery, Dunkirk, NY (group exhibition)
Oxford Gallery, Rochester, NY, *The Nude*
Stavaridis Gallery, Boston, MA, *Doug Anderson, Alfonse Borysewicz, Lawence Carroll, Russell Floersch, Stephen Mishol, Alberto Rey, Randolfo Rocha, Doug & Mike Starn, Lowell Vesch* (group exhibition)
Kipp Gallery, Indiana University of Pennsylvania, Indiana, PA, *Alumni Invitational Exhibition*

1987

Hallwalls Contemporary Art Center, Buffalo, NY, *Western New York Invitational Slide Registry*
Art Dialogue, Buffalo, NY, *Director's Choice Exhibition*
Oxford Gallery, Rochester, NY, *Recent Works: Juan Cruz and Alberto Rey*
Bethune Gallery, Buffalo, NY, *An Awe-Inspiring Show of Visual Thespians*
Art Dialogue, Buffalo, NY, *Art Parts Invitational Exhibition*

1986

Oxford Gallery, Rochester, NY, *Oxford Artists*
Pyramid Art Gallery, Rochester, NY, *Artist-Invite-Artist*
Sunship Communications Center, Buffalo, NY, *Artist and Models Annual Invitational Exhibition*

1985

Bethune Gallery, Buffalo, NY, *Politica and Art Exhibition*
Oxford Gallery, Rochester, NY, *Three New Artists: Jackie Felix, Malik Maliki, Alberto Rey*

JURIED GROUP EXHIBITIONS

1998

Spaces, Cleveland, OH, *Regional Forecast–*

1994

Anderson Gallery, Buffalo, NY, *Pre-sent*
Erie Art Museum, Erie, PA, *71st Annual Spring Show*

1993

Albright-Knox Art Gallery, Buffalo, NY, *In Western New York 1993*

1992

Anderson Gallery, Buffalo, NY, *X Sightings*

1990–1991

Albright-Knox Art Gallery, Buffalo, NY, *In Western New York 1991*
Albright-Knox Art Gallery, Buffalo, NY, *Western New York Exhibition*

1988–1989

Adams Memorial Art Gallery, Dunkirk, NY, *Access Annual '86* (group exhibition)

1987

Adams Memorial Gallery, Dunkirk, NY, *Performance Installation*
Artist Gallery of Western New York, Buffalo, NY, *Dixon-Gemperlein-Rey*
AAO Gallery, Buffalo, NY, *Best of Show,* group exhibition

1986

AAO Gallery, Buffalo, NY, *Fourth Annual Art Expo*
Adams Memorial Gallery, Dunkirk, NY, *Access to the Arts Annual Juried Exhibition*

1985

Artmart, Buffalo, NY, *Persona, PERSONA: Brent Scott, Alberto Rey, Mark Blech*
Memorial Art Gallery, Rochester, NY, *Finger Lakes Art Competition*
Gallery at 24, Bay Harbor, FL, (group exhibit)

1984

Mutiny, Coconut Grove, FL, *Mutiny II Art Exhibition* (group exhibition)
Los Angeles International Art Competition, Los Angeles, CA
Cambria County Center for the Arts, Johnstown, PA, *Cambria County Group Exhibition*
William Penn Memorial Museum, Harrisburg, PA, *William Penn Memorial Museum Annual Exhibition*

1983

Pittsburgh Center for the Arts, Pittsburgh, PA, Pittsburgh Society of Artists Exhibition
Southern Alleghenies Museum of Art, Johnstown, PA, *Allied Artist 51st Annual Juried Show*, Shirley Gaynor Honor Award/Honorable Mention
Undercroft Gallery, Pittsburgh, PA, *Undercroft Gallery Painting Exhibition*

1983

Allied Artists, Johnstown, PA, *Print, Photo, and Drawing Exhibition*, First Prize and Honorable Mention
Hoyt Institute of Fine Arts, New Castle, PA, *Hoyt National Painting Show*, Grumbacher Award
Three Rivers Art Festival, Pittsburgh, PA, *Three Rivers Art Festival Exhibition* (group exhibition)
Southern Alleghenies Museum of Art, Johnstown, PA, *U.S. National Art Exhibition*, Merit/Purchase Award; selected into Permanent Collection

VIDEOS AND SCREENINGS

2013

Biological Regionalism: Horseshoe Lake, Monroe, Louisiana, USA, Color Video (1:09).

This video was created for a site-specific installation at the Masur Museum in Monroe, Louisiana. The video documents a dead tree, as it slowly moves back and forth against the current of a stream during a period of uncommonly high-water conditions in northern Louisiana. The *Biological Regionalism* series tries to reestablish connections to the fish and the landscape that are characteristic to a region through the use of traditional and contemporary media. In so doing, I also hope to create a venue from which to begin dialogues between historical and contemporary theories of aesthetics, social development, and environmentalism.

Acquired by Masur Museum, Monroe, LA, in 2013.

Biological Regionalism: Black Bayou, Monroe, Louisiana, USA, Color Video (3:15).

This video was created for a site-specific installation at the Masur Museum in Monroe, LA. The video captures the life that unfolds in a bayou only when visitors leave that specific environment.

Acquired by Masur Museum, Monroe, LA, in 2013, and by the Extremaduran and Latin American Museum of Contemporary Art, Badajoz, Spain, also in 2013. Video screened at the Masur Museum, Monroe, LA, and at the MEIAC, Badajoz, Spain, also in 2013.

Biological Regionalism: Reiter Creek, Sheridan, New York, USA, Color Video (five 1:30 videos), 2012–2013.

The videos present a 180-degree view of a specific site on the stream as steelhead migrate upstream to spawn.

Permanent Collection of the Museo Extremeño e Iberoamericano de Arte Contemporáneo, Badajoz, Spain.

Screened: 2013, Extremeño e Iberoamericano de Arte Contemporáneo (Extremaduran and Latin American Museum of Contemporary Art), Badajoz, Spain, *Alberto Rey: Exploratory Aesthetics*.

2010

Biological Regionalism: Lower Falls, Genesee River, Rochester, New York, USA, Color Video (1:36:30).

This video and two eight-foot paintings were created as part of as a site-specific installation for the Fourth Rochester Biennial at the Memorial Art Gallery, Rochester, NY. The artist explores the migratory pattern of a Lake Erie fish species (steelhead trout) and the historical depictions of the Genesee River.

Screened: 2010, Grand Gallery, Memorial Art Gallery, Rochester, NY.

Biological Regionalism: Ellicott Creek, Amherst, New York, USA: III (Bottom Panel), Color Video (1:30:12).

Biological Regionalism: Ellicott Creek, Amherst, New York, USA: II (Middle Panel), Color Video (1:36:30).

Biological Regionalism: Ellicott Creek, Amherst, New York, USA: I (Top Panel), Color Video (1:30:34).

These underwater videos and two eight-foot paintings were created as part of a site-specific installation for the Lightwell Gallery at the University of Buffalo, Buffalo, NY. The artist explores the migratory pattern of a Lake Erie fish species (largemouth bass) and the history and fragility of Ellicott Creek that borders the campus.

Screened: 2008, Lightwell Gallery, Center for the Arts, University of Buffalo, Buffalo, NY.

2008

Biological Regionalism: Big Mary's Creek, Vesuvius, VA, May 8th, Color Video (5:30).

The video was created as part of a residency at Washington and Lee University, Lexington, VA. The artist explores the state's indigenous fish species, brook trout, and fragility of the environment at Big Mary's Creek, Vesuvius, VA.

Screened: 2008, Washington and Lee University, Lexington, VA.

2007

Biological Regionalism: Atlantic Cod, B/W, (10:00).

The video was created for a residency at the Peabody Essex Museum in Salem, MA. The artist provides a brief overview of his *Biological Regionalism Series* while providing a brief history of the Atlantic cod and its influence on the economy of New England.

Screened: 2007, Peabody Essex Museum, Salem, MA.

2006

Primal Connections, B/W Video (18:40), 2006.

The connection between nature and culture seems to have been lost, as most of our social and economic reliance has moved to an urban setting. Our culture has developed outdoor recreational activities, zoos, and pets as a way to reconnect with our innate need to be closer to nature. This film investigates one attempt to reconnect.

Screened: 2008, Washington and Lee University, Lexington, VA; Rochester Contemporary, Rochester, NY.

2013, Acquired, Extremaduran and Latin American Museum of Contemporary Art, Badajoz, Spain.

Screened: 2013, Extremaduran and Latin American Museum of Contemporary Art, Badajoz, Spain.

2005

Great Lakes Tributary, New York, United States, March 12th, 2005, Color Video (5:28).

Screened: El Museo Francisco Oller y Diego Rivera, Buffalo, NY.

Los Jardines de la Reina (*The Queen's Gardens*), Cuba, July 10th, 2004, Color Video (5:40).

2005, Acquired, Permanent Collection of the Art Museum, University of Virginia, Charlottesville, VA.

Screened: 2008, Washington and Lee University, Lexington, VA; 2005 El Museo Francisco Oller y Diego Rivera, Buffalo, NY.

2005

An Unkept Promise, B/W Video (19:00).

Alberto Rey's family fled Cuba in 1963. Alberto was three years old when they found political asylum in Mexico. Thirty-five years later he returned to Cuba for the first time. *An Unkept Promise* chronicles the emotional complexities of his trip, why he promised himself never to return, and the invitation that makes him reconsider.

Screened: 2010, Memorial Art Gallery, Rochester, NY;

2010,University of Buffalo, NY; 2008, Mary Baldwin College, Staunton, VA; 2008, Washington and Lee University, Lexington, VA; 2007, Cleveland Institute of Art, Cleveland, OH; 2007, Chautauqua Institution, Chautauqua, NY; 2005, Dead Center Gallery Film Festival, Oklahoma, City, OK; 2005, Burchfield Penney Art Center, Buffalo, NY.

2013, Acquired, Extremaduran and Latin American Museum of Contemporary Art, Badajoz, Spain.

Screened: 2013, Extremaduran and Latin American Museum of Contemporary Art, Badajoz, Spain.

2004

Waters off of Caribbean, Cuba, B/W Video (66).

The hour-long footage documents the waters off of Caribbean, Cuba. This small island, off the eastern coast of Cuba, was a popular site where the *balseros* used to set off on their rafts to catch the Gulf Stream to Florida. The video tries to capture what the *balseros* would see on the beginning of their often tragic voyages.

Permanent Collection of the Burchfield Penney Art Center, Buffalo, NY.

Screened: 2010, Memorial Art Gallery, Rochester, NY; 2010, University of Buffalo, NY; 2008, Mary Baldwin College, Staunton,VA; 2008, Washington and Lee University, Lexington, VA; 2007, Chautauqua Institution, Chautauqua, NY; 2007, Cleveland Institute of Art, Cleveland, OH; 2005, Burchfield Penney Art Center, Buffalo, NY.

2013, Acquired, Extremaduran and Latin American Museum of Contemporary Art, Badajoz, Spain.

Screened: 2013, Extremaduran and Latin American Museum of Contemporary Art, Badajoz, Spain.

2001

Seeing the Dark (shot on B/W 16 mm film, edited on video). (6:30).

The short film captures Alberto Rey's first return back to Cuba after thirty years. The film relates how he decides to stop creating paintings about his nostalgic interpretations of his homeland.

Screened: 2010, Memorial Art Gallery, Rochester, NY; 2010, University of Buffalo, NY; 2008, Mary Baldwin College, Staunton,VA; 2008, Washington and Lee University, Lexington, VA; 2007, Chautauqua Institution, Chautauqua, NY; 2007, Cleveland Institute of Art, Cleveland, OH; 2001, Marvel Theater, State University of New York at Fredonia, Fredonia, NY.

2013, Acquired, Extremaduran and Latin American Museum of Contemporary Art, Badajoz, Spain.

Screened: 2013, Extremaduran and Latin American Museum of Contemporary Art, Badajoz, Spain.

EXHIBITION PUBLICATIONS

Gracia, Jorge, *Painting Borges, Art Interpreting Literature,* Volume 1, Number 1, University of Buffalo Art Galleries, Buffalo, NY, 2013.

Wolff, Cori, *Evolution/Revolution*, Buffalo Arts Studio, Buffalo, NY, 2012.

(I+E)2. CAB, Centro de Art, Burgos, Spain, 2011.

Cavanagh, Cecilia Rosemary, *Painting Borges. A Pictorial Interpretation of His Fictions*, EDUCA, Buenos Aires, Argentina, 2010.

Biological Regionalism: Ellicott Creek, Amherst, New York, USA, Lightwell Gallery, Center for the Arts, University of Buffalo, Buffalo, NY, 2010.

Alberto Rey: Life, Death and Beauty, Staniar Gallery, Washington and Lee University, Lexington, NY, 2008.

Drifting Sideways and Up, Dinah Ryan, Principia College, Elsah, IL, 2005.

A New Naturalism: Biological Regionalism, Johanna Drucker, UCLA, Los Angeles, CA, 2007.

Engaging Ambivalence: Alberto Rey's The Aesthetics of Death, Marc Denaci, St. Lawrence University, Canton, NY, 2008.

11.22.08, Burchfield Penney Art Center, Buffalo, NY, 2008.

Gateway: Space, Place and the Transformative, Ted Pietrzak, Burchfield Penney Art Center, 2008.

What Is Western New York Art? Nancy Weekly, Burchfield Penney Art Center, 2008.

Complicit! Contemporary American Art and Mass Culture, Art Museum, University of Virginia, VA, catalog essays and podcast, 2007

"Earth Day Programs," *P/E/M Connections*, Peabody Essex Museum, Salem, MA, March/April, 2007.

"Back to Nature: Alberto Rey's Explorations Take Him to Spiritual Places Where Art, Culture and the Environment Converge," *P/E/M Connections*, Peabody Essex Museum, Salem, MA, January/February, 2007.

Gracia, Jorge and Lynette Bosch, "Negotiating Identities in Art, Literature, and Philosophy: Cuban Americans and American Culture." University of Buffalo, Buffalo, NY, 2006.

Grachos, Louis, Kristen Carbone, and Douglas Dreishpoon, *Beyond/In Western New York*, Albright-Knox Art Gallery, Buffalo, NY, 2005.

Drucker, Johanna, *Alberto Rey: New Naturalism* Abud Foundation for the Arts, Lawrenceville, NY, 2005.

Vanco, John, Suzanne Proulx, and Lynette Bosch, *Alberto Rey—Piscatorial Investigations*, Erie Art Museum, Erie, PA, 2005.

Metz, Don and Lynette Bosch, *Art on the Hyphen: Cuban-American Artists of Western New York State*, Burchfield-Center Art Center, Buffalo, NY, 2005.

Licata, Elizabeth, *Big Orbit Gallery: Ten Years of Spin on Western New York Art*, Anderson Gallery, Buffalo, NY, 2002.

Prosek, James, *Trout Encounters*, Adams Art Gallery, Dunkirk, NY, 2001.

Bosch, Lynette, *Alberto Rey—Cuba: Image or Reality*, Bertha Lederer Art Gallery, State University of New York, Geneseo, NY, 2000.

Drucker, Johanna, Martin Kruck, Sean Donaher, and Sara Kellner, *My Private Addiction to Lies*, Big Orbit Gallery and Hallwalls Contemporary Art Center, Buffalo, NY, 2000.

Cusack, Nancy, *Uncommon Perspectives: Artists from the Caribbean*, South Shore Art Center, Cohasset, MA, 1999.

Nieves, Marysol, *Histories (Re)membered: Selections from the Permanent Collection of the Bronx Museum of Art*, Paine Webber Gallery, New York, NY, 1998.

Channing, S., S. Kellner, and M. Horne, *Regional Forecast*, Space 101, Pittsburgh, PA; Hallwalls, Buffalo, NY; SPACES, Cleveland, OH, 1998.

Santis, Jorge, *Breaking Barriers*, Museum of Art, Fort Lauderdale, FL, 1998.

Talley, Dan, *Silence and Darkness: Alberto Rey*. Kutztown University, Kutztown, NY, 1997.

Bosch, Lynette, *Crossing Borders*. St. Lawrence University, Canton, NY, 1997.

Bosch, Lynette, Past Cuba: Identity and Identification in Cuban American Art. Thomas Walsh Gallery, Fairfield University, Fairfield, CT, 1997.

Marysol Nieves, *Amidst the Silence: Enrique Martinez Celaya and Alberto Rey*. Bronx Museum of Art, Bronx, NY, 1996.

Markle, Greer. Alberto Rey—Cultural Iconography. Schneider Museum of Art, Ashland, OR, 1995.

Olsen, Sandra. Alberto Rey—The Incongruence of Memory. Castellani Art Museum, Niagara University, NY, 1995.

Isaacs, Susan. *1994 Critics Residency*. Hallwalls Contemporary Arts Center, Buffalo, NY, 1994.

Brutvan, Cheryl. *In Western New York, 1993*. Albright-Knox Art Gallery, Buffalo, NY, May 1993.

Talley, Dan. *Alberto Rey*. INTAR, New York, NY, April 1993.

Kellner, Sara. *The 2nd Skin*, Hallwalls Contemporary Arts Center, Buffalo, NY, September 1992.

Talley, Dan. *Wit and Wisdom: Humor in Art*. Forum Art Gallery, Jamestown, NY, May 1992.

Brutvan, Cheryl. *In Western New York, 1991*, Albright-Knox Art Gallery, Buffalo, NY, May 1991.

Talley, Dan. *Personal Territory—Artists of the Southern Tier*. Centre Gallery, Olean, NY; Forum Gallery, Jamestown, NY; Burchfield Art Center, Buffalo, NY, January 1991.

SCHOLARLY PUBLICATIONS

2012

Painting Borges: Philosophy Interpreting Art Interpreting Literature, Jorge J. E. Gracia, State University of New York Press, Albany, New York, 2012,

"Drawing (on) Borges," *The New Centennial Review* 11, no. 1 (Spring 2011).

Cuban-American Literature and Art: Negotiating Identities, Isabel Borland and Lynette Bosch, State University of New York Press, Albany, New York, 2009. "Memories of Others: Ana Mendez and Alberto Rey," Isabel Alvarez-Borland, *Review: Literature and Arts of the Americas* 42, no. 1, 2009.

2008

Identity, Memory, and Diaspora: Voices of Cuban-American Artists, Writers, and Philosophers, Gracia, Jorge J. E., Lynette Bosch, and Isabel Alvarez Borland, ed. State University of New York Press, Albany, NY, 2008.

2004

Cuban-American Art in Miami, Bosch, Lynnette, Ashgate Publishing, Lund Humphries, Hampshire, UK, 2004.

2002

Memoria. Artes Visuales del Siglo XX (Memory. Visual Artists of the 20th Century), Vives Gutierrez, Maria Cristina, California/International Arts Foundation, Los Angeles, CA, 2002.

2001

ReMembering Cuba: Legacy of a Diaspora, O'Reilly Herrera, Andrea, University of Texas Press, Austin, TX, 2001.

1994

New American Painting, Number Two, Steven T. Zevitas, ed.; Elisabeth Sussman, curator. Open Studios Press, Needham, MA, 1994.

Index